Edith Summerskill

A Woman's World

HEINEMANN : LONDON

William Heinemann Ltd
LONDON MELBOURNE TORONTO
CAPE TOWN AUCKLAND

First published 1967

© Edith Summerskill 1967

Printed in Great Britain
by Cox & Wyman Ltd,
London, Fakenham and Reading

Contents

1

A Doctor's Daughter

I cannot record that my first memory of life on this planet was a particularly joyful experience. Indeed, if I had been old enough to assess the situation I might well have asked myself wistfully whether this very short span – for I must have been two or three years old – was to represent my full life term; or whether I was to join all those other infants and toddlers interred in our cemeteries in the nineteenth and early twentieth centuries.

The fact is that my earliest recollection was of extreme discomfort. I was puffing and wheezing under a canopy which had been erected under the direction of my father and which he called a tent. A kettle with a long spout standing on the trivet of a blazing coal fire discharged a steady jet of steam into the tent. If I had heard tell of hell at that early age I might well have asked myself whether these conditions could be any worse than those with which the sinner was threatened in his after life. The heat seemed unbearable for I was swaddled in flannel. A flannel nightie with some kind of flannel undergarment was supplemented by the periodic application of poultices to my chest.

People peeped into the tent to see how I was faring; my mother, my aunt, who had been called in from another part of London to help with the night nursing, and every now and then – when there was a lull in the stream of patients downstairs – my father would leap up the stairs two at a time to look at me.

He would feel my pulse, take my temperature or give me a dose of medicine and make no attempt to conceal his anxiety.

There was no need to adopt a jolly bedside manner to allay the patient's fears for the patient had no conception of the meaning of death. Indeed, to breathe called for so much effort and concentration that this seemed to occupy all my attention and I had neither the energy nor the desire to cry.

The gas light turned low emitted a slight hiss and all conversation was conducted in a whisper. Suggestion and countersuggestion was made. Had I too many blankets or too few? Was there anything in the theory that some fresh air might do good? My father soon scotched this query of my aunt. 'Don't be stupid, Alice, there's a pea-souper outside.'

Occasionally a maid in a well-starched cap and apron which crackled as she moved would silently creep in with a scared expression and ask if anything was wanted. She would attend to the fire and then make a second journey with a scuttle of coals which she had carried up two flights of stairs from the cellar below street level. In the course of her expedition she would glance sideways at the tent and try to catch my eye with a little encouraging half-smile, but I was in no mood to exchange nods with Lizzy.

After 'surgery hour' my father would come up and sit by my side while my mother and aunt had some supper in preparation for the night vigil. My father's anxiety stemmed not only from the natural fears of a parent over the illness of a child; as I was to discover in later years, he was tormented by the thought that this attack of bronchitis could have been prevented and that for some inexplicable reason – he alone was to blame.

I was born in Doughty Street, Bloomsbury, in 1901 when the Clean Air Act had not been conceived and indeed the belching chimneys of London were looked upon as something which had to be borne with resignation. My father would complain endlessly of the polluted air and attribute the recurrent attacks of bronchitis of both my brother and myself to the fog. Although he always endeavoured to find the answer to some of the less obscure medical problems he did not envisage the day of smokeless fuel and the zoning of the country into areas where black smoke would be prohibited.

Undoubtedly those London winters led him to give special consideration to diseases of the chest and he would read with intense interest articles in the medical journals on bronchitis and tuberculosis. During my illness there was great talk of 'building me up' before the next winter. There was no question of my being a delicate, thin, weedy little girl who needed extra milk and food. I was a big, fat, bouncing girl always overweight through the building-up process which had been firmly established since the day I was born. Three large meals a day, a pint of milk, a hot bath and bed at six sharp was the unvarying formula until I verily believe that school homework alone compelled my parents to amend the time-table.

I dwell on this apparently insignificant aspect of my up-bringing because I believe that my bronchitis was caused in great part by over-feeding and that my father's passion for preventive medicine (at a time when nutritional disease was extremely prevalent) had contributed to this condition. I was the youngest of three children, two girls and a boy, and it is hardly surprising that a conscientious doctor should strive to protect his family so far as was within his power and knowledge of contemporary medicine. The death-rate among children from infectious diseases was high. Diphtheria was dreaded and broncho-pneumonia following measles a commonplace. Small-pox was responding to vaccination and the smallpox boats on the Thames of the nineteenth century were no more. Bovine tuberculosis attributed to infected milk, fatal in some cases and with its various manifestations, meningitis, and joint infections which left permanently stiff limbs, was accepted with a degree of fatalism. The most common form of nutritional disease, rickets, accompanied by crooked legs, seemed to be the rule rather than the exception in some families, particularly in industrial areas.

Later in my life when I contested a parliamentary election in the north of England and found bandy legs accepted as though it were a hereditary complaint, I used to feel highly indignant that society had permitted a condition which led to preventable widespread deformities. However, when I spoke of this to some of my northern friends, they would generally laugh and look at me a little curiously. 'Their father and mother had bandy legs,' I was told. 'It must be a family complaint.'

My father did not laugh. I often visited patients with him when I was a girl, and after leaving a poor home he would say,

'Did you see the tin of milk on the table? That provides sugar and milk for the tea and sets the pattern for the diet. No wonder half the children have rickets.'

These visits with my father were undoubtedly the strongest single influence in my life. They made me wish to take up medicine, to give immediate help to the sick. And they made me wish to help in the long-term – removing by political action some of the causes of malnutrition and consequent ill-health. In other words, they made me a socialist as well as a doctor, and took me to the House of Commons.

In the affluent society of today nutritional diseases are not apparent. Tucked away, however, in the little rooms which serve as homes for many of our old people, there are those who through poverty or disablement are unable to feed themselves adequately, but the misshapen limbs of the rickety child are no longer seen on the streets to prod the conscience.

My father was a dedicated doctor who found his fulfilment in ministering to the poor and sick. Those were the days when women had large families, were denied adequate rest and accepted a prolapse of the uterus, varicose veins and varicose ulcers as an inevitable accompaniment of middle age. Indeed they were often worn out before the age of forty.

When I was a medical student my father would show me the healed leg of an overburdened working woman with the same enthusiasm and satisfaction as an artist would exhibit a choice painting at the academy.

'Tell my daughter,' he would say, sitting back in his revolving chair, 'what your leg was like before treatment.' Then the woman, occasionally giving my father a glance of profound devotion, would describe in detail how she had come to him many months before with a large, foully-discharging, evil-smelling varicose ulcer which he had patiently treated, week after week, until it slowly contracted and finally healed. The tragedy for both of them was that they knew that with her large family and long hours of standing at the sink or washtub, possibly taking in other people's washing, the chances were that the condition would recur and that my father's time and patience would once more be in demand. Nevertheless, for the time being she was restored to comparative health and they rejoiced together on the successful outcome of months of patient effort.

My father would demonstrate with what celerity a large speculum could be introduced into the vagina to treat an erosion of a woman complaining of a constant backache; or, a pessary inserted to support a prolapsed womb. The contraceptive pessary for women was unheard of in those days otherwise he would have been equally adept in fitting one.

Always solicitous concerning the complaints of the housewife and mother he often recalled a midwifery case to which he was summoned during his first assistantship in Grantham and which had left an indelible impression. He was a Yorkshireman, qualified in 1889 at the age of 21 at the Leeds medical school soon after the employment of unqualified doctors was prohibited. In fact his predecessor at his first practice was the doctor's coachman who was sent to take a patient's temperature, feel the pulse and generally to assess the urgency of a call before troubling the doctor.

My father visited his patients on horseback and one winter's night he received an urgent call to a confinement at a farmhouse deep in the countryside. After a long and hazardous ride he found himself at a derelict house surrounded by neglected farmland. In a room lit by candlelight he found an old gamp who had been trying to deliver the mother for two days; and in a basin beside the bed was a baby's arm. The ignorant woman had been tugging on this with such violence that she had torn it from the child. The mother was semi-conscious and soon after my father had delivered her she died.

The high maternal and infantile mortality rate of the day caused him to indulge in frequent diatribes against the authorities for not ensuring a higher standard of midwifery. It was not until 1902 that midwives were registered and indeed not until about 1924 that unqualified women were prohibited from attending confinements. While great progress has been made in the pharmaceutical field nevertheless it is the improvement in elementary hygiene which has been chiefly responsible for the reduction in the high morbidity and mortality rates of the last century.

When I was a medical student my father took me to a

midwifery case attended by an unqualified woman of about seventy. I would call her an old gamp if that term were not associated with the partaking of alcoholic refreshment to while away the waiting hours of labour. My father's old nurse would not dare to take a drop of anything stronger than tea; she was only too well aware of my father's views on this subject.

When we arrived we found the patient in full labour and the kettle was singing away on the hob of the coal fire. My father never took risks. 'Nurse, wash up please,' he said. He knew that the title 'Nurse' was the highest compliment he could pay her. The old woman turned to me and with a toothless smile said 'Your father is funny; you know I never washed before a confinement until I met him. Only after.'

Then with rather an embarrassed laugh she turned up her sleeves above the elbow and pouring some water from the kettle scrubbed her gnarled old hands. 'Arms as well,' said father. She turned with a half-wink to me and then obeyed. Until her death she believed that this washing ceremony was some curious obsession of my father's which had no rational basis, but she deemed it easier and economically more desirable to humour him than resist his demands. Years had elapsed since Pasteur had warned the world of the harmful effects of invisible germs, but like most pioneers his warnings remained unheeded for many generations. Meanwhile women in childbirth all over the world continued to be sacrificed because the most elementary precautions against infection failed to be observed.

My father came to St Mary's hospital for a post-graduate course and at a party he met my mother and subsequently decided to settle in London. My mother, an energetic woman, always identified herself with the practice like most sensible doctors' wives, and this is indeed even more necessary today in the absence of adequate help in the home.

She came from a large family who lived in a rambling old house near the Crystal Palace and who derived all their pleasure from a close association with the musical festivals of that massive Victorian institution.

The Victorian 'musical evening' served to equip my mother with the skill and knowledge necessary to organize entertainments designed to raise funds for hospital and other medical causes, for in those days Voluntary hospitals were entirely dependent on public charity. She even wrote a little fantasy called 'The Wishing Well' but when a patient in the world of the theatre suggested that the standard was high enough for commercial production, my Victorian father, who was inclined to regard all people professionally connected with the stage as 'rogues and vagabonds', put his foot down. Years afterwards my mother would still quote this as an illustration of the position of women completely dependent on their husbands for financial support.

I attribute my horror of spiders to a Christmas entertainment organized by my mother in which I was cast as Little Miss Muffet. At the age of three or four, arrayed in a long frock with a web embroidered on my tummy, with a stuffed black velvet spider sitting in the middle, I would recite the nursery rhyme placing special emphasis on the last line; the audience, clearly unconvinced that such a big Miss Muffet could be 'frightened away' by a spider, thought it all highly amusing. However, my husband is under no illusion. He knows that my cry for help means that there is a spider somewhere in the offing and he dispatches the offender without indulging in any psychological dissertation.

My mother's energy was considerable but the customs of her day offered little outlet other than the management of her home and the organization of money-raising efforts for medical charities. No doubt this pent-up energy was responsible for the thoroughness with which she conducted her household affairs, never failing to notice if some item of furniture had not been polished or some speck of dust had not been removed from the mantelpiece.

My mother was just and fair to the procession of maids who provided the domestic labour in our home, but she demanded such a high standard of work that I was always conscious of the misdirected energy of so many young women who were part of my early environment. Sometimes as a very small girl I crept down to the kitchen, where a bright fire would be burning in the highly polished black range, to find a girl vigorously scrubbing the kitchen floor or the large kitchen table which was white and worn from years of similar treatment from strong young arms. This process was repeated every day, and woe betide anyone if my mother descended the stairs and found that the work had been skimped.

An older girl was generally in charge of the cooking but her daily directions were given by the mistress of the house who never failed to exercise the most detailed supervision, for according to her standards the bottom of a saucepan should be as spotless as the inside.

It was in my mother's absence that I occasionally ventured into the kitchen and saw what pranks these high-spirited girls could get up to. I was lifted on to the kitchen table and encouraged to sing songs and do a little dance to the accompaniment of roars of laughter from the maids. I suppose my fat little legs, tightly encased in knickers trimmed with embroidery which these girls had themselves goffered with hot irons, amused them. My frocks always seemed to be too short or too tight, for I grew out of them all at an astonishing speed. After a few encores the maids would throw their arms around me, hug me, and press their rough red cheeks against mine. I have to admit that my adventures in the kitchen were not disinterested; I had a motive which was not entirely concerned with bringing some life and laughter into the lives of the maids, although I thoroughly enjoyed these excursions. After my little performance on the table my eye would wander to the highest shelf of the huge wooden dresser attached to the wall; there, well out of the reach of children, stood a jar of boiled sweets, for my father's views on the protection of children's teeth were translated into a strict rationing of sweets. The bottle of sweets kept out of our way, yet in full view, was a constant reminder that good conduct might result in a very pleasant reward. At the risk of discovery by my mother it was an understood thing that my little song and dance merited this reward. Poor girls! Separated from their homes and families, imprisoned in a London house from which they were only permitted to escape for a few precious hours each week, how they must have longed for the only means of securing their liberty – marriage. And how, in their artless way they must have yearned for a family of their own with whom they could laugh and romp without fear of some reprimand.

I must have been quite young when the proximity of these girls served to stimulate thoughts on their unenviable lot. In their position I would run away, I thought. But where to? There was no work near their homes and their parents would not welcome another mouth to feed; besides, to run away from their 'place' would mean to forfeit a reference and who would engage them without a reference?

However, despite my concern for their welfare, most of these girls left us only to get married, generally to one of the trades-men who conducted the preliminaries of courting at the back door. On the assumption that a child's attitude to life can be determined, in part, by the influences brought to bear in the first years of life, I am inclined to reply to those who have asked me how and where I acquired the confidence to address a public meeting, 'On a kitchen table with a most appreciative audience of two who laughed and applauded my efforts whether in song or verse.'

Occasionally more help was introduced into the household in the shape of a middle-aged woman, a spinster or widow, who was entirely dependent on her own earnings, but who had 'seen better days'. She had probably been supported by her parents until their death, when she had been compelled to fend for herself or, in the case of a widow, when her income ceased on the death of her husband.

If she had been fortunate enough to have had some education with perhaps another language, she could style herself a gover-ness and enter homes where the most rudimentary education sufficed for the girls of the family. The women who resided with us for various periods would no doubt today be classified as 'mothers' helps', for their chief function was to care for the children and keep them out of mischief. Their position in the household was always a little ambiguous. The maids were conscious of their powerlessness and were not prepared to 'put themselves out for them', and the mistress no doubt was ever vigilant lest they usurp her maternal functions. These women had a profound sense of dependence; they had lived for years under their fathers' or husbands' roofs, ministering to their wants and tolerating without question a subordinate position. Although they had never worked outside the home they could

not be charged with indolence for they had toiled for their
parents or husbands in homes totally devoid of modern labour-
saving devices, in houses, it would seem, designed and furnished
to provide the maximum amount of work for a patient woman's
hands. The kitchen, the children and the church were acknowledged to be a woman's sphere and the opportunity for other
work was strictly limited by custom and prejudice. Even typing
was considered to be a man's work and the Civil Service were
reluctant to admit women as typists – or typewriters as they
were called. Ridicule was the weapon most effectively used
against those women who demanded the right to a full education
or expert training in some field for which they felt they had a
special aptitude. A woman who was prepared to challenge the
conventions knew that she would pay a heavy price, for she
might alienate men, even her father and her brother, and a
possible suitor would find her independent spirit wholly un-
attractive.

Her mother tended to uphold the conventions for reasons of
her own. The husband-hunting mother of whatever period is
too swiftly condemned for the methods she adopts to secure her
daughter an eligible partner; it is only she, a woman, and not
her husband or her sons, who know how compelling is a
woman's conscious or subconscious desire for children.

Nevertheless, a woman like Elizabeth Garrett Anderson,
determined to follow her strong inclination for a medical career,
defied the man-made conventions of her day and announced to
her family that she wished to become a doctor. According to
Elizabeth's biographer, 'her mother retired to her room for a
fortnight and wept because she knew that she had given birth
to an unnatural daughter'. Her wealthy father, to his credit,
having overcome his initial shock, sought help from his doctor
friends but received a rebuff even if they did not seek to ridicule
the whole idea. Later the men students pelted Elizabeth with
rotten tomatoes and barricaded the examination room against
her when she sought to gain admittance. It was not surprising
that the more timid of her sex stayed at home patiently tolerating
an existence which often denied them both fulfilment in marriage
and employment outside the home.

Miss Collins was one of these. She came to us having cared

for her parents, and when her father died shortly after her mother's death, his pension ceased. Her brother and sisters, all with large families, had no extra room in their houses for her, even if they had been able to pay her pocket-money for her services in the home.

The selfishness of some old people who exploit the love and kindness of their single daughters is difficult to understand. Where is the natural affection of these parents? How can they endure year after year watching an unselfish daughter give her time and energies, day and night, tending to their wants while she is denied the joy of companionship and entertainment outside the home?

Miss Collins answered an advertisement of my mothers asking for somebody to help to care for three boisterous children. On arrival we children came to the conclusion that this demure little mouse-like creature of indeterminate age, with her sweet, grave face, could soon be quelled by our united efforts. I should say here that my sister Daphne was the quietest of the three and adopted a certain responsible attitude to our affairs while my brother and I would, on occasion, gang up together if we thought circumstances merited it.

We calculated that Miss Collins would be fair game for practical jokes and her capacity for exercising any form of discipline never occurred to us. However, there are methods other than those of the disciplinarian for handling active, mischievous children, and it was not long before Miss Collins exercised her power over us. Whether it was a deliberate policy or not it succeeded, for she was a superb story-teller, and having our meals alone with her provided a captive audience who revelled in her fascinating narratives. We roamed the world with her, climbing mountains in Switzerland, visiting fascinating towns in Italy, getting lost in the alleys of mysterious cities in the Orient, or making a hazardous journey up the Amazon. We had adventures in every continent and on every sea, and when we were wrecked on a desert island we always finally escaped on a raft. The chief participants in these adventures were always two girls and a boy bearing a curious resemblance to ourselves. So realistic and colourful were her stories that when I journey round the world I sometimes experience a little disappointment that the places I visit are not as exciting as I anticipated.

Miss Collins would put me on her lap with her arms around me for I was the youngest. Daphne and William would sit on hassocks at her knee, all listening intently, only interrupting if we thought there had been some illogicality in the development of the story.

If that little woman had dreamed of children and a home and of travelling to distant parts she at least experienced a vicarious satisfaction during the time which she spent in our home.

Then suddenly she disappeared and we were told that she had gone to live with a brother or sister. I was inconsolable for a time. What wonderful qualities are possessed by these unselfish, single women who have been denied complete fulfilment solely because the number of potential mothers outnumber that of men.

It must have been my sympathy for the Miss Collinses of this world – as well as my mothers succession of maids – that helped to turn me into an ardent feminist. When much later, for instance, I took up the cudgels for the 'National Council for the Single Woman and her Dependents', I was thinking of our dear Miss Collins.

There were other events in my childhood which helped to determine my outlook on life. When my father decided that the family should move from the centre of London to the more salubrious country air on the outskirts of the town, we welcomed this decision with whoops of joy. He arranged to enter into partnership in a practice in Seven Kings, Essex, which, with the neighbouring Chadwell Heath, represented a rural paradise to our eyes after the streets of Bloomsbury.

This change in our lives marked my father's entry into the world of politics. He was an admirer of Gladstone and a portrait of his political hero adorned our walls; we were well aware that any question about Gladstone's activities would incite my father to give a short exposition of his policy and justify his more unpopular activities. For a professional man to give his allegiance to the Gladstonian Liberals was a mark of true radicalism. Later indeed when I joined the Labour Party, my father recognized that social progress was safe in the custody of my

Party, particularly when the National Health Service was introduced.

I have already mentioned the tragic mortality rate among babies and small children which was in a great part attributable to gastro-intestinal infections. One hot summer evening a mother brought a dying baby wrapped in a shawl and suffering from the unmistakable symptoms, to my father's consulting-room. She was heartbroken for she had lost another baby with a similar complaint. My father never tried to disguise from the people the social causes of some of their ailments. He believed that his contribution to their political education might at least stimulate a few of them to recognize that the social and physical ills from which they suffered were in a large measure preventable and could be ameliorated by political action. On this occasion, because the hot summer had aggravated the conditions responsible for infantile diarrhoea, he spoke strongly. He told the woman that unless a small baby was given clean milk and food it would become ill and he added that the flies from some of the evil-smelling manure dumps were contributing to the trouble. 'The Council should take action,' he said. 'Well, why don't you get on the Council and see that it is done?' wailed the woman. 'That's just what I will do,' replied my determined and irate father. A by-election was held in Seven Kings Ward on 27 April 1905 and my father stood for election.

Then began one of the most curious one-man party contests, for my father had only one plank to his political platform. 'If you vote for me, I will clean this place up for the benefit of yourselves and your families,' was his promise. He certainly created an impression. Small boys regarded this tall man, making the strange assertion that there was some relationship between flies on a manure heap and a baby's illness, as a great joke and they followed him in the street calling 'Summy-e-kill and Summy-e-don't'. I have often wondered why at my own election my political opponents have not invented a similar cry.

The Ilford Recorder of 14 April 1905 noted in the editorial columns that: 'Doctor Summerskill has entered the municipal arena at Seven Kings in order to do battle with the plague of flies and the smells which vexed the souls and worried the bodies of the inhabitants of that district during last summer.'

My father, without a political machine of any kind at his disposal, failed in his courageous attempt. His partner and many of his patients, who included some Councillors and their families, did not regard this excursion into politics at all favourably. Indeed many went so far as to assert that his 'folly', as they called it, would damage the practice seriously, for a patient could have no confidence in a crank. On the other hand, the poor, particularly the women, regarded my father as a hero who had defied authority and taken up the cudgels on their behalf. Subsequently my mother assuaged the feelings of many of the former critics by producing successful 'Cantatas' which contributed quite considerable sums to the local hospital.

She was intensely loyal to my father and her answer to any criticism of him was always, 'If you believe a thing is wrong then you should say so.' She never subscribed to the view that discretion might be the better part of valour in any circumstances, and she firmly believed that to fail to denounce injustice was the essence of moral cowardice.

While later in life in the clash of party politics I found her precept an unfailing source of strength, nevertheless it was a different matter for a child with its immature judgement to make dogmatic assertions. I have been banished from a classroom on many occasions, and directed to sit outside the door for daring to contradict my teacher on some question because I believed that she was mistaken. Most teachers unfortunately find life much easier if children bear some resemblance to peas in a pod.

One feature of that election which contrasted sharply with my own political jousts was the form of transport my father used. Cars were still in their infancy and beyond the means of country doctors, and my father used a 'Victoria', a carriage with open sides and a coachman mounted in front high above the occupants. I would often accompany him on his visits, and on a warm sunny day enjoy being gently carried round the country lanes to the accompaniment of the driver's loving commands to his horse.

But I have never campaigned in one, except in 1954 when the Fawcett Society decided to protest against the failure of the Government to introduce equal pay and, in order to emphasize this anachronism, the women Members of Parliament of all parties rode in ancient carriages which had been stored in various parts of London. Irene Ward, the Conservative Member for Tynemouth and I occupied an old Victoria and as we trotted round Parliament Square to St Stephen's Entrance, I sat back with a sleepy contentment as the old coachman's skilled hands manœuvred the horse through the heavy traffic. The sun shone, Big Ben looked benign, and I privately recorded that there was much to be said for the gentle unhurried pace of a horse-drawn vehicle. Indeed, I felt very much at home.

As the coachman handed me out at St Stephen's Entrance he asked: 'Do you remember when you were last in this carriage, Dr Edith? This was your father's carriage and I was his coachman in Seven Kings. Although you always wore two bows in your hair, you were a bit of a tomboy. Do you remember falling out of this carriage in a lane in Chadwell Heath?'

After a few happy carefree years spent at Westgate-on-Sea – carefree for us children – it was decided that we should move back to London.

My father said that it was a sad commentary on our society that he and his family were economically dependent on disease that therefore they must return to a big city. He had conducted a small practice besides helping to establish a clinic for the tubercular in Margate, and this had served to strengthen his view that preventive medicine offered the most satisfactory approach to disease both for patient and doctor. He believed that a system was basically wrong in which the poorest, by reason of their poverty, were deprived of treatment in the early stages of a disease.

Our stay by the sea had been marred for me by one incident at the Church of England village school where we had been sent after an enjoyable but, in my father's view, risky few terms at the Convent des Oiseaux. I had been banished to the cloakroom for talking and had taken myself home. When my mother sent me back to apologize, the headmistress, without giving me a chance to speak, gave me a stroke of the cane on each hand. I knew nothing about the sadistic impulse but I sensed that this woman would find the exercise more to her liking if I cried. 'Don't cry. Don't cry,' I said to myself. My hands were clenched and as the class commenced I opened them and peeped at the red weals on my palms.

I had always been surrounded by affection and this isolated incident did not inflict any psychological trauma; at least I hope not. It did, however, have one lasting effect. It taught me the real meaning of the misuse of power, for that small black figure with her yellow face and twitching lips showed no mercy; she was not prepared to allow the victim one word in her own defence, whether it transpired that the defence was valid or not. This was the important lesson that I learnt from my first and last dose of corporal punishment.

2

Home Life: The Seeds of Feminism are Watered

On our return to London my father established a practice in Lee, South-east, and my sister and I were sent to Eltham Hill School. It seemed to me that my carefree childhood had vanished and now I had entered on a period of my life when examinations dominated the lives of children and parents talked of preparations for the future. Not that I was averse to talking about the future. I found life – its various activities and future prospects – of absorbing interest, and no doubt this was in part due to the physical proximity of people who were closely concerned with the comedy and tragedy of existence.

Our home life was not isolated from that of our neighbours for our sitting-room communicated with the waiting-room and the consulting-room, and it was customary for the various members of the family to stroll through to chat with my father after consulting hours and thereby meet patients waiting for medicine or having a gossip with the dispenser. We learned through the patients all about the activities of the neighbourhood and, if such a thing as class consciousness existed, at least we were unaware of it.

The grammar school I attended did its best with the teachers at its disposal but then as now the most striking shortage was in the science subjects. I was fortunate in having a brother two years older than myself who helped me with my Chemistry, but with a certain reluctance; he would never believe that my ignorance was due to any shortcomings on the part of the teacher but only to my failure to pay sufficient attention in class. My mathematics teacher, Miss Canter, was a brilliant woman but I never liked figures and it was only due to her wonderful devotion to her job that I succeeded in passing in mathematics in the London matriculation examination, a hurdle which had to be cleared if one was to enter London University.

Little Miss Canter, physically tiny and angular, but with a needle-sharp brain, would stay after school hours, sitting beside me at a desk, intent upon bringing my Geometry and Algebra up to matriculation standard. And I would go home conscious of my debt to her, but above all, with a sense of guilt that I had been the cause of this wonderful woman arriving home late night after night. I could not visualize then the empty rooms or flats which awaited many of the single women teachers and the lonely isolated lives they led. It was not until years afterwards when I had a daughter of my own and I invited one of her dedicated teachers to a meal at the House of Commons, that she confided to me how lonely and empty are the home lives of many single women employed in our schools. Teachers get a little tired of mixing with each other outside school and the girls' parents, afraid of what they often wrongly believe is the teacher's intellectual superiority, rarely offer them hospitality in their own homes. One of my regrets is to have failed to have discovered where Miss Canter lived after her retirement. My only explanation is that after leaving school I sincerely believed that Miss Canter must have sighed with relief that she no longer felt obliged to spend some of her spare time coaching me, and that the very last thing she would have desired was to have me call upon her.

I suppose I was a boisterous, noisy, talkative girl because whenever I give the prizes at a girls' school and identify the gym mistress, I seem to hear the voice of my gym mistress at school admonishing me with 'No horse play, Edith, *please*.'

While I was still at school the 1911 Health Insurance Act was introduced and there was a tremendous outcry from doctors who were bitterly opposed to 'the encroachment of the State'. For years my father had been critical of a system whereby the sick poor were compelled by virtue of their poverty to delay seeking medical advice until it was too late. This particularly applied to women and children, because the mother who handled the limited housekeeping money would be reluctant to call in a doctor until she was convinced that home medication had failed.

The proposed Insurance scheme provided medical care only for those earning under £400 a year and did not include the dependants in the family, but at least it was the first step in the right direction. However, the hostility from certain elements in the medical profession was very great; although those doctors who regarded the scheme not only as a means of helping the patient but also of providing the doctor with some measure of economic security, endeavoured to convince their fellow medical practitioners of the wisdom of the proposal. After surgery hours my father called a meeting of the neighbouring doctors and successfully persuaded them to support the new service.

Another campaign which my father followed with considerable satisfaction was the struggle for women's suffrage, and whenever some incident hit the headlines he would comment, 'The franchise is all very well, but we must also establish the economic emancipation of women.'

This was incomprehensible to me at the time, but it certainly influenced me later and at least I was increasingly conscious, as the years passed, that my mother did not envisage me simply as a housewife. Time and again when I would peep into the kitchen and she was there, she would say sharply: 'You are not wanted here; go upstairs and get on with your work.'

I don't know how she expected me to cook if I never learned, but I can only presume that she never anticipated a time when there would not be an ample supply of domestic labour. I recall that I had only one cooking lesson in my life at school, when I was taught to make coconut pyramids. Mine were a little burnt but I ate the lot on my way home. Years later, when I found it necessary to be able to turn out at least one satisfying meal in an emergency, I asked a friend what was the quickest and at the same time a tolerably attractive meal one could prepare. She advised the omelette and let me into the secrets of good omelette making. That teaching has apparently proved successful if one can judge from my husband's culinary taste.

Whenever we visit a restaurant whether at home or abroad, and he is left to make a decision, he asks the waiter 'What omelettes have you?' The more feline of my readers may comment, 'Poor man, he knows nothing else.' I would reply that for the most part other women have cooked for him, women who have devoted time and energy to the art but apparently either my effective lesson or my husband's loyalty has not destroyed his taste for omelettes.

When my mother used to direct me to go upstairs she was indicating my bedroom where I always worked. My father believed that whenever possible the strain on the circulation should be relieved and that bed provides an ideal place for reading.

To this end he bought my brother and me each a bed table which could be adjusted to hold books and papers. I found this a most satisfactory arrangement because it enabled one to enjoy an even temperature instead of sitting in front of a gas fire and suffering from partial overheating. I have adopted the same methods of work in my adult life although on occasion it is a little difficult to explain to strangers that, although I am enjoying the best of health, I appear to spend most of the morning in bed.

It was some years before I realized that my father's feminism was not entirely an intellectual exercise. My paternal grandfather was a wool merchant with a family of five children, three boys and two girls. The only one of my father's sisters whom I knew well and who was a frequent visitor to our home was Aunt Eleanor. She was a good-looking woman two or three years younger than my father to whom she bore a striking resemblance. She was widely read, a ready talker and indulged in an astringent wit which highly amused my father, but was not regarded very favourably by my mother who, in the course of the years, had been the victim of her sister-in-law's sallies.

Wit of this kind is rare in women, for to be successful the perpetrator must be aggressively minded and prepared to wound. Undoubtedly to my childish eyes and ears Aunt Eleanor was a most unusual woman and highly regarded by her brother. My father had told me that while it was accepted that the boys in his family should be educated and trained for some business or profession, it was the custom for girls, denied any serious education, to receive a small amount of pocket-money pending the advent of some young man prepared to ask for their hand in marriage.

My father saw this cruel convention accepted in his own home, and it grieved him to see one of his sisters bearing a striking resemblance to himself, with a first-class intelligence far superior to any of the sons, denied a higher education. Nevertheless, no exceptions were made by his father. The times demanded one treatment for boy children and one for girls irrespective of their potential intellectual gifts.

Every vacation my father would return home from his medical school and there see his brilliant young sister trying, but failing, to devote herself to the only creditable occupation, namely, that of dressing herself attractively and arranging her hair in order to attract the eye of an eligible husband. Her sister, also highly intelligent, succumbed to convention and married, but Eleanor stubbornly refused to comply. No doubt she used that devastating tongue too freely in the presence of possible suitors and frightened them off, and they failed to realize that while the girl might be above their heads intellectually and be difficult to handle during the courting period, nevertheless, she would have made a most exciting wife and mother.

However, Eleanor did not marry until in her middle age, but the memory of that frustrated girl denied the right to fulfil herself or even the means to earn her livelihood, never faded from my father's mind. He had decided that there should be no similar discrimination in his own family, consequently he showed an undisguised eagerness in following the activities of women who succeeded in work outside the home.

The First World War swept aside many of the old conventions and the 1919 Sex Disqualification Removal Act opened the doors of Parliament and all the professions with the exception of the Church. The wholesale slaughter of young men made it imperative that medical schools should accept women in order to ensure an adequate supply of doctors. Therefore there was little difficulty in securing a place for me in King's College and subsequently at Charing Cross Hospital for my medical training.

Some time after the war Charing Cross Hospital closed its doors to women and later like other hospitals agreed to accept only a small quota. All kinds of curious excuses have been given for this, but the only logical one that could be accepted without question, namely that women had failed to make efficient doctors, is not among them. So powerful are the forces of prejudice and custom that they have prevailed despite the shortage of doctors, and now in her extremity Britain has to rely on Commonwealth doctors to maintain her medical services.

3

Medical Student 1918

I was seventeen in October 1918 when I began my studies in Chemistry, Physics and Biology at King's College. I was tall, with a well-washed round face untouched by cosmetics, which had only one redeeming feature, to my mind, and that was a well-defined dimple in my cheek which was revealed when I smiled. As I seemed to find much to laugh about no doubt my only claim to any attractive feature did not pass entirely unnoticed.

When my father first took me to interview the Dean after leaving school, I wore my hair in a pigtail down my back. I understood that women students were expected to wear their hair up and therefore I clumsily wound this pigtail round my head and secured it in place with a number of hairpins. I wore black cashmere stockings, heavy school shoes and clothes which had been provided for week-end wear as an alternative to my school uniform which I normally wore five days a week. Nothing was added to my wardrobe which I had not already worn in my schooldays except a packet of hairpins. I accepted this without question and felt very well turned out having discarded my school uniform.

When I became a medical student I was given £1 a week. This was expected to cover all my meals in town, lunches, teas, stockings, hair do's, and all incidental expenses. Until I was qualified my clothes were bought by my mother. A new frock was an event and only purchased if my wardrobe showed distinct signs of wear and tear. My husband enjoys recalling that it was my black cashmere stockings which first caught his eye. Although I would often long for a little more pocket-money and more glamorous clothes I never felt any sense of resentment. While my father was not a wealthy man no doubt he could have afforded to give me more; perhaps his views on the subject were unconsciously influenced by his knowledge of the amount of pocket-money given to his sisters. They received sixpence a week until they were married.

The first term's work at King's College appeared to my mind to be little more than an advanced standard of school work with some boys of my own age added to our classes. I attended every session whether theory or practical, took copious notes and returned home immediately after the last lecture to a meal followed by homework.

It was during a physics lecture on the morning of 11 November that a messenger hurriedly entered and whispered to the Professor. A normally shy, reserved man, his face was suddenly wreathed in smiles and he turned to the class and announced, 'An armistice has been signed; you are dismissed.'

We leapt from our seats and yelling with excitement and relief poured out into the Strand. The pent-up agony of the First World War was shared by the whole nation and my generation were especially sensitive to the appalling casualty lists. Young servicemen friends would visit us before leaving for the front and cynically toss a coin to decide whether they would return to see us again. My brother, a source of constant anxiety to us, was serving as a 'surgeon probationer' on a submarine despite the fact that he had not yet reached his finals at Guy's Hospital. The armistice marked a rapid transference of young men still officially in the Services, to the Universities in order not to waste any more precious academic time. Our lecture-rooms filled with sophisticated young officers in uniform, khaki, Navy or Air Force blue, who looked very striking by contrast with the raw boys so recently emerged from the schoolroom. It was scarcely surprising that these men found some difficulty in settling immediately to academic work and every concession was made by the authorities in cases where 'civvy life' was found difficult to assimilate.

The silence of the lecture-room hitherto broken only by the

voice of the lecturer, the scratching of pens or a discreet cough, was now often desecrated by some amusing aside which a Serviceman found irresistible. My attention was diverted and I made no attempt to hide my enjoyment if I heard any comment which appealed to me. On the other hand the ex-Servicemen themselves found me a source of amusement. Never in the trenches had they envisaged a girl with a well-washed face and a plait fixed with ugly hairpins round her head. The boldest would enjoy himself by tapping my shoulder when the lecturer's back was turned to the blackboard and whispering, 'Forgive me, Miss Summerskill, but does this belong to you?' and offering me a hairpin which had fallen on the floor. My propensity for scattering hairpins became a kindly joke, so without informing my family I visited a little hairdressers' shop off the Strand, had my hair 'bobbed' and daringly purchased a little book of *papier-poudre*, a Victorian innovation designed to be applied to the face by ladies on those occasions when an overheated room called for some discreet application to the skin.

The hairdresser cut, shampooed and curled my thick hair and I attended a lecture that afternoon with a massive 'bob'. In the course of a dry exposition on some aspect of chemistry a note was passed to me. 'I shall miss the hairpins but I like the new you. The three little maids have a similar hair-style. I have two seats for *The Mikado* tomorrow night. Will you come and see them with me?' I looked around and there was the smiling face of one of our attractive Servicemen in Air Force blue. Could he possibly know, I thought, that I had never been to a West End theatre, only pantomimes at Christmas. Should I reveal that I simply do not know what he means by the 'three little maids' and that *The Mikado* is just an unfulfilled dream to me?

This introduction to Gilbert and Sullivan was followed by other invitations from our Service students starved for so many years of the colour and music of the theatre. They were also in possession of a gratuity from a grateful country which seemed to be burning a hole in the pocket and consequently, as I was assured so often, I was helping them to spend in the best possible way what might otherwise be wasted. I frequently visited the Opera, the Ballet and all the little theatres in the Strand, recklessly cutting my lectures in favour of matinées. My youth and inexperience prevented me from taking this new and exciting life in my stride, and combining it with an amount of work adequate to the demands of an examiner. Consequently my work suffered to such a degree that I failed my examination in June. My father would accept no excuse. He was well aware that I had undergone some kind of metamorphosis for I made no attempt to hide the fact that I went to the theatre and dances with our ex-Service medical students; indeed, they visited my home and consequently my parents knew that they were pleasant, cheerful young men with no ulterior motive.

Nevertheless, my father was quite irrational or so I thought; after all I had, as a wartime measure, entered King's College at seventeen when the usual age was eighteen, and therefore it could scarcely be argued that I had wasted much time. I wanted to explain, but I was tongue-tied in his wrathful presence, that I was still the same eager, questing young woman desirous of becoming a doctor but I had been diverted for a short time by the novelty of London life, and that none of the young men meant more than just pleasant companions. My father's disapproval was such that he cancelled my seaside holiday as he considered that in the course of the year I had enjoyed sufficient relaxation. I shut myself in my room with my books, took the first medical in September and passed.

On reflection, this reaction of my Victorian father might have been expected. His own life appeared to be one of unrelieved work. A singlehanded general practitioner never experiences the glorious sense of being free of responsibility. He is called out at night often unnecessarily, has fixed consulting hours morning and evening and is available for domiciliary visits at all other times. If he does arrange a holiday he must find a *locum* who can be trusted to conduct the practice, for the principal is still responsible for the actions of his deputy. When my father was not working he rested in order to conserve his energy. He had no organized leisure and theatre visiting would not only involve late nights but also the necessity of providing a deputy in his absence. He was abstemious, and only cider was permitted to be brought into the house; this stemmed from his experiences at the hands of an early Victorian whisky-drinking, tyrannical

father whose behaviour during frequent attacks of gout terrorized the household. My father did not hide from his patients
his objection to alcohol. One of his most devoted patients whom
he visited regularly, was a prosperous publican suffering from
cirrhosis of the liver who, after my father had finished his
examination, would offer him some refreshment. A refusal was
anticipated and both doctor and patient parted good friends.
My father used to tell me that if he had accepted the offer on
any single occasion, he was convinced that his patient would
have lost confidence in him.

My father had no time for what he called the 'slacker'; men
and women must make their contribution to the community
in some form or other, otherwise they merited his contempt.
Having tea in the House of Lords and listening to comments on
various aspects of sport and the manifold ways in which a man
can use his leisure hours, I often reflect on the unremitting toil
of the conscientious family doctor.

However, even the routine of a doctor's life is interrupted
occasionally. Among our patients was a Civil Servant who had
a secret obsession; he believed that he could discover a formula
guaranteed to break the bank at Monte Carlo. He was not
insane for he was an exemplary worker, but all his evenings
and week-ends were directed to working on his 'method'. He
would hoard his money during the year, much to the distress of
his long-suffering wife and then disappear to Monte Carlo
during his annual vacation to test his theory, and his frequent
disappointments far from curing him only seemed to whet his
appetite to try yet again next year. He had bought himself a
roulette wheel and a green cloth and night after night the wheel
was spun and he recorded the numbers.

My father was called in at intervals of increasing frequency
to see the wife who was understandably suffering from a nervous
condition attributable to her husband's obsession. Finally, in
desperation, she asked my father to tell her husband that if he
did not give up this abnormal way of life she would leave the
home. My father did as he was bid and was agreeably surprised
to find that the ultimatum distressed the husband and he reluctantly agreed to his wife's terms. But, he said, he must get rid
of the wheel. 'I shall never be able to restrain myself if I know

B

that it is in the house. Take it away – anywhere you like, doctor,' he pleaded. And so it came about that one day my father arrived home with a roulette wheel and a green baize cloth, all of which fitted very well on to our long Victorian dining-room table. From then onwards, every Sunday evening, our dining-room resembled a private gambling club although only the family and a few friends were present. I should hasten to add that the amounts which changed hands at the end of the evening were insignificant. Years afterwards when I invited Jeffrey Samuel – my future husband – to visit our home for the first time, I suggested supper on a Sunday night. My husband is a Welshman brought up in a Nonconformist home and I had forgotten about our roulette sessions so it was not without amusement that I observed his expression when I introduced him to my father who was in charge of the game for the evening.

It was customary for students at King's College who were attached to Charing Cross Hospital to attend lectures given by members of the staff on pet subjects other than medicine. One night, with two of my friends, we went to hear a talk on 'Old London'; as I found it a little dry I made some audible comments to my friends. Immediately, there was a command from a senior student behind, 'Be quiet or you will have to leave.' And so I heard my future husband's voice for the first time. Subsequently he invited me to have tea in the Strand Fuller's, a favourite haunt of students, and very successfully erased that first formidable impression. However, it was not until we were strolling along the Victoria Embankment one summer evening and he sang in a glorious Welsh tenor: 'I'll Walk Beside you', that I told myself that it would be exceedingly pleasant to have that voice near me for the rest of my life.

My future husband had a very limited allowance but this did not prevent us from enjoying the shows at the Coliseum and the little theatres in the Strand. With other students we would toil up to the gallery of the Coliseum where a seat cost 6d. and in a bout of extravagance enjoy a pit seat in the Strand for 2s. 6d.

4

Marriage: Some Thoughts on Marriage and Childbirth

In 1925 about a year after I was qualified I developed an illness, accompanied by a low daily temperature, which baffled my father and his medical friends; accordingly I was sent to Charing Cross Hospital where a full investigation could be conducted.

I found myself in the charge of a house physician, qualified at the same time as myself, in whom I did not have complete confidence and I felt I was amply justified in this when long afterwards I was told by my husband that she had informed him that the differential diagnosis was between typhoid and lymphatic leukaemia, both of them near fatal diseases. I recovered without any final diagnosis having been made, apart from some form of influenza which had failed to clear up following a period of overwork.

During my illness Jeffrey and I had talked about marriage and it seemed to us that at twenty-four and twenty-nine we ought to know our own minds. Marriage is not a state into which a man or woman should enter lightly; it is the most important decision which one is called upon to make in life, for the right or wrong partner can determine one's future.

In my own case I felt complete confidence in the outcome; we had known each other for six years and our compatibility flowed from a difference in temperament but a similarity in tastes and sympathies. I regard the act of marriage as a contract undertaken by two people who are in complete harmony and who have arrived at a stage when after careful consideration the decision to live together for the rest of their lives represents the climax of a very loving association.

For this reason I consider that an engagement period, widely publicized and marked by the exchange of a ring, as inimical to a free and unfettered decision which can be reassessed in the light of events. I believe that it is a mistake for young people to commit themselves to an engagement long before a marriage is contemplated or presents a practical possibility. A man and woman must be free to make the most important decision with which they will be confronted in their lives without having to look over the shoulder to see the reaction of their neighbours and friends, if they wisely decide to change their minds before the irrevocable step is taken.

No doubt the acquisitive instinct combined with commercial pressures will continue to uphold the present conventions. The wise girl, however, should question whether the acceptance of a ring and the consequent commitment it implies, is conducive to the most honest appraisal of the chances of a successful marriage, or whether, it does not rule out second thoughts. The breach of promise case stems from this custom, and I can think of no action more basically insincere, than one conducted with the maximum publicity, for damages for a broken heart by a young woman who must already loathe the man who has rejected her.

As it is probable that now the number of boys is in excess of that of girls the breach of promise case will die a natural death; let us hope so.

Jeffrey and I, having decided that the moment had arrived, saw no reason to delay our wedding. I went to London, bought a dress in beige chiffon and a hat and shoes, and together we found a ring of platinum inlaid with diamonds. The wide gold conventional wedding ring had to my mind always smacked of some primitive survival.

Whenever we attend other people's weddings my husband and I are fortified in a belief that undoubtedly our arrangement was the ideal one. Both Agnostics, we were concerned lest his family who were devout, with one brother-in-law a vicar in the

Church of England and another a minister in the Methodist Free Church should be hurt by our rejection of the conventional marriage service. I was also reluctant to have our wedding solemnized in a register office for the ceremonies I had attended in those places unlike those of today had always been associated in my mind with rather squalid surroundings. We arrived at a happy compromise. As Jeffrey could not leave his hospital until the day before the wedding my father and I obtained a special licence and a brother-in-law performed a short service in a little church made beautiful with flowers skilfully arranged by my mother. We had a delightful lunch of about twelve relatives and friends and later went down to the hot sunny shore and bathed from the sands which had so enchanted me in my childhood. And we stayed where we were in the house at Westbrook where my parents were spending the summer for two weeks instead of rushing off to a strange place for a honeymoon; after all we did propose to spend the rest of our lives together and there was plenty of time for adventure.

In the nineteenth century my husband's family (originally farmers) had played a prominent part in developing Llanelly, where his grandfather built ships and later participated in founding the tin plate industry. My father-in-law captained his own sailing ships and no doubt recurrent shipwrecks and the loss of his brother at sea had something to do with his encouraging his own sons to enter other professions.

At the time of our marriage my husband was a medical officer in a mental hospital, Peckham House in South London. He had a special talent for dealing with the psychiatric patient and as he often commented shrewdly, 'My mind is the kind which understands the working of theirs.'

Peckham House was a private mental hospital which provided accommodation for paying patients; however, as the treatment of the mentally sick improved the London County Council used some of the accommodation for the care of the poor and mentally ill. I was a frequent visitor to the hospital – indeed it provided a background for our courting – and we never failed to join in the Christmas festivities for many years after my husband had left.

The Board of Control paid regular visits and their advent

was often marked by some little incident which was discussed in the staff rooms until the next visit was due. On one occasion a rather pompous representative, who kept his bowler hat firmly planted on his head throughout his tour of the wards with the doctor, arriving at the padded cells inspected one where a well-educated, elderly woman completely nude sat and stared at him. Suddenly she shouted, 'Don't you know that its good manners to take your hat off when you meet a lady?' It is a mistake to think that a certified patient can be forgetful of the courtesies of life.

When we were married it was suggested that we should live in a house adjoining the hospital but I, already mindful of the needs of a possible family, hankered after the heights of North London. And so we found a house in Finchley where our son was born and I experienced 'twilight sleep' and the expert ministrations of Everard Williams an obstetrician and my former teacher from Charing Cross Hospital. Since that time I have ardently campaigned for analgesia to be available for all women who want it. James Simpson who first gave a woman an anaesthetic at childbirth was denounced by his medical colleagues for the use of chloroform as being dangerous to health, morals and religion; nearly a hundred years later poor women were denied the use of analgesia. This was partly due to the fact that the bulk of midwifery practice was in the hands of midwives, who were considered insufficiently qualified to administer anaesthetics.

But in 1932 the British College of Obstetricians and Gynaecologists undertook to conduct an investigation into the matter. The published result of the experiment caused a sensation, for while the College regretfully concluded that, at the present stage of our knowledge, chloroform should not be used by midwives acting alone, it recommended that the giving of gas and air in an apparatus invented by Dr Minnitt was a safe and satisfactory method of inducing analgesia.

It occasioned general dismay on the part of the public and the most progressive section of the medical profession to find that the British Medical Association did not welcome this recommendation wholeheartedly. One doctor putting the case bluntly expressed the view that, 'this recommendation could

mean another nail in the coffin of the general practitioner'.
Many people, both lay and professional, had been persuaded
that the attitude of the Association arose from its desire to
protect mothers in childbirth from the harmful effects of an
anaesthetic.

Of course the midwife of the twenties bore no resemblance to
the woman who attempted to deliver a child by pulling on the
arm, the Mrs Gamp, portrayed by Dickens, who with her snuff
and her bottle of gin, 'went to a lying-in or a laying-out with
equal zest and relish'.

When I entered the House of Commons in 1938 this aspect
of our maternity services distressed me, and in order that the
public should be reassured I asked the Minister of Health on
27 July 1939 whether his attention had been drawn to the
resolution passed by the British Medical Association deprecating
the use of an analgesic by midwives; and whether, with a view
to countering any ill-effects of this resolution, he would make
a statement to reassure the public as to the complete safety of
the administration by midwives.

Mr Elliot was clearly sympathetic to my attitude and made
an answer of unusual length in order that the general public
should fully understand the position.

Eleanor Rathbone, the Independent member for the combined English Universities, a very fine woman who, when I
first entered the House, had given me invaluable advice based
on her long experience of public life, put a supplementary
question. She asked whether the Minister of Health would
undertake that this merciful practice of allowing midwives to
administer an analgesic would not be interfered with by the
selfish attitude of a certain section of the medical profession who
expressed their views the other day?

The Minister of Health answered: 'It cannot be interfered
with; that is the ruling of the Central Midwives Board which is
the statutory authority.'

After this interchange Eleanor Rathbone and I had a long
chat in the Women Members' Room. She was much older than
I, and experienced in the ways of the House, and knew that
reforms such as the one I had just ventilated would not come
unless every opportunity was seized for focusing public attention

on the matter. A native of Liverpool and the first woman member of the Liverpool City Council she had devoted a great deal of time and energy to the question of family allowances which she considered of paramount importance to the over-burdened mothers of large families.

I asked her what should be my next step in this new campaign. Sitting back and holding her spectacles which were attached to her neck by a long silver chain she said, 'Always remember this; twenty-five years generally elapses between the inception and the fruition of a new idea.' But I reminded her that nearly a hundred years had elapsed since Simpson had given a woman an anaesthetic at childbirth, and still women could say after their confinement, 'The pains of hell got hold upon me.' This reluctance of certain elements in the medical profession to support wholeheartedly the recommendation of the British College of Obstetricians and Gynaecologists led me as an immediate step to write my first book *Babies without Tears*, the case for analgesia at childbirth.

There were those who tried to discredit 'twilight sleep' by asserting that it affected the child at birth. Of course only the trained man or woman, whether in charge of a midwifery case, or in the operating theatre, should be permitted to give an anaesthetic. Provided instruction is given by an expert there is little to fear.

Certainly if one can judge from the roar which my nine-pound son emitted soon after birth there was no indication that the painless childbirth which his mother had recently experienced had affected his vocal powers.

His loud cry was the signal to my husband, sitting on the stairs, that his first child had arrived in a rude state of health.

I find it difficult to understand why women wish their husbands to attend the last stage of childbirth. The presence of a husband or mother, or other near relative, can afford great comfort in the early stages, but a woman does not present a very pretty sight at the end of the ordeal and personally I would prefer to leave the final stages of labour to the imagination, even in the case of a doctor-husband.

I am inclined to think that there are some young husbands who, anxious to compensate for some great human experience which they are denied, find some vicarious satisfaction in witnessing a childbirth. It is a little similar to the reaction of the male members of some primitive people who retire to bed when a baby is expected.

It would seem that the middle of the twentieth century has ushered in bottle-feeding as a normal practice, and the breastfeeding mother is regarded as a 'square', to use the current expression, for those who do not conform to new-fangled notions. If the trend continues I suppose in the dim and distant future the breast could become a vestigial structure.

The woman who works outside the home may well protest that the whole economy of the home is geared to her earnings, and that the experts assure her that the modern baby foods are equal in nutritional value to breast milk. Nevertheless, I believe that the mother and child are denied a great emotional experience if the opportunity to feed a child is lost.

While there is no proof that a child suffers physically if it is fed on artificial milk, nevertheless, this is the great opportunity for a mother and child to revel in the closest association, and even if it is impossible for the psychologist to assess whether the child does, or does not, benefit, I believe that the experience for the mother is of inestimable value. Apart from the deep sense of satisfaction she experiences at the time, this intimate contact establishes a relationship so powerful that a love and a sense of responsibility for her child is generated which is unquenchable. For this reason I welcome the attitude of those concerned with the care of the unmarried mother who advise that breast-feeding should not be encouraged in mothers who have agreed to adoption. It would be heartrending for a girl to have to part with her baby on economic grounds after having experienced the satisfaction of feeding her child herself.

Without any doubt, feeding my own children was one of the most satisfying of my many satisfying experiences.

5

First Steps in Politics: Some Thoughts on the Place of Women

Through all these years I had given much thought to questions concerning mothers, children and the inferior position of women. But it was not until 1933 that these ideas took me into politics, and even then it was what I may call the back door.

One morning in 1933 during surgery hours my telephone rang and the Medical Officer of the Wood Green Urban District Council, the area in which I practised, telephoned me. He invited me, on behalf of the Maternity and Child Welfare Committee to join the Committee as a co-opted member. Both national and local politics had, until the 1919 Sex Disqualification Removal Act, been conducted almost exclusively by men, and even some *ad hoc* committees dealing with matters concerned with the welfare of women and children were composed of men. The 1919 Act did not appreciably change matters, for custom and prejudice die hard and it was not easy to persuade male selection committees to nominate women candidates. In many areas this is still the case but at least time has modified the attitude of some younger men towards those women anxious to serve in the political field.

Even some of the most prejudiced male councillors, prodded no doubt by more enlightened officials, acknowledged that women could have views which might prove useful in the administration of the Maternity and Child Welfare Act of 1918.

Nevertheless, how was it possible to use their services if the normal channel through nomination and election failed to function? It was deemed necessary therefore to introduce a measure, opposed to all democratic principles, which enabled a local authority to by-pass the electoral machinery, and empower it to co-opt two women, with special knowledge of the subject, on to the Maternity and Child Welfare Committee. And so it came about that I said to the Medical Officer of Health 'Thank you, I shall be very pleased to serve', and forthwith entered the world of politics. I had on numerous occasions spoken on various aspects of preventive medicine which included of course the care of the mother and child; and I learned that a fairly effective speech was like dropping a pebble into a pond, the ripples travelled quite a long distance.

My husband and I have never been associated with any political party other than the Labour Party. My husband was born in Llanelly, a place with a strong radical tradition, and after many years of Liberal representation in Parliament, it changed to Labour.

The industrial conditions in South Wales were notorious and unemployment so widespread that the General Strike of 1926 stemmed from the general discontent of the miners. The plight of the miners' families compelled girls to seek work in domestic service in the big towns for lack of any light industry suitable for women in the mining valleys.

My husband's uncle, a doctor, practised in Llanelly and my husband, accustomed when at home to giving his successor some help, had an opportunity of observing the physical and moral deterioration of the industrial workers. While his parents had always been firm supporters of the Liberal cause, my husband recognized that Liberalism had failed to measure up to the problems of industry; therefore the Labour Party should be given an opportunity to demonstrate how far its policy could alleviate conditions.

In the twenties and thirties I had learned in the consulting-room the effects on the family of long-term poverty and hunger, and that the first aid provided by our social services was as effective as putting a plaster on a running sore; it seemed that

only national planning could effectively deal with the widespread unemployment. With a few medical friends my husband
and I received the hunger marchers from South Wales and the
industrial areas of the North in halls in various parts of London.
Their physical condition was pitiable and their stories of long-
term unemployment and the demoralization of whole communities horrifying in a highly organized society where certain
sections enjoyed unlimited wealth. The urgent need to introduce measures to ameliorate the lot of the people in the depressed areas became the theme of my early speeches. I argued
that this could only be effected by political means, through the
Labour Party, which had a well-considered policy, unlike the
two outmoded parties, the Conservatives and the Liberals, who
had failed to adapt their policies to the grave unemployment
situation.

There was little difficulty in securing the rapt attention of an
audience, because a speaker on behalf of the Labour Party concentrated on the basic needs of the family: food, housing,
employment and security in old age; for these were the
controversial topics of the day.

The powerful influence of men like George Lansbury and
Jimmy Maxton and many other pioneers stemmed from their
ability to speak with absolute sincerity on conditions with
which they were familiar because they had lived among the
poor. My knowledge was, I felt, almost first-hand, for the
ordinary people had flowed through our home for many years,
consequently there was no suspicion that I might be just a
middle-class 'do-gooder' remote from the real lives of the
working people.

One of my close friends was Fred Messer, the Labour Member
of Parliament for South Tottenham, a great propagandist,
whose eloquence and whimsical humour delighted the people
in his own and neighbouring constituencies. He was largely
self-educated. Reading occupied his spare time and he de-
voured books on law, politics and social administration, combining this with his social work for the people of South Tottenham. His wise counsel and unfailing championship of the poor
and needy had led the South Tottenham Labour Party to

select him as their parliamentary candidate, and he was returned as their Member by a large majority in 1929. They were
confident that this indicated a permanent swing to the left, but
the 1931 National Government election proved the fickleness
of the electors when even South Tottenham rejected its doughty
Labour champion. This was a blow for the Messer family for
their income ceased with the dissolution of Parliament. Fred
Messer showed no bitterness; he felt that the people had been
the victims of a gross deception and that it was understandable
that they should change their allegiance, on being informed
by the Conservatives that their Post Office savings would be
imperilled if they voted Labour. There was nothing for it but
for Fred to re-educate his flock and show them the error of their
ways, and this was most effectively done at open-air meetings.
He would often ask me to accompany him, and on Saturday
nights we would stand on a box at the corner of Green Lanes
and St Ann's Road, Harringay, opposite the Salisbury public
house. Occasionally we would have a third speaker to relieve
us, because the meeting could well last two to three hours if a
sizeable crowd collected. Indeed at closing time the meeting
might be joined by some loquacious individuals whose knowledge of politics was nil, but who had persuaded themselves
with each successive drink that they were citizens of outstanding
merit.

In the course of the evening as Fred or I was speaking, the
door of the bar would be pushed open from within and two,
or three grinning men would appear and point at us; they would
withdraw for a few moments and bring others from inside to
behold this, to them, excruciatingly funny spectacle. I suppose,
Fred Messer, shorter than average, and I, taller than average,
standing in turn on a box exhorting the crowd, which during
the early evening only consisted of a handful of Labour stalwarts, may have presented a picture calculated to appeal to the
sense of humour of a 'four-ale' bar on a Saturday night.

However, nothing deterred us; we regarded these oafs as
being beyond the political pale, therefore not worthy of our
notice. The meeting always wound up with questions. Then the
smart Alec in the crowd, egged on by his pals, would endeavour
to embarrass the speaker by plying him with questions which

had no relevance to the subject; or somebody with a chip on his shoulder would demand to know the answers to his particular personal problem. I always knew that in the event of some individual being aggressively offensive the crowd would be on our side.

Although it seemed that my speeches, based on my knowledge of the lives and needs of the ordinary people and spiced by an occasional anecdote, were received with appreciation, I decided that my limited knowledge of economics and Marx should be remedied. Consequently, I acquired three volumes of Marx from the library and various books on economics. This caused me to question my qualifications as a political propagandist, for I found the economists pursuing lines which were totally at variance with each other; and Marx such heavy going that I would fall asleep after a chapter.

I confided this to Harold Laski. He replied, 'If you find anybody who says he has read and digested the three volumes of Marx then you know that he is a liar. Only a few men in the world have done that.' I learned that economics was not an exact science and that the most erudite men would analyze the economic ills of the world and arrive at totally different conclusions. Moreover, they never seemed deterred by failure; it is this aspect of the economist which baffles me; he never confesses to having made a faulty diagnosis and a wrong prognosis or an equally false assumption as to the initial causes of some economic collapse.

Those trained in an exact science feel a little bewildered by the assertions and counter-assertions of so-called trained economists. Governments still pin their faith to some new economic nostrum which is produced periodically by some bright young man. Only time proves that his alleged magic touch is illusory. Parliament has heard many members in their time expound the economic problems of the country and it is striking how very few succeed in holding the attention of the House; politicians are a little sceptical of those whose opinion has hitherto only found support among their own coterie.

In 1934 Fred Messer asked if I would like to contest the Green Lanes Ward of Harringay at the forthcoming Middlesex County Council election. He hastened to add that the Conservatives had always held it and that it was regarded as a hopeless seat for Labour; I was being offered the vacancy he explained because no man wanted it and if I refused then the seat would go by default.

I did not hesitate; I accepted. I had become resigned to the fact that sex played a most important part in determining the eligibility of a candidate whether in local or parliamentary elections. I was a woman, and therefore at this stage of our social progress, I had to accept the fact that my reproductive organs were what decided my political future, not my experience, knowledge, intelligence, or indeed any other qualification which should commend a potential candidate.

The Green Lanes Ward consisted of long rows of terrace houses belonging to working people of the artisan class. Fortunately for me I had firm friends in the various sections of the Tottenham and Wood Green Labour Parties, together with some grateful women patients living in the Ward. I led this magnificent little band of women up and down the hilly roads of Green Lanes knocking on every door; we confined our case to the social problems of the family and the power invested in the Middlesex County Council, which, exercised in a humane and generous manner, could alleviate the lot of many unfortunate people.

We met with some rebuffs, particularly from men, who I suspected felt that our activities outside the home might put ideas into the heads of their wives. The selfish husband experiences great satisfaction in possessing a wife who is always at his beck and call, constantly at her post when he returns, whatever the hour, and anxious to minister to his comfort.

The thought, that she might ever hanker after interests outside the home or give a thought to the welfare of those other than himself and his family, not only alarms him, but he views the whole prospect with extreme distaste. The main sufferer would be himself and any inconvenience or discomfort even of the most trivial nature is anathema to him.

Consequently even the sight of women in a canvassing squad suggested a veiled threat to the creature comforts of some of the men who opened the door to us. On the other hand there was the warm human response of the politically minded man who

on seeing our Labour pamphlets promptly said, 'You're wasting
your time calling on me. I'm with you.' Nevertheless, this was
a Tory ward, and it had been drummed into me by old hands
at electioneering that it is the policy that counts and not the
personality of the candidates, and that therefore, whatever
personal contacts we made, our chances of success were remote.

It poured with rain on the day before the election, but heed-
less of the conditions we marched forth. Weary by now I made
the unforgivable blunder of knocking on the door of a known
Tory supporter. Fuming with suppressed annoyance he opened
the door and shouted 'Go and look at yourself, do you think
anybody would vote for you.'

I took a long look at my bedraggled appearance when I
returned home, at my hair plastered round my shining face,
and for the first time I agreed with a Tory. My appearance did
not inspire the least confidence.

It seemed that there were those who took a different view.
To my relief, and to the delirious delight of my supporters we
won with a very healthy majority, and my husband and I had
the magnificent experience of being dragged in our car from
Tottenham Town Hall back to the Green Lanes Committee
Rooms. A well-to-do supporter presented us with a bottle of
champagne, and as many as possible drank to the health of the
Labour Party.

Ted Willis, an active and eloquent member of the South
Tottenham Labour League of Youth made a great contribution
to that victory and was one of the young stalwarts of the Party
who helped to pull the car. In 1964 when he entered the House
of Lords as a Labour life peer I had the pleasure of being one
of his sponsors. He gave me a beautiful champagne glass which
he said had been scrounged as a souvenir by another member
of the League of Youth on that memorable night. While I
appreciated his friend's gesture in returning the glass I was
quite sure it did not belong to me. On the one hand we could
never have afforded such lovely glass at that period of our
marriage, and further it was more likely that cups were used
by most of us for I would not have tempted providence by
anticipating victory.

The next election of the Middlesex County Council called for less strenuous efforts for I was returned unopposed.

Meanwhile, between the elections I spoke in the Guildhall on a number of topics concerned with social legislation. On one occasion I spoke with some passion on the gross exploitation of our nurses and demanded that their salaries should be increased and a forty-eight-hour week introduced.

The Victorian attitude, still much in evidence was exemplified by an elderly man just in front of me who jumped to his feet and cried, 'Don't listen to this woman; she's a revolutionary. If you make this concession, she will be coming and asking for silver baths for the nurses next.' The philosophy of this member was shared by many. They believed that a woman's vocation should provide sufficient satisfaction irrespective of the conditions of her service. I suspect, however, that that irate Tory was more concerned with the prospect of an increase in his taxes if we did do justice to the nurses.

The question of Equal Pay was raised very frequently by women speakers; most men treated the matter lightly and with some amusement, contenting themselves at an annual confer-ence with approving a resolution calling for the rate for the job. They seldom recognized at least publicly, that there was any relationship between political and economic equality unless the work being exploited happened to belong to their own sex.

Hannen Swaffer, the journalist, sent me a scribbled verse during a meeting in which I had raised the matter; it read:

> To Edith
> Altho' the words I have to say
>   Are never meant to vex
> A woman's only chance of equal pay
>   Is change of sex.
>
> H. S.

But equal or not women were becoming more and more interested in public affairs. In the thirties, The Friends' Meet-ing House, in Euston Road, was the most popular place for large indoor meetings concerned with social questions like the High Maternal and Infantile Mortality rates; the case for Painless

Childbirth; Disarmament and Collective Security; all of which commanded a large audience of women not necessarily affiliated to any political party. Trafalgar Square offered ample accommodation for outdoor meetings the size of which could not always be predicted; furthermore, topics of urgent national importance could be ventilated there with the maximum publicity.

Many years later, in 1957, Trafalgar Square saw one of the most inspiring meetings I have addressed; it concluded a march for women only to protest against Nuclear Weapon Tests, and nearly all the women wore black coats or black sashes. They were there because the fall-out from these tests was responsible for contaminating milk, which in turn affected the bone marrow of children with the attendant risk of a grave increase in lymphatic leukaemia. The *Manchester Guardian* of 13 May 1957 reported:

'Undeterred by heavy rain, women marched from Hyde Park to Trafalgar Square yesterday afternoon in a demonstration organized by the National Council for the Abolition of Nuclear Weapon Tests. As they assembled, a loud peal of thunder heralded the downpour and for the fifty minutes of the march down Park Lane, Piccadilly, and the Haymarket, the rain did not cease. Many of the women wore black sashes over their plastic raincoats, others were in complete mourning, and many carried home-made banners reading 'Stop The Tests', and 'Save Your Child'. Some of the women had come in contingents; there were twenty-five from Watford who have been lobbying the House of Commons, under the leadership of their prospective Labour candidate, Renée Short, continuously since Wednesday, and Friends from various Quaker centres, readers of *Peace News* and teachers from the London area. At one point it was possible to see that the march stretched the length of Haymarket and contained between 1,500 and 2,000 women. In Trafalgar Square, Mrs Joyce Butler, M.P., Miss Vera Brittain, Mrs Steele (wife of the Quaker who is planning to immolate himself in the Christmas Island explosion), and Dr Edith Summerskill, spoke to a crowd of three thousand. They were greeted with clapping from the men who were in sympathy with their aims but who had not been allowed to join the march.

The first of the women speakers said that they represented ordinary housewives and mothers who were not Communists or fellow-travellers, but who wanted the Government to stop the tests on Christmas Island in the interest of humanity.

'Miss Brittain, the authoress, who followed said that after a visit to the United States she knew that Americans were looking to this country for a lead "Britain has not lost her soul nor her moral authority," she said, "I appeal to you with all my strength to give a moral appeal to the United States and to the world."

'Dr Summerskill who criticized the Press for not having given publicity to the demonstration said that, "radiation from the bombs would have the effect of rendering women sterile and it was the maternal function which determined a woman's whole approach to life".'

I criticized the Press because there was a widespread feeling that to oppose nuclear tests and nuclear warfare could only be playing into the hands of the Soviet Union who were engaging in repeated tests; consequently it was assured that any demonstration must be Communist-inspired and did not warrant Press coverage. Whereas this demonstration of women in a November downpour was in fact a protest of mothers against the folly of polluting the atmosphere with fall-out, which the most eminent scientists of all nationalities warned provided a hazard to health and even life itself. But this is looking ahead, and some of those Trafalgar Square meetings in the thirties were in their different way quite as dramatic.

6

Some Elections: Birth Control:
Marie Stopes

Shirley, my red-headed, cream-complexioned daughter, was born painlessly in 1931. My tripartite existence, which encompassed politics, medicine and my family could only be sustained by securing help in the home of a kind which left no doubt in my mind that when I was away my children were receiving the care and affection which would be an adequate substitute for my own.

When my son was about a year old Agnes Wakeford, a red-cheeked plump little Scottish girl of twenty-two, entered our household, and now many many years later she is a treasured friend living not far away from me and Shirley and showing a consideration for our welfare equal to that which she lavished on us all when the children were small. The only occasion I remember on which she remonstrated with me about my behaviour was when I tried to insist on dieting after feeding my last child for eight and a half months. This she considered tantamount to neglect; I should wait until the nine months had elapsed she insisted. I meekly acquiesced.

All through the years Nana has stood on guard over her charges and, during the six years of war and the subsequent evacuation from London, she seldom had relief; although this could well have been available, she never left them until I could go and take charge during her annual holiday. Service of this kind is rare these days; for this reason many professional women with families find it difficult to pursue their professions after a family has arrived.

The secret of our successful relationship lay I think, in a capacity to co-operate and enjoy the children together without either experiencing a twinge of jealousy. Night after night I would ring up from the House of Commons, when the children were suffering from one of the childish complaints and receive a reassuring report from Nana.

I was fortunate also in having a doctor husband who was devoted to his family and who generally lunched at home, except during his Army service. Consequently, the children were in touch with their father during the day.

This day-to-day contact has always seemed to me important and I have never favoured boarding-schools. I find it difficult to understand how people with a pleasant home, and a congenial family life can send a child to a strange school where, even assuming the parents know the head master or mistress, frequent changes in the staff may result in some inefficient or undesirable individual playing an important part in their child's environment. A home where the parents are separated or divorced may well prove unsuitable for a child and boarding-school may be considered as a possible alternative; I cannot think of any other reason why parents should deny a child home life during its most sensitive years.

With my rear safeguarded as it were I could take an increasing part in politics in those years of great change at home and abroad. My first opportunity to contest a parliamentary election came in 1934. A by-election was pending in the Conservative stronghold of Putney owing to the death of the sitting Member who had a majority of 21,146. Even with this kind of majority a by-election offers an excellent opportunity to a young inexperienced candidate because the Party headquarters' machine goes into action on her behalf. Moreover, supporters from other constituencies are free to come and help and if it so happens that the by-election coincides with some national controversy then the contest assumes a special interest and the outcome may be regarded in the nature of an opinion poll.

Although Labour's chances in Putney were considered negligible nevertheless there was no shortage of potential candidates anxious to be considered, for the short list. The man selected was the author of a book which the National Executive Committee of the Labour Party had decided might diminish the chances of the Party at the election. Consequently his candidature was not endorsed. Many members of the Putney Labour Party supported the original choice and resented what they considered was the puritanical approach of the National Executive. Nevertheless, they agreed to convene another selection committee and to compile a second list of candidates. My telephone rang one evening and I was asked if I would allow my name to be added to the list. The Agent of the Party had on some occasion heard me making a strong appeal for Labour support in a near-by borough and it occurred to him that I might be approached.

The large number of men anxious to be considered for a candidature generally ruled out a woman's chances. I could only assume that the local Party having taken umbrage at the rejection of their first choice decided to shock Transport House, the headquarters of the Labour Party by including even a woman on the short list.

The selection was made on a cold misty autumn night and on arriving at the Party rooms at Putney I found the national agent, Mr William Shepherd, standing on the pavement; from this I gathered he was *persona non grata*. I felt instinctively that as he looked at me he was considering the electoral chances of a woman and that he had concluded that I would probably lose the deposit. As one of seven or eight on the list I waited my turn clutching a little speech which I had carefully prepared, fearful that I might forget certain points to which the Committee might attach particular importance.

When I was ushered into the packed, smoky room I saw a crowd of friendly faces peering at me with some curiosity through the haze, for I was the only woman who had been chosen to appear before them.

I had met some of them on other occasions and this gave me confidence. I pushed the speech into my pocket, told them about myself, how and why I joined the Labour Party and what fundamental changes I considered should be made in our social services. On foreign affairs, I believed that our future safety could only be guaranteed by supporting an international body empowered to settle disputes, and consequently it was imperative that nations should be prepared to surrender some measure of their national sovereignty. I then returned to an adjoining room with the other candidates and waited for the voting to take place. Very soon the door opened and the secretary beckoned me. I was chosen.

The succeeding campaign was chiefly remarkable, from my point of view, for the support I received from the women in North London who had rallied round me in my Middlesex County Council contest. They travelled in motor-coaches and we descended on Putney, in fact, as we had done in Green Lanes. They objected only to canvassing West Hill, Putney, where it was reported that the butlers were inclined to be hostile; or course there is no stronger Tory than a British butler. I, therefore, undertook to tackle the butlers and I found as my supporters alleged that they were hidebound politically.

I attach great importance to a complete canvass but, in an area like Putney, it was not so easy to persuade women to come to the doorstep as it is in a poorer part of London. In order to encourage them to listen to me I had a record played called 'Little Old Lady Passing By' and I followed this with a short speech through a loud speaker in each street. This melody has a great appeal which apparently few women can resist; it was relevant except that at thirty-three a politician can scarcely be labelled 'old' and I was certainly not 'little'.

My opponent, Mr Marcus Samuel, a wealthy banker, did not find canvassing housewives to his taste with the result that his majority dropped by over 18,000 votes and I lost by 2,663 only.

One profoundly satisfying aspect of this campaign was the opportunity afforded me of proving to the Party hierarchy that women candidates had a vote-catching potential at least equal to men if not in some cases superior. It is a fallacy to believe that women lose votes on grounds of sex; on the contrary women voters if thoroughly canvassed are prepared to support a woman because she is more conversant with the problems of the home. And I have never known a politically minded man vote against a woman candidate because of her sex.

At this election I also met large numbers of people from Fulham who crossed Putney Bridge to help me. These Party supporters had the opportunity of seeing me in action and prompted no doubt by this experience invited me a few years later to contest another by-election following the death in 1938 of the Conservative Member for the West Fulham constituency. I adopted the same methods as I had done in Putney and this time succeeded in being returned to the House of Commons.

However, before this I had a quite different experience in the General Election of 1935. Immediately after the Putney election the Labour Party executive of Bury, Lancashire, approached me and asked if I would accept nomination. I was advised that an industrial constituency would provide me with an experience unlike any which I might encounter in London and furthermore the chances of winning Bury for Labour appeared very promising.

Except for an occasional speaking engagement I knew little of the industrial North and I accepted the invitation of the warm-hearted Bury Labour Party fully believing that their attitude reflected the sentiments of the working people of the town.

I very soon learnt that there were political, social and religious factors in the industrial towns of the North which do not obtain in London, where local public opinion is slow to express itself and where sectarian influences make little general impact.

As a modern young doctor, I favoured the planned family on economic, social and humane grounds. I believe that a pregnancy should be a condition brought about after careful consideration and not as a result of some hasty, ill-considered act, the possible consequences of which might be bitterly regretted immediately afterwards. I regarded Marie Stopes's pioneering work among the poor women of London with admiration and I visited her birth control clinic in Whitfield Street and watched the work in progress. She was subject to the vilest abuse, her enemies implying that her own morals must be suspect otherwise she would not devote her life to work opposed to the laws of nature. It would appear that all over the world nature unchecked has led to widespread disease and premature deaths.

Certainly uncontrolled reproduction has been responsible for untold numbers of preventable deaths of mothers and infants.

Now that the high birth-rate threatens the balanced economy of some countries, desperate remedies are being introduced to bring it within bounds; the contraceptive pill, despite the fact that it has not been adequately tested and pronounced free from serious side effects, is distributed indiscriminately in some countries.

The Graefenberg Ring, which was denounced by health authorities as being harmful to the mother, is now being reintroduced in another guise, although its capacity to irritate the soft membrane lining of the uterus is little less than that of the discredited Graefenberg Ring.

Birth control is now no longer a subject which must be talked about in hushed tones; neither does it have a salacious connotation; it is regarded as a means whereby prudent families and governments keep their numbers related to their means.

The Catholic Church, however, has for centuries condemned the use of contraceptives on religious grounds and a Catholic using any method of birth control other than the so-called 'rhythm method' is guilty of a grievous sin. With the change in world opinion and the obvious need to check the rising birth-rate of countries like famine-ridden India, younger generations of Catholics challenge the authority of the Church and limit their families by more certain means than the 'safe period'.

Successive Popes have been faced with evidence submitted by their priests to the effect that, if the authority of the Church is to be upheld, then some authoritative pronouncement on birth control in tune with current trends should be made. However, custom, prejudice, and the dominance of a bigoted minority in the Church has delayed any clear lead being taken by the Vatican.

Although in London my views on these matters were known and I had contested a local and a parliamentary election without having them challenged by the Catholic Church, I was to discover that the attitude of Catholics in the North whose ancestral roots were in Ireland was another matter. There was a large Catholic population in Bury, and occasionally, in the months before the 1935 General Election, I was asked by one or two people what were my views on birth control. I never sought to evade the issue. I told them that as a woman doctor I believed that pregnancy should not be forced upon an already overburdened mother and that parenthood called for careful planning both for the sake of the parents and the children. I quoted statistics which revealed that the infantile mortality rate was higher among large families in the poorest parts of the country and that the maternal mortality rate rose after the fourth child.

In 1935 the General Election campaign opened peacefully. Although I missed my small army of London Labour women, we went into battle with a resolute body of workers, who felt strongly that a town like Bury with its low-paid workers, back-to-back houses, and limited social services should have 'gone Labour' many years ago. There had been only one brief period, following a three-cornered fight, when Bury had been represented by a Labour Member.

I was opposed by a Liberal, Dr D. Johnson and my Conservative opponent was Mr Alan Chorlton, an engineer. I took a little furnished house in Bury for the family; my husband, having acquired a *locum* for the duration of the election, gave his invaluable help as my good companion, car driver and morale booster. The campaign, which in the initial stages was satisfactory, was well advanced when persistent rumours reached me that canvassing against me was being undertaken by certain Catholic organizations and that their main attack was on the birth control issue. At no time had I ever made a public speech advocating birth control in Bury; the subject was not mentioned in Labour's political manifesto and consequently it was irrelevant to the election.

It was clear that a whispering campaign had been started to discredit me in the eyes of poor Catholic men and women who had responded to my appeal on political grounds, but who would be prepared at the last minute on the instruction of the Church to change their allegiance. Five days before polling day I was asked to receive four Catholic priests who claimed to represent the Catholic Church in Bury. The officials of the Party, my husband and myself were present at the interview. The priests did not mince matters. They told me that they understood that I believed in birth control and that as this practice was opposed to the teachings of their Church they felt that they must advise their members not to give me their support. On the other hand, they recognized that many of their people were attracted to the political policy which I had expounded and therefore they had come to make me a proposition. If I would give an undertaking not to teach any woman birth control in the future they were prepared, from the pulpit, on the following Sunday, to advise their people to vote for me, and they estimated that the number of votes would be approximately five thousand. One of my young officials, white with suppressed anger, looked at me and said: 'Shall we kick them all down the stairs Dr Edith?'

I said that I found it difficult to believe that in 1935 four men, apparently well informed on social affairs, could in the name of religion come to make such an inhuman suggestion and furthermore stoop to exploit a parliamentary election in order to secure their ends. I absolutely rejected their proposition. There was silence for a few moments.

Then I looked at one of the priests who wore an unkempt beard and who seemed to regard me with complete detestation bordering on hate and said: 'This proposal of yours is medieval in conception. Your attitude suggests that if you had the power and the opportunity you would put me on the rack in order to secure your ends.'

The bearded one answered. 'Yes I would. You deserve it.' I asked them to leave the premises.

The following Sunday the congregation were told to support the Conservative candidate and the last few days of the election were spent by my supporters, saddened and ashamed at this appalling manifestation of bigotry, canvassing against the well-organized Catholic Church.

After the result, which I felt certain would spell defeat there were cries of 'Down with Popery'. The next day we left; never to return to Bury.

My London political advisers had certainly not deceived me. There were factors in elections in Northern constituencies undreamt of in London, but I do not think that even they could have anticipated how different these factors would turn out to be.

A powerful supporting team had come from London to speak for me in Bury including George Lansbury, Aneurin Bevan, Hannen Swaffer and on my return they advised me to put my experiences on record in the *New Statesman and Nation* for the benefit of the candidates who might unwittingly be drawn into a similar web.

I did so and in my account of that discussion with the four priests told how I instanced the case of a woman exhausted from tuberculosis, to whom a further pregnancy might mean death, and would most certainly aggravate the disease. 'Was it not immoral to withhold from her such information as would prevent such a contingency?' I asked. To my utter amazement they replied that there could be no immorality comparable with that of sexual immorality. I was unable to decide which was uppermost, their ignorance or their impertinence, when they asked why I did not devote myself to improving the housing conditions of the poor. In their zeal (or it may have been convenient) they had forgotten the Labour Party's fight against strenuous Tory opposition to slum clearance in Manchester.

It struck me as pitiable that four celibates, living in a world of monkish unreality, should attempt to discuss a sociological matter of which they have, admittedly, no knowledge.

I ended my letter with this barbed shaft: 'As a footnote, it is perhaps enlightening to add that the Tory and Liberal candidates (with families of two and three respectively) satisfied the priests that they had no sympathy with "family planning". It would seem that in their case a beneficent Providence achieves the same results as "birth control" does in mine!'

Twenty years later I found that some of my staunchest friends and supporters in my constituency of Warrington were devout Catholics who knew all about my previous experiences and did much to erase any painful memories.

Family planning has never ceased to be one of my interests and I well remember my first invitation to lunch with Marie Stopes.

A pioneer seems to develop eccentricities; these may provide further evidence that she is prepared to defy conventions in promoting a cause which to her transcends all other considerations. This applied to the woman who devoted her life to the birth control movement. Her clothes and her hair always suggested that while she recognized that the community would expect her to be adequately clothed and coiffed, nevertheless this was a waste of precious time and must be achieved as expeditiously as possible.

One always had the impression when speaking to her that her thoughts were on important matters which only she could appreciate and other people were too stupid or bigoted to understand. This conviction is a great solace to a pioneer faced with an opposition buttressed by the moral censure of a section of society. It also provides support and succour when friends express doubt as to the wisdom of pursuing a certain course. Complete confidence in one's cause and a determination to achieve it is the most effective protection against the bigotry and inhumanity of those determined to discredit the one who dares to challenge customs and observances sanctified by religion.

Marie Stopes's courageous denunciation of the unplanned family which spelt poverty and misery to the children, and ill-health and unhappiness to the mother was opposed by the Catholic Church. They regarded her crusade as a threat to their authority over the family. To the salacious and prurient it offered an opportunity for perpetrating obscene jokes which were abhorrent to a cultured woman. Inevitably this cruel persecution told on the victim. Marie Stopes would repeat over and over again to anybody prepared to listen, that she had lost her first child in a nursing-home through the deliberate careless-ness of a Catholic nurse.

At no time did I give any credence to this story; however, the belief was firmly rooted in her mind and no amount of argument on my part would persuade her that obstetrical complications, unrelated to an act of deliberate negligence, may have accounted for the death of the child.

Her second husband, Humphrey Roe, was a patient, under-standing man, whose admiration for his wife's pioneering work, and the moral courage which enabled her to defy her adver-saries, had attracted him to her in the first place. He devoted a large part of his income to financing her birth control clinic in Whitfield Street off the Tottenham Court Road.

Those who hold strong beliefs on certain subjects are inclined to adopt a rigid attitude on other matters which they feel they are qualified to pronounce upon, and another subject on which Marie Stopes felt strongly was smoking.

Marie Stopes lived in a rambling old house where she enjoyed entertaining her friends. My husband and I welcomed our first invitation there because we were both anxious, among other things, to see how this remarkable woman conducted her domestic affairs. Although the charming small son of our hostess was at the table the conversation inevitably turned to birth control and a lively interchange of ideas took place on the next steps calculated to educate the public in the use of birth control clinics. One woman guest, renowned in the journalistic world, anxious no doubt to secure a little copy, and aware that birth control in the thirties was not hot news, asked Marie Stopes what she thought about the legalization of abortion. She was silenced immediately. 'I do not allow such a matter to be mentioned in front of my son,' was the answer.

Then at the end of the meal Mr Roe asked my husband – they were the only two men present – if he would like to smoke. Anticipating my husband's acceptance, Marie announced crisply that under no circumstances would she allow smoking in the living-rooms and that they would have to go outside. As it was a chilly day she suggested that they should go to the greenhouse; and so the two men rose and took their pipes to the inhospitable conservatory.

At the time my only reaction was one of shocked surprise at what appeared to be an act of gross discourtesy. No doubt my displeasure was accentuated by the knowledge that my husband would be denied taking part in the ensuing conversation, which I knew he would have enjoyed. On further reflection I had to admit that Marie Stopes had only been manifesting the courage of her convictions once more.

The Victorians, living in houses such as the one Marie Stopes had acquired, knowing little of the aetiology of cancer of the lung, had for aesthetic reasons forbidden smoking in most of the living-rooms. More recently, although statistics have proved an undoubted association between smoking and cancer of the lung, smokers consider it their inalienable right to pollute the atmosphere in defiance of the non-smokers.

It is recognized by the transport authorities that the non-smoker should be given protection in a bus, and the smoker banished to the top and more non-smoking carriages provided on railway trains; nevertheless an apparently well-mannered man will envelop strangers or his relatives and friends alike in a cloud of smoke without the slightest compunction. Is he unaware of his offensive behaviour or of the silent resentment of the non-smoker at this manifestation of selfishness and lack of consideration? I have never found an answer to that question.

A method of campaigning rather different from that of Marie Stopes was one which I met on my first visit to the Soviet Union in 1932 when I visited health clinics, where elementary hygiene was taught by displaying posters, many of which were so impressive that I brought some home as being worthy of consideration by the British health authorities. One showed a family sitting in a room with mother mending; a toddler on the floor; children sitting at the table playing and the whole enveloped in a haze of smoke for which father, sitting reading a paper, was responsible. The caption gave a warning that polluting the air in this fashion was detrimental to the health of the whole family.

Marie Stopes, a Doctor of Science, knew a great deal about preventive medicine and the obvious connection between the contents of the atmosphere and the condition of the lungs. She saw no reason why two cigars or pipes which gave pleasure to two people should be allowed to contaminate the air breathed by six people and a child, and of course she was right. However, how many of us would allow our convictions to banish our guests to the greenhouse after a very enjoyable lunch?

When faced with this problem today, with a forced jocularity, I do inform my guests that we do not keep any cigarettes in the house; I hasten to explain that it seems to us the very negation of hospitality to encourage your guest to develop cancer of the lung. My good intentions are not always appreciated, for the compulsive smoker invariably asks me if he can smoke his own cigarettes. Consequently, I find myself not only enveloped in smoke, but with the even greater discomfort of knowing that in the eyes of this visitor I have failed in a hostess's first duty, that of providing for the needs of her guests.

7

The House of Commons: Speeches on Cancer and Tuberculosis

It was in 1936 that the West Fulham Labour Party, seeking a Labour parliamentary candidate asked me to appear before a selection committee. This gave me considerable satisfaction for I recognized that the invitation stemmed from my work in the neighbouring constituency of Putney.

However, I was feeling very sore about the treatment I had received at the hands of the priests in Bury. Therefore my speech to the selection committee commenced and finished with a warning that, if they chose me, the same thing might be repeated; consequently I ought to be regarded as a political untouchable in a marginal seat which had never been won before by Labour in a straight fight.

This was greeted by laughter, but my warning, after my searing experience, was not intended to be treated lightly. Despite this they chose me, but in my second speech to the meeting I emphasized that my acceptance was conditional on an assurance from the local Catholic priest that the kind of persecution from which I had suffered in Bury would not be repeated in West Fulham.

I lost no time and next morning I called on the priest. I told him the whole story. A pleasant, young, intelligent-looking man, he listened gravely and assured me without qualification that such a thing could not possibly happen in a neighbourhood where he exercised any power; in fact he was sure that nowhere in London would the Catholic Church conduct itself in such a manner.

In view of this assurance I wrote to the West Fulham Labour Party and accepted their offer of nomination. In 1938 I contested West Fulham successfully at a by-election. I held the seat in the three following General Elections in 1945, 1950 and 1951 when a redistribution of seats took place and the West Fulham constituency ceased to exist.

My Conservative opponent in West Fulham in 1938 was the very popular good-looking local coal merchant, Charles Busby. His coal carts emblazoned with his name in large letters filled me with apprehension for the importance of the service that he supplied must I thought give him an advantage which I could never overtake.

However, Labour triumphed and I had the exhilarating experience of taking my seat at Westminster as a by-election victor. The only other woman on the opposition side of the House was Ellen Wilkinson. Ellen, 4 ft. 11 in. with a mass of fiery red hair and an equally fiery eloquent tongue, had, despite her sex, succeeded in establishing herself as an able trade union leader. Subsequently as the indomitable Member of Parliament for Jarrow she led the hunger marchers to London. She was the brilliant child of a poor family whose struggles to provide for them adequately were often retailed by her.

When I entered Parliament my son Michael was eleven and tall for his age. Ellen was fond of children and she would look up at Michael and say: 'If only I had been given the opportunity to drink fresh milk every day I would be as tall as you.'

There was only one room for women Members, with an adjoining smaller room which boasted a small iron Victorian wash-stand with a tin basin in which stood a jug of cold water. After a chilly wash one pulled out the plug and the water flowed into an iron bucket standing underneath. The Conservative women (Mavis Tate, Nancy Astor, the Duchess of Atholl, and Joan Davison), Ellen and I accepted this crude arrangement without complaint and indeed with some amusement, and it was not until Jenny Adamson came into the House and demanded modern 'ablutions' that a change was made. Nobody, other than women Members, were allowed to use our limited

c

accommodation and the rule was strictly observed. The Duchess
of Atholl, looking a little like a Victorian governess would, on
changing her frock, present her back to the half-open door to
enable her maid, standing in the corridor, to fasten the numerous small buttons which only the maid's practised hand could
manipulate. Lady Astor and Mrs Tate were outspoken feminists
and Nancy never tired of telling us what a very unpleasant time
she endured as the first woman in the House, following her
husband's elevation to the peerage and her subsequent election
to his Plymouth seat. She alleged she suffered most at the hands
of Winston Churchill who had opposed women's suffrage and
consistently snubbed the first woman to take her seat. I cannot
vouch for the truth of her favourite story, that when, after many
years, she asked Winston Churchill why he had cut her, he
retorted, 'When you came into the House I felt that you had
entered my bathroom and I had no sponge with which to
defend myself.' She replied, 'You're not handsome enough to
have worries of that kind.'

I have observed that a story travels quickly round the Palace
of Westminster, and, when finally the person to whom it is
attributed is taxed with it, he often replies that that is the first
time he has heard it.

Be that as it may, on my first day in the House I was astonished
to observe Lady Astor who sat on the corner seat of the second
bench below the gangway, flick Winston Churchill who sat
immediately in front of her, contemptuously on the head with
her order paper. She regarded him then as a discredited
politician and I suspect never forgave him for past slights. He
turned round fiercely and castigated her. I should have liked to
have heard how he responded to her flippancy. Those were the
'dark and lonely' days when Winston Churchill had few close
friends with the exception of Robert Boothby, Duncan Sandys
and Brendan Bracken, who after a speech of his would ostentati-
ously rise to indicate support and follow him out of the
Chamber.

I was astounded at Nancy Astor's crudity; she was completely uninhibited and her running commentary on her life,
her friends and her family were almost embarrassing to her
listeners. Her language was such that a trade union member

accustomed to the language of the pits or heavy industry would think nothing of responding with expressions equally earthy.

Soon after I took my seat the Spanish Government invited Ellen Wilkinson and me to visit the refugee camps which sheltered the women and children, for the Spanish Civil War was attracting world-wide attention and the Republicans were having to contend with powerful foreign forces. Unfortunately Ellen developed influenza and I had to go alone. I met the Spanish Foreign Secretary, Señor Del Vayo, in Barcelona and he described the appalling plight of the increasing number of refugees, and after I had visited some camps it was clear to me that he had not exaggerated the case. Not for the first time I ruminated on the tragic helplessness of mothers and children driven from their homes by war.

I had just retired to bed one night in Barcelona when I heard a bomb fall. It sounded rather close. 'This is it,' I thought and I was comforted in the knowledge, as I have been on other occasions when it seemed that the chances of survival were uncertain, that the family, guarded by Nana, were together. However, it was an isolated incident and the next day I went behind the lines on the eve of the crossing of the Ebro battle and at first hand witnessed the cool courage with which soldiers, dedicated to a cause, can face possible death and disablement with a smile and a joke.

On my return to London I found a cable from the USA asking me to go over under the auspices of a relief organization to tell the Americans about the conditions of the ordinary people in Spain. This was my first visit to the USA and my first introduction to the organization of a lecture tour, unpaid of course, which included addressing universities and women's clubs during the day, public meetings at night and travelling overnight by train to the next assignment. In between I enjoyed the generous and overwhelming hospitality of the people. I wilted and resolved that in the future when I visited this great adolescent, uninhibited country I would ask for a copy of the itinerary beforehand.

Parliament, with its conventions and protocol, seemed a little like a boys' school which had decided to take a few girls. Woe betide the new-comer who forgot the rules. Fortunately I had acquired the capacity from early childhood to mix easily with patients of all ages and both sexes. When as a medical student I used to visit patients with my father whoever answered his knock would be informed, 'The patient is lucky today, he has got two doctors', and with a confidence born of familiarity with the home and its occupants he would enter with me following close behind. Then up the stairs, into the sick room, with a hearty assurance to the patient that he was indeed lucky to have two doctors. Laughs all round would follow because everybody knew I was still a student.

This early conditioning enabled me to mix freely under all circumstances. In the male community of the Commons and Lords I found no difficulty in establishing friendly relationships. I was more bewildered by the building which houses our legislature and it took me six months to grasp the geography of the Palace of Westminster and to find my way about the hundreds of rooms and miles of passages. I decided that it was no good standing shivering on the edge of the debating pool but that I would plunge in quickly and get the first shock over. Consequently I made my maiden speech on the Budget in April 1938 and then decided to assimilate the atmosphere thoroughly by listening day after day to debates until the place became as familiar to me as my own home. My speech was elementary and to the point and on reading Hansard the next day I found it fairly comprehensible. This surprised me for I experienced my full share of first-night nerves, and my chief recollection is of Mavis Tate's face as seen through a mist.

A woman speaker rarely burns much midnight oil on inventing aphorisms or flights of oratory; her biological structure may have something to do with this approach to speech-making. Nature has planned her primarily on strictly utilitarian lines and her functional sense rejects the superfluous.

I admired a speaker, capable of quick and witty repartee, and it took me a little time to learn that brilliance of this kind which often led to the injection of malice into a conversation did not necessarily indicate wisdom.

Those who say they dislike the House have never deliberately accustomed themselves to it. The silent Member is to be found spending his time in the various rooms ancillary to the Chamber; consequently he fails to acquire the habit of speaking. Captain Edward Fitzroy, the Speaker in 1938 when I entered the House, bore a strong resemblance to my father, and he ruled the House with a rod of iron. If he did not finish the questions down on the Order Paper for the day, we were reprimanded for asking too many supplementaries. If one was to judge by the way he occasionally reproved Eleanor Rathbone I do not think that he approved of women in the House. One cannot blame subsequent Speakers for failing to exercise such a strict discipline for I do not believe that the House would tolerate such firm handling today.

His successor, Mr Clifton Brown, a complete contrast to Captain Fitzroy, was a charming man. He asked me to read his feminist speeches and gave me a slip of paper on which he had written the references in various Hansards in order that I could look them up in the Library. After this we were firm friends and I found no difficulty in catching his eye if I wished to speak. The late Speaker, Sir Harry Hylton-Foster, deserved the sympathy of the House. An able lawyer, he was chosen during a Conservative period of office and was invited by the Labour Government to continue, despite the fact that there was a considerable number of Labour Members who felt strongly that the time had arrived to choose a man from the Labour benches. I always felt that he worked under considerable strain. Of one thing I am quite certain I am entirely unsuited to fill the office of Speaker. To pronounce on a delicate situation arising from the clash of party politics so as to satisfy everybody is entirely beyond my powers. I would find it very difficult to hold my tongue at a moment which called for some relevant intervention.

However, this comment is entirely superfluous for at least another twenty years must elapse before the House of Commons is prepared to accept a woman Speaker and thus the complete equality of the sexes. Nevertheless, a woman Member of the House is never subject to any adverse discrimination. As a Member she enjoys not only all the rights and privileges of the House, but the loyalty and support of every other Member irrespective of party in the event of any infringement of these privileges.

I saw an example of this when a new Irish Member, Mrs Patricia Ford, in her ignorance of the customs of the House, was prevailed upon by the *Daily Express* newspaper to write a chatty article on her experiences. She described certain personalities and how, during an all-night sitting, she had peeped into a room where Mrs Bessie Braddock and I were having forty winks, and how the sound of our snores rent the air. I am afraid this was a little piece of journalistic licence for Bessie Braddock and I were not together at any time in that room during that night. To the outsider this may seem a light-hearted piece of fun, but the House knows that the standards of Parliament can only be protected if the Members are permitted to conduct their lives within the precincts of the House without interference by individuals or the Press. This article was clearly a breach of privilege. The matter was raised in the House and Mrs Ford without reservation and with the full approval of the Members, apologized. This was a matter concerning three women and the only object of the article was to poke fun at two of them; nevertheless, a packed House took the matter very seriously indeed because it represented a breach of privilege and a Member's rights had been infringed.

The standard of House of Commons humour can be Fourth Form. It was customary for men to wear top hats but, when speaking, to uncover their heads and place the hat on the seat. The first occasion on which I saw the House rocking with laughter was when a speaker, one of the few men still following this custom, sat down on his hat.

When I qualified as a doctor in 1924 I was entered in the Medical Register as 'Edith Summerskill' and this entry remained unchanged after I married. Subsequently after a few tedious arguments with returning officers I contested elections in that name. This was entirely in order, because a candidate is entitled to fight an election in the name by which she is publicly known.

When, however, I was returned to Parliament a question was raised, unofficially, as to whether I could take my seat, as a married woman, in my maiden name. As I was the first woman who had sought to do this, no precedent had been established. Sir Stafford Cripps, K.C., a former Attorney-General in the

Labour Government, was deputed to discuss the question with me.

It was not without some secret amusement that I found myself confronted with a brilliant lawyer, a little out of his depth in questioning me on a matter which he had never encountered before. There was no statute law or regulation, and little custom to guide him, for only a few married women, at that time, had entered Parliament.

I helped Stafford Cripps when he returned to those shadowy figures behind the scenes whose prejudices had prompted them to ask him to raise the matter with me. I asked him whether a death certificate would be invalid if I signed it in any other name but Edith Summerskill? He had to admit that it would.

'Well,' said I, 'if the General Medical Council considers that I am competent to undertake professional work, calling for a high sense of responsibility, without changing my name on marriage, why should parliamentarians be more obdurate?' This clinched the matter and Stafford Cripps had nothing more to say. It seemed that both he and the Chief Whip, William Whitely, bore me no ill-will for they were my sponsors when I was sworn in.

Shirley and Michael also took my name and Shirley on being returned for Halifax entered Parliament in her maiden name.

Young male newspaper reporters are never tired of investigating this aspect of my marriage. They have no scruples about asking my husband questions calculated to irritate some men. The 1966 Election and Shirley's return to Parliament prompted a reporter from a local paper, the *Hampstead and Highgate Express* to telephone Jeffrey to ask him what he thought about 'this flaming feminism'. My husband answered, according to the newspaper report, 'A man doesn't change his name when he marries, so why should a wife change hers? If my wife had asked me to change my name, I might have protested. I can't see any logical reason for a woman to take her husband's name.' He went on, 'It's quite unfair for the children always to take on the name of the father. I was glad to make my small contribution to redress the balance.'

In the twentieth century, actresses, who have established themselves in their own names, retain them after marriage, yet young women who have built a great reputation for themselves in sports still lose their identity on marriage to some man who is entirely unknown to the public. It is significant that all these women are very young, perhaps the older and more sophisticated professional women are more capable of handling those young reporters, who feel that to fail to adopt your husband's name is an affront to their own ego.

It did not take me very long to get into my stride in the House of Commons. It so happened that the Government introduced a 'Cancer Bill, 1938', and this gave me an opportunity of expressing my views on the position of the housewife of modest means denied any right to free medical treatment unless she was working outside the home. Walter Elliot was Minister of Health, and no doubt some of my indignation flowed from the knowledge that he was a doctor and therefore he should use his knowledge and authority to challenge the old order.

On the Second Reading of the Bill I observed, 'I look upon this as a niggardly method of treating a tragic problem. We find armaments research and industrial research being subsidized while medical research has to go on year in year out on insufficient means. The poorer you are the more likely you are to die from cancer. It is a horrible commentary on our society that the incidence of cancer in the generative organs of women increases with increasing poverty. . . . The rich woman gets treatment immediately whereas the poor woman has to postpone treatment. What is the barrier between the poor woman and the doctor? The barrier is an economic one; that is the answer. You will be told by many people that the housewife does not want to know the truth, but the real reason is that the housewife will economize on every penny. She will have some symptom but she will put it off because she knows that the money is necessary for feeding her children . . . The average housewife is a most unselfish creature. She often postpones getting medical treatment until it is too late.

'What is the Minister going to do? I can assure him that in the industrial areas the smallest medical fee is too high. . . .

How is the Minister going to get her to the doctor before she is sent to the radium centre? I suggest that you have to get rid of the economic barrier between the patient and the doctor. What I am going to suggest – I know the Minister of Health has gone to sleep.'

Mr Elliot jumped to his feet: 'I have heard every word of the Hon. Lady. I am listening very carefully to all she says. I do not agree with any of it, but I am very carefully listening to what she says and it is a little hard that she accuses me of sleeping.'

Dr Summerskill: 'If the Right Hon. Gentleman agrees with nothing that I have said then I can assure him that he does not understand the problem. . . . He does not understand the people. . . . The only solution of the problem, the only long-term solution, is to introduce a State medical service in the country so that the people can have a free health service just as they have free education. I know that there is nobody on the Government benches who will listen to that. It is a kind of Utopia but we know that that Utopia will probably come during the next ten years. My final word – I shall not bore the Right Hon. Gentleman any longer with these unpleasant details – is that he should consider including the dependants of the insured person under the National Health Insurance Act, so that these women may have an opportunity of consulting a doctor in the very important first stage of the disease.'

In 1939 I had a further opportunity in a debate on Tuberculosis to emphasize the importance of introducing a comprehensive National Health Service which would include the women and children and so enable them to obtain advice and treatment in the early stages of a disease.

During my visits to North Wales on holiday with my family I had often discussed the high tuberculosis rate with local people and I was shocked to learn with what fatalism they accepted the situation. They appeared to regard it as an act of God not as an omission on the part of the local authorities to provide better houses and adequate accommodation in sanatoria.

In 1939 the long-awaited report from a Committee convened to investigate Tuberculosis Services in Wales, presided over by Mr Clement Davies, was published. The revelations it made shocked the country and the report was debated in the Commons.

I spoke, although it was strictly a day for Welsh Members.

'I ask the forgiveness of my Welsh colleagues for intervening in this debate which is purely a Welsh matter, but I feel that they will realize that in my case there may be special circumstances because I have the great good fortune to have a Welshman for a husband. From my very close association with Wales I claim to have made a particular study not only of Welsh culture but of the social services which obtain in Wales today. I think that if the Hon. Member who conducted this inquiry also conducted an inquiry on the same lines in England or Scotland, the English and Scottish Members also might have cause for alarm and surprise. . . . While the report has directed the attention of the House to the gross neglect of certain small authorities, it is in my opinion a glaring indictment of the Ministry of Health and the Board of Education. What impressed me most during the debate was the extreme complacency of the Minister himself in the face of this alarming report. I want to know why it is that no immediate action has been taken and why in the face of the result of this inquiry which occupied two years, the House is told again that it must be content with another Conference, further inquiries and letters from the Central Government to local authorities. . . . We are told in the report that there is evidence that the local authorities in some districts have taken no action in regard to the disinfection of houses which have already housed tubercular people. It is well known that in a house in which a tubercular person has lived, six weeks after the death of the patient, the walls of the room in which the patient died have been scraped and the dust has been found still to contain virulent tubercle bacilli. The report reveals that there are houses throughout Wales which are never disinfected after the death of a tubercular patient. Is the Minister of Health going to content himself with another inquiry and leave these disease traps to infect the next innocent occupants? There is only one paragraph in the report – the only paragraph which I will not endorse – which contradicts what might be regarded as the housewifely attainments of the

Welsh woman. On the one hand we are told that she is an excellent housewife who keeps a hovel which is little better than a pig-sty in order, but on the other hand we are told that she is much too fond of the tin-opener when feeding her family. Welsh housewives are perhaps – and I say this after due consideration – the best cooks in England and Wales; in fact I believe their pastry cannot be beaten even by that of the Yorkshire housewife. Therefore I cannot believe that the bad nutrition which obtains in many families is due to Welshwomen using the tin-opener. . . . In the report it says that 40 per cent of the cows give a positive reaction to the tuberculin test. It says that those authorities who are giving innocent children in the schools infected milk of this character are callous – I would say criminal. Something must be done immediately about cleaning the milk supply of the country. . . .

'The report says that in one village the sanitation is in the same condition as when the Romans left it in A.D. 400. . . . The sewage is still discharged untreated in its crude state into the river; the privies are still emptied into the garden where the pump stands. We are told that because of a certain fatalism in Wales the people refuse to leave their homes and enter a sanatorium and that is why there are 16 per cent of patients dying of tuberculosis in institutions in Wales and 34 per cent in England. The reason is that there are not sufficient beds in Wales. . . . In Cardiff the patients are ready and eager to go to a sanatorium but when the report was drawn up nearly five hundred could not find beds.

'I believe that another factor which militates against patients going into a sanatorium is the fact that immediately they are admitted the Public Assistance grant is decreased. Grants to the dependants of a tubercular person should be taken out of the hands of the Public Assistance Committee and administered on a much more generous scale. I want to draw attention to the importance of early diagnosis. In Wales in 1936 of the new adult patients found to have tuberculosis half were advanced cases and 58 per cent were people between fifteen and thirty-five. There can be no question that the best approach to this disease is to facilitate early diagnosis. The incidence among the young women is extremely high in Wales. The young married

women in Wales have between them and the doctor an
economic barrier. One of the finest methods of preventive work
that the Minister could do in order to reduce the morbidity and
mortality rate from tuberculosis would be to include the dependants of the insured worker under the National Health
Insurance Act. This is a very urgent reform and one which in
Wales, where there is so much poverty and distress, would be
very welcome.'

Ten years later the National Health Service was introduced
by the Labour Government and women and children dependants
of the insured worker were no longer debarred from obtaining
early treatment on account of poverty. But before this happened
the people of Britain had to go through six years of war.

8

The War Years: Women at Work

On the day that war was declared I was listening to the recital of the emergency regulations while my thoughts wandered to my family and the changes which must inevitably take place in our family life. The children would have to be evacuated. My husband, I knew, although he was forty-three, would join up in the R.A.M.C.; his detestation of Hitler and all his works was so profound that he had already told me that in the event of war he would offer his services. In that event I would help to take over his work in the family practice.

As these thoughts were racing through my mind, a Conservative Member beckoned me behind the Speaker's chair, a place where it is customary to have a short chat.

He suffered from arthritis and he had often asked me for a prescription which he could send to have made up by the chemist in Bridge Street. As I approached him I felt very sorry for him. Personal problems at this time were bad enough, but to have some chronic illness superimposed was a trial which I had been spared. 'Well, this news does not help you,' I said sympathetically. 'Is the pain bad today? Would you like a prescription?'

'Oh, no, this time it has nothing to do with me. I want to help you. I have a sister in Canada with a lovely estate; I want you to choose four children from among your friends and send them with Michael and Shirley to be looked after there until the end of the war. I can promise you that they will want for nothing; she can provide good nurses and governesses and the best of everything. And I should be honoured if you would allow me to arrange the passages.'

I was quite overwhelmed. Apparently the small contribution which I had made to this old man's comfort had prompted him to make this generous offer. No doubt he was astonished that I did not accept forthwith, for the horror stories of German preparedness against our comparative defencelessness were being spread freely. Such a thing as sending my children to another country, among strangers at such an impressionable period of their lives did not enter my head. However, I thanked him, said I would discuss it with my husband and telephone him that night.

Another Member also wanted a word with me, Sir Jocelyn Lucas, the Conservative Member for Portsmouth South, a famous breeder of Sealyhams, realized that he must reduce his kennels in war-time when people would be too preoccupied with getting sufficient food for themselves to find extra food for pets. Sir Jocelyn asked me if I would accept one of his Sealyhams for the children. While recognizing his very kind thought, I refused his offer; I could not contemplate adding a dog to our family responsibilities.

On returning home I told the family what had happened. Nana looked apprehensive. 'Well, Nana, what do you feel about this? Would you like to go to Canada with the children?'

Nana almost broke down. 'Oh, no, please don't send us. If we were torpedoed, I can't swim; I might be able, in a life-belt, to hold one child up but do you think I could hold two?' I was glad to find that there was absolutely no support for breaking up the family by sending the children abroad. Then I told them quite casually about Sir Jocelyn Lucas's offer of a Sealyham and how I had refused it. Immediately there was a howl of protest. How could I be so unfeeling? Poor dogs; they must have good homes in war-time and our home could take at least one. I appealed to Nana. I knew she had once told me that she would do anything for children, but she was not quite so attracted to animals. Michael and Shirley turned to her for support and of course she succumbed. So I had two phone calls to make, one refusing the generous Canadian offer and one to Sir Jocelyn telling him that I had changed my mind. And so Happy joined our family, was evacuated with the children, cared for devotedly by Nana, and beloved by us all until he died of old age.

My constituency, West Fulham, was heavily bombed and Lord Haw Haw, the notorious William Joyce, who had lived in Chelsea and Fulham, would warn us on the radio during his periodic broadcasts that that night such and such an area in Fulham would be hit. Our people jeered. Families were bombed out time after time and we used school halls to accommodate them during the night. As I walked among them, old women, who had been completely dispossessed perhaps for the third time, would shout, 'Are we downhearted?' and the answer would come back in a roar, 'No.' Never at any time did one person suggest that we could no longer 'take it'.

After the fall of France it seemed to me that it was rather incongruous that a woman like myself could have a husband in the army, children evacuated, but be entirely defenceless, if the moment arrived when instructions went out that everybody must resist to the uttermost.

A few other like-minded women and I founded Women's Home Defence. This consisted of a body of women of all ages, shapes and sizes, who would be prepared to learn to shoot in defence of their country. Already women were permitted to join the Home Guard but only in a non-combatant capacity. They could cook, type and soothe the tired warrior, but in the event of hostilities nobody knew exactly what their function would be, if it came to fighting on the beaches and in the streets.

It seemed logical that these women should be taught to use a rifle even if there were not, as we were told repeatedly, enough to go round. In the event of a male Home Guard being killed then his rifle should be used by whoever was near him at the time, irrespective of sex. We could not in these circumstances expect the enemy to be scrupulous about the sex of his opponents. Hitler did not differentiate in the gas ovens. This new conception of women's role in the event of an invasion was not confined to London. Groups of Women's Home Defence were formed in most of the big towns and first-class, experienced ex-Service men offered their services as instructors. Sympathizers lent the London group The 'Empire', Coventry Street, in which to have recruiting meetings and a large room near by was available every Saturday afternoon for instruction. While the capacity of the women was indisputable and they became first-class shots, we were not unaware of our incongruous appearance. Lying on their tummies in the Coventry Street room, handling vintage rifles, were women of all ages, fat and thin, blondes, brunettes and grey, married and single, clad in breeches, trousers or skirts, yet all fully determined that 'they shall not pass' if they could help it.

As the movement grew I went to see successive Secretaries of State for War and asked them to allow women in the Home Guard to receive instruction in how to handle a gun even if there were not enough to go round. My first advances were treated with scant respect. It takes some time for a man to jettison his peace-time conception of women and adjust his thinking to the demands of an all-out effort to win a world war.

Sir James Grigg, a Civil Servant who had been promoted by Churchill to be Secretary for War, was extremely unpleasant and when I met him a little later by chance in the central lobby and broached the subject again, he said, 'I don't want to hear any more about your bloody women.'

As a former Civil Servant he had never been able to adjust himself to the House of Commons and his manner at the dispatch-box could be equally offensive, although 'bloody' would have been regarded as an unparliamentary expression. It was not surprising that a little later the House turned its thumbs down on this gentleman.

In December 1942 I visited Manchester to open thirteen local units of Women's Home Defence; I said, according to the *Manchester Evening News*: 'Let us make no mistake; there are still Government departments controlled by Rip Van Winkles who are unconscious of the tremendous change which is taking place in public opinion towards women. We must waken them to realities, for the 1950 world for women can never be built by men with 1850 prejudices.'

I persevered and, as the international situation darkened and women demonstrated in every field their capacity for undertaking work hitherto performed by men, the attitude of the War Office changed. With the appointment of Captain H. D. Margesson, later Lord Margesson, I was accorded an entirely different reception when I tackled him on the subject. He thought that it was a practical proposition and he promised to give it his blessing.

The average man's conception of a woman's capabilities is formed by his experiences in his own home where his wife and his daughters set a pattern of behaviour; consequently war calls for a tremendous readjustment of preconceived ideas. For a woman to work outside the home disturbs some men. They privately believe perhaps that their wives may be subjected to unwelcome advances; consequently there is a conflict between personal desires and the needs of the country.

I presume that it was in order to set the minds of such husbands at rest that in 1942 the Government convened a committee to inquire into the conditions of the Service women. I was asked to serve with some other women, among whom were Baroness Elliot, then Mrs Walter Elliot, Mrs Mary Stocks, now Baroness, Miss Thelma Cazalet, M.P., and Miss Violet Markham. Visiting the various units of the A.T.S., W.A.A.F. and W.R.N.S. was full of interest, but I never quite understood how, by paying a visit to an officers' mess at lunch-time and making a cursory tour of a camp one bright summer day, one could discover anything adverse about the sex life of the girls. We discussed every aspect of their lives with the senior officers but, quite rightly, these women showed a commendable loyalty to their charges.

It was very satisfactory to learn that in the event of a girl becoming pregnant in the Services, she was well cared for during the ante-natal period. Arrangements were made for her confinement, and after the baby was born and, provided she could make the necessary arrangements, she would be permitted to return to her unit. This humane and moral approach to a very old situation marked a change in attitude. The question was often asked in a mixed unit, who was to blame, the man or the woman? Or both? Whatever the answer it would be grossly unfair to punish the woman only. Though that is the practice in peace-time, the harsh realities of war help people to see this age-old problem in its proper perspective.

In Richmond at an anti-aircraft unit, I asked the Commanding Officer whether the marriage rate was lower in a unit where

the women did work which called for intelligence and the men
were valued for their muscle and brawn. The Commanding
Officer laughed. 'On the contrary,' he said, 'I think that it is
higher here because there is such a strong mutual attraction.
The man admires a girl's brains and the fact that he is not her
intellectual equal simply appears to stimulate her maternal
instinct.' He added, 'I'm an old regular. If anybody had told
me before the war that I would be in command of girls, I would
have replied that in that case I would resign. For me, war is a
man's pastime. However, having seen my girls in action, if
someone came along now and threatened to take only one away,
I would threaten to tender my resignation.'

At Aldershot in a mixed Sergeants' Mess I asked a male
sergeant how he felt about having meals at the same table with
women. He was a tough regular and I anticipated some protest,
although it might be delivered in a manner calculated not to
offend me. He replied simply, 'Look at these tables with white
cloths and flowers. They are not put there today for your
benefit. We have them every day; it makes it seem like home.
that is my answer.'

The Report of this inquiry emphasized the difficulty of
arriving at any firm conclusion regarding the sexual activities of
the women in the Services. We summed it all up in one sentence,
'Chastity has no gossip value'.

Ernest Bevin, the Minister of Labour in the war-time Coalition Government was never tired of praising the woman
industrial worker. He said that her nimble fingers were capable
of fine work which men could not perform. Indeed, he added,
if men had this special attribute they would be demanding a
bonus.

He invited me to join a Committee convened to consider
matters of particular concern to the woman in the industrial
field and questions relating to the conscription of women. A
difficult question to answer was whether we should call up
prostitutes. While it seemed unjust that a woman, and a lazy
one at that, who was profiting by the war situation, should be
exempt, nevertheless, was it in the interests of the Service man
that we should permit a prostitute, possibly with some latent
venereal infection, to join the Services?

We decided that if a woman declared that she was a con-
victed prostitute then she should be exempt from service. Some
of the Committee doubted whether even a prostitute would be
prepared to reveal her occupation in this way, but we need not
have been under any illusions. The prospect of regular work
under strict military discipline did not appeal to the prostitutes
and they had no hesitation in declaring their list of convictions.

I used to believe that unemployment was the root cause of
prostitution; I have to admit that the experience of the war
years and the full employment of the post-war years has changed
my view of the matter. The necessity to introduce the 1959
Street Offences Act in order to clear the streets of prostitutes
called for some very hard thinking on the problem; I believe
that what all prostitutes have in common is a fundamental
laziness which makes regular work anathema to them and
undoubtedly this has been proved during the war years and
the post-war years when a variety of work was available for
women.

Ernest Bevin always recognized that a woman working outside the home was called upon to do two jobs. He therefore asked
employers to remember this and give special consideration to
women who had household responsibilities. Ernest Bevin's
mother was the bread winner and she had a hard struggle to
rear her family; her son never seemed to have lost his admiration
for a mother and those like her who bravely shouldered these
heavy responsibilities.

In response to an invitation to write a pamphlet on the
various jobs open to women in war-time I wrote *Women Fall In*
with a preface taken from Mr R. C. Menzies's speech, broadcast
in London in 1941. He said:

'If some questioner were to say to me quietly "What is your
outstanding impression of Britain today?" I should think of
many things. . . . But my answer to the question would still
unhesitatingly be the courage, the action, the endurance of
Britain's women. Wherever I go I see them and I marvel at
them. Is it possible to believe that not long ago we called them
"the weaker sex"? No man born of woman could ever have
doubted in his heart the courage of woman; her uncomplaining

fortitude, her acceptance of the unexciting role, her patient
planning to overcome difficulties. . . . And then the war came
with all its stupendous demands upon manpower and what did
we find? Women conducting vast organizations; women in the
uniform of the Navy, the Army and Air Force. Women at Fire
Brigade stations in blue overalls, always ready; women driving
great vehicles; women digging in the fields; women wielding
hammers and riveters in factories; women at their gentle work
of nursing the sick soldiers; women working in the hospitals in
the middle of air raids; women doing their turn of fire watching
in their own suburban streets as the incendiary bombs rain down
and, last but not least, that forgotten but splendid woman the
housewife, who copes with rationing, with shortage of foodstuffs
and who not infrequently goes short herself so that her man and
her children may be fed. The vast movement of women into
the service of the nation doing these things and a hundred
others is spectacular. It marks the beginning of a new era.'

This speech was made by a hardheaded Australian politician
who, deeply impressed by what he saw, used this occasion to
give deserved praise to the women of Britain. I have no doubt
that he believed that woman's massive contribution to the war
effort and to the salvation of Britain's economy at that critical
time, would usher in a 'new era'. He did not define precisely
what his conception of a 'new era' was; but in the light of his
previous remarks I take it that in the future, women's work was
to command a greater respect and appreciation from the
country. Twenty years after the war and those stirring words
the 'new era' has yet to materialize. Women are still denied the
rate for the job in industry. They may be engaged in precisely
the same process as men employed in the same room, but their
generative organs and not their skill determine their rate of pay.
In the event of an employer failing to pay a male immigrant
the rate for the job an official strike will be called, but the
failure to pay the wife, sister or girl friend the rate is ignored by
men who have fought for trade union principles. The nimble
fingers of women still do specialized work which men are unable
to perform, but this is categorized as 'women's work' and therefore commands only a low rate of pay. Women have raised their

voices individually and collectively in the unions where they form the majority without success.

Both Shirley and I have asked questions and made speeches on this injustice but to no effect. It would seem that while a national emergency evokes universal eulogy of women's contribution to the war effort, these high-sounding phrases are forgotten directly an armistice is signed.

I believe if men of the stature of Ernest Bevin and Arthur Deakin had survived they would have honoured their debt to women. There are too few men with the moral courage to defy those whose ego finds satisfaction in the knowledge that both in the home and the factory women are exploited economically.

Yet another theme on which I began to campaign in earnest was the importance of clean milk. In the early days of the war children were evacuated to country districts where some farmers expressed contempt for the means employed in most large towns to ensure that the milk was safe for consumption. They persuaded country folk and visitors that milk straight from the cow provided the perfect beverage unequalled in health-giving properties.

On 5 October 1939 I asked the Minister of Health whether, in determining what is a suitable reception area for children in country districts, investigations are made concerning the cleanliness and safety of the local milk supply. On receiving an unsatisfactory reply I asked the Minister whether he would not agree that a daily dose of tuberculous milk is surely more dangerous to health than the possibility of an air raid at some future time. I had evacuated my own children to the West Country and it was necessary to call on two dairymen before I could find milk which I considered safe for human consumption.

Shortly before the war we had all stayed in a small hotel in a seaside resort in Devon. On arrival I had asked, as was my wont, where the milk came from, and whether it was straight from the cow. The proprietor, anxious to please, assured me that it was. That evening I visited the farmer to make my own investigations and was horrified by the filthy condition of the farm. On returning to the hotel I gave instructions that all milk was to be boiled until I could find some other source of supply.

That same evening the son of the proprietor returned from

London where he had been to have 'treatment' and I observed on his face a patch of lupus, or tuberculosis of the skin, attributable to tubercular infected milk. I told the father the cause of his son's complaint and the following day the local farmer, almost in tears, came to see me and begged me to say nothing more about the relationship of milk and tuberculosis, otherwise he would be ruined. I agreed on condition that I would communicate with the local Medical Officer of Health, who would get in touch with the appropriate authorities to ensure that in the future the farmer's herd was tested and the milk pasteurized.

9

The 1945 General Election: Impressions of Clement Attlee

The busy war years were made yet busier when I was included in a parliamentary good-will mission to Australia and New Zealand in 1944. And then the 1945 General Election was upon us – the first for ten years.

When I learned that my opponent was to be a handsome Spitfire pilot called Laddie Lucas, I felt that my chances of victory this time were remote. Londoners quite rightly worshipped the men who had defended them for many consecutive nights of heavy bombing, young men who had been prepared to face almost certain death rather than allow the Germans to occupy Britain. Laddie Lucas was a great friend of Douglas Bader, the legless pilot who continued flying despite his disability.

During the election Shirley, aged fourteen – who shared to the full Britain's admiration for our fighter pilots – came to me and asked: 'Mama, Laddie Lucas is speaking with Douglas Bader tonight; would you mind very much if I went to listen to them? I think Bader is a very brave man.'

'Of course,' I replied, 'I don't mind.' I minded to the extent of thinking that if my own daughter was captivated by the glamour of the Air Force, what chance had I of persuading the thousands of voters, equally grateful to these wonderful young men, to vote for me.

I thought that I was justified in putting a picture of my

husband in uniform and the children on my election address, and it was not until a few days before the poll, when Winston Churchill drove through Fulham with Laddie Lucas sitting on the hood of the open car and my women helpers ran from their work in the Committee Room and waved and yelled a welcome to the former Prime Minister and the Conservative candidate, that my customary optimism began to desert me. When the women returned to the Committee Room I told them of my misgivings. They laughed ever more loudly. 'Don't worry Dr Edith. We cheered them, but that doesn't mean we're going to vote for them.' Well, such is the unpredictability of politics that I trebled my majority.

The Labour Government with its massive support in Parliament represented the strength of the feeling in the country and we were fortunate in having Clement Attlee, an experienced parliamentarian with a fund of common sense, as Prime Minister. He had a deceptively mild manner which was wont to astonish people. His choice of a Government was followed with intense interest by the old hands, but as a young Member I listened in a detached manner to the tea-room chat about the possible choice of this or that individual.

When Willy Whitely, our chief Whip, put his head over my shoulder in the Members' dining-room one lunch-time just as I was about to begin my meal and whispered, 'Clem would like to see you at Number 10,' I thought immediately that the Prime Minister had been stricken with some sudden illness and that in the emergency a message had been sent across to the House for a doctor. I looked at Willy and said, 'Is it urgent?' He smiled and replied, 'Well, not very, but I should go now if I were you.'

As I walked along Downing Street I began to think of other possibilities. Could it be that Clem had some job for me? I waited in the hall of Number 10 and within a few minutes I was called into the Cabinet Room where the Prime Minister, all alone, sat puffing at his pipe. He said, 'Sit down, Edith. I have been thinking that you might do well as the Parliamentary Secretary at the Ministry of Food. With your knowledge it should suit you. I think that you and Ben Smith would make a good team. What do you say?'

I replied: 'Thank you very much, I should like that.'

'Well, that's settled then. Good-bye,' and he shook hands. Within a few minutes of arriving at Number 10 I was out in Downing Street again with the difference that now I was a Junior Minister.

Clem Attlee has always been a man of few words and whatever the situation his laconic style has never deserted him, and before I go on to describe my work at the Ministry of Food, perhaps I may be allowed a short digression about him.

Clem likes telling the story of a visit he made which involved him in a long and exhausting journey to an Eastern country to address a conference. He spoke for fifteen minutes because, as he explained afterwards, he cannot bear tedious repetition and already there had been a spate of seemingly endless orations. His hosts thought that he must be ill, but he assured them that he felt very well and had simply expressed in a few succinct sentences some fresh thoughts that had occurred to him after having heard the previous speakers.

Women study men closely and, like the rest of my sex, I observe a man's reactions to circumstances and make my deductions about his character and personality. While conspiracies, successful and not so successful, have encompassed Clement Attlee, never, in his political life, has he been guilty of disloyalty; the interests of the Party are always his first consideration. Attlee's success in climbing the political ladder which finally took him to Number 10 Downing Street can be attributed in a great part to his devotion to the Labour Party and an unquestioning acceptance of decisions regarding policy and organization providing they had majority support.

He served the Party for years patiently and without ostentation, but by good fortune he had chosen to work in an area where the overwhelming numbers of Labour supporters assured him of a safe seat which returned him to the House of Commons as one of the most able of the little band of opposition members after the 1931 landslide.

Clem Attlee never engaged in malicious gossip; never sought the limelight and never manœuvred to further his own ends. His extreme modesty and shyness combined with his tiny figure and unimpressive physical appearance tempted Hugh Dalton, a man with a huge frame and a mischievous sense of humour, to refer occasionally to 'that little man'. However, the little man, emulating the tortoise, passed his rivals; and the very nature of his negative qualities ensured his final success. His modesty and shyness had prevented him from enjoying a full social life and thereby being drawn into gossip and petty controversies about personalities and events. He had offended none, either by word of mouth or by pulling strings in order to achieve some coveted post. He had so few enemies that the attempt by a tiny minority after the 1945 Labour victory to displace him proved abortive.

Clem Attlee has none of the defects of the small man who desperately seeks to compensate for nature's failures. Even on his physical shortcomings he likes to make some terse comment. 'The fact is,' he told me, 'I was starved at school. I went to bed hungry night after night.' Underfeeding of boys at boarding-schools was not unusual and it seems in keeping with the description that Attlee wrote about his boyhood at Haileybury. 'At that time there were two baths for eighty boys, the rest using zinc "toe pans". Sanitary needs were supplied by three rows of earth closets illuminated in the evenings by one feeble gas jet in each row.'

Clem Attlee did not develop any pronounced inhibitions; he is at his best with young people and they seem to have the effect of evoking some of his best oratorical efforts. My family was honoured by one of these gems at Shirley's wedding. In August, 1958, in the crypt of the House of Commons, she was married to John Ryman, a barrister whom she had met at the University Labour Club at Oxford. Members of Parliament enjoy the privilege of having their children married or christened in the tiny Crypt Chapel which, so it is said, had been used as a stable by Cromwell's men and later was restored to its pre-Reformation beauty.

After the ceremony we returned to Pond House, our Highgate home where, with supreme optimism, I had arranged for a reception in the garden. Plans of this kind can fail disastrously because their success is entirely dependent on the vagaries of an English summer. My daughter's wedding day resembled mine in one important respect; the sun shone throughout the day and even the cake was finally brought out to be cut in the garden.

Clem Attlee toasted the bride and bridegroom. Shirley had

taken her medical examinations from Somerville before going to St Thomas's Hospital, and her husband had read law at Pembroke. Spread over the lawn were many of their Oxford friends including my son Michael and daughter-in-law Florence who had also met at Oxford, and who subsequently presented us with three lovely grandchildren. Throughout the afternoon Clem Attlee, himself an Oxford man, with his wife Violet had sat under the flowering catalpa tree, puffing his pipe and contemplating the scene with evident enjoyment. Then when the moment arrived he rose and gave the perfect speech on modern youth; his theme was that they looked different and appeared different in their approach to life from those of his own days, yet fundamentally their aspirations were very similar.

This short address was the superb contribution that I would have wished for had I been able to make a choice. Wedding receptions mean different things to different people. Some judge them by the ceremony, the clothes of the bride, the guests, or the food and drink. I and probably most politicians wait for the speeches. A short speech which indicates that the speaker has given some thought to his theme, expressed with sincerity and modesty, is the recipe for success at a wedding. On this occasion Clem revealed himself to be a kindly, understanding man, not bored on a hot August day by yet another wedding, but stimulated by his genuine love of youth. He spoke with a great appreciation of their important place in the community, when anyone might have forgiven an elderly man for making a few platitudinous comments on marriage.

In Parliament he was well aware of tea-room plots and counter-plots which surrounded his administration and which derived from jealousies and rivalries masquerading as plans for a fundamental change in policy. His unruffled reaction to the activities of these gentlemen and their disloyalty showed that his knowledge of psychology was the source of his strength. He quietly observed the unrestrained, emotional protests of Aneurin Bevan, together with the more devious manœuvrings of his henchmen who used Aneurin as an effective and eloquent spokesman. Many loyal members of the Party surveyed the scene more in sorrow than in anger; it was recognized that these manœuvres of the spurious Left were a betrayal of the millions of honest simple men and women who had given of their time and energies to help to build the Labour Party. The noise and fury did not derive from intellectual conviction but unfortunately many Members were deceived by the political antics of the Bevanites into believing that they represented the true word; and that Clement Attlee with his middle-class origins and his apparently mild manner had betrayed the revolutionary spirit of the Party. What nonsense it all was. Clem Attlee had come into the Party, not because he personally had anything to gain by making the rich less rich and the poor better off, but because for many years he had studied the whole basis of our society from the vantage-point of a hostel for boys of which he was Warden in the East End. He worked his passage in the Labour movement as a propagandist, a local Councillor, a Labour Mayor and a Labour Member of Parliament for Limehouse in the East End of London where George Lansbury, a neighbour, was never tired of commending his zeal and selfless devotion to the movement. For years, never sparing himself, he undertook the back room work of the Party, from framing resolutions to writing pamphlets.

I have never seen at close quarters men manœuvre for position in business, but from newspaper reports one can only assume that the primitive instinct of self-preservation becomes perverted into an insatiable desire for power. In politics the same appetite for power leads some men to jettison all those loyalties which in their youthful idealism they had cherished.

Attlee was an astute politician; he recognized when some action calculated to displace him would succeed. In 1955 we addressed the Durham Women's Gala together; after the traditional walk through the town, we were having tea, when an afternoon newspaper was brought to us confirming the news that Hugh Dalton was resigning from the Shadow Cabinet on grounds of age. Dalton had always been a great admirer of Hugh Gaitskell and it was general knowledge that he would like to see him as leader of the Party. When Attlee read this he passed it to me and said, 'Well, this may be the end.'

Within a comparatively short time of that dramatic occasion, when Herbert Morrison found himself second to Aneurin Bevan and last in the race of the three contestants, the Parliamentary

Labour Party chose Hugh Gaitskell as leader. Attlee, who had listened quietly to the result congratulated the new leader, and rose and left the room followed by his faithful and loyal colleague, Arthur Moyle, his former Parliamentary Private Secretary.

10

At the Ministry of Food

Becoming a Minister must be a harrowing experience for
somebody who has no knowledge of the subject matter with
which his department is concerned. In the nineteenth century
the business of foreign affairs and the treasury dominated
parliamentary debates. Having regard to the number of
potential Foreign Secretaries in the House it would seem that
now, as then, a personal opinion in the field of foreign affairs
suffices. On finance, economists differ, and so the poor Minister
cannot be blamed if the views of his advisers, which he echoes
in the House, are proved to be unsound. However, with the
advent of the twentieth century and the Welfare State, a
number of Ministries, Health, Agriculture, Fisheries and Food,
Housing and Local Government, National Insurance and Industrial Injuries, were established which call for a certain
expertise in their parliamentary representatives. Briefing from
a well-informed Secretary is important, but the supplementary
question charged with special knowledge cannot be always
anticipated and this is when the newcomer to the dispatch-box
can reveal an abysmal ignorance if he has failed to do his homework. At least I took comfort from the fact that I knew a good
deal about the work of the Ministry of Food, which was then
under constant attack. It was chiefly concerned with providing
the population with a balanced diet and consequently it was
our duty to ensure that not one of the nutritional diseases could
be laid at our door. At the outbreak of the war, and for some
years afterwards, the Government took control of all the

essential foodstuffs of the country. In order to establish a harmonious relationship between the Civil Service and the trade, we invited representatives of the various divisions of the food industry to share the responsibility of administration with their opposite number in the Civil Service. It might have been thought that this admixture of commerce and the Civil Service would have been disastrous, having regard to the different approach to life of the introverted Civil Servant and the businessman. On the contrary this novel arrangement enabled each to examine the other at close quarters and both found the experience exhilarating.

On my first day at the Ministry I was told that it had been arranged for me to visit various places concerned with food production and distribution, accompanied either by the commercial head in charge of a particular division or the Civil Servant. Each morning as we set off I was joined by a pleasant man who introduced himself, but never indicated whether he belonged to the world of commerce or the Civil Service.

I observed after trial and error that the Civil Servant generally wore a black trilby and carried an umbrella and the businessman a bowler hat. However, I soon learnt that this was an over-simplification. I asked my guide one morning how long he had been in the Civil Service. Far from being affronted he replied that he was in trade. I took another look at the trilby and noted that it looked rather new. Was this sartorial innovation some small token of his respect and growing affection for the Civil Service? When I learned that I was expected to address conferences of businessmen associated with a particular food trade, I said bluntly that I did not think that I was capable of such a thing. The only conferences I had addressed were concerned with medical, educational and political matters. I envisaged a conference of hard-headed businessmen utterly contemptuous of my ignorance of trade and determined to catch me out with some technical question. However, there was no alternative; it was part of the job.

My first appearance was before the sweet confectionary trade and Mr Mackintosh and Mr Cadbury, the aristocrats of the business, accompanied me on the platform. The department gave me a brief, but, having a sweet tooth, I thought I would open up with a reminder that I had always had a close personal interest in their products. Moreover, as I have always had a liking for liquorice I thought it only fair to say that while Mr Mackintosh and Mr Cadbury had played some part in my life, nevertheless I would at some time like to meet Mr Percy Bassett. There was a roar of laughter and from the back row up jumped a charming little plump man who called out, 'Here I am; I'm Percy Bassett.' After that everything was easy.

Quite fortuitously I had a similar experience at the 'Soft Drink' luncheon at the Savoy which followed a business conference. As the wife of a Welshman, I said that Idris lemon squash always found favour with me, for I pictured it being dispensed by a tall, dark Welshman with a perfect tenor voice. Laughter greeted this, and up rose a tall, handsome man who said: 'Here I am and I *can* sing.'

After these two experiences I looked forward to trade meetings as a light relief from the fierce exchanges of the political arena.

As I had always advocated better food and less medicine as the correct approach to healthy living, the Ministry of Food suited me. The department buzzed with activity. Parliamentary questions have an alarming effect upon Civil Servants; they are obsessed with the idea that a question is an implied criticism of themselves. The fact is that although some questions in the House are of general concern, most questions are put by Members who have some special or constituency interest in the matter. Consequently a Member's chief anxiety is to reach his own question. This is why a Speaker need not be too reluctant to demand that there should be fewer supplementary questions; he would have the support of the whole House.

Immediately after the war great disappointment was expressed because rationing could not be discontinued; and the ration book, symbolizing the inadequacies of the Government, became a favourite topic for newspapers hostile to the administration. It was impossible to dispense with the ration book because we had always imported approximately 50 per cent of our foodstuffs and consequently our home reserves had been drastically depleted during the war years. Furthermore, other countries were in the same plight and one important source of our beef supply, the Argentine, was courted assiduously by other nations who normally were self-sufficient in meat. If, therefore, British people were to be given a balanced diet, that is a diet containing the correct proportions of protein, fat and carbohydrate, we had to look elsewhere for our meat or fish which provided the protein or body-building element.

South Africa offered us a fish which was popular in their country. It would provide an effective substitute for meat and we jumped at the opportunity of securing our much-needed protein. Our nutritional experts regarded this as an excellent solution to our problems and in those initial discussions nobody raised any objection to the proposition.

It is said that a rose by any other name would smell as sweet; nevertheless, I am convinced in retrospect that if this fish had been called by some name calculated to please the ear and stimulate the gastric juices, we should have been more successful in our venture. The fact was that it was called Snoek, pronounced 'Snook'. We were so pre-occupied with our success in finding a nutritionally adequate food that it never occurred to us that its name would prove unpopular and suggest unpalatability to the British ear.

I was given the task of persuading the women of the country to buy Snoek for the purpose of supplementing the rations. From the storm of abuse which greeted my efforts one would have thought that the Ministry was trying to force some inedible, unwholesome concoction into the family larder. At least I derived some comfort from the knowledge that most of the protests at our public meetings came from a noisy element calling themselves the Housewives League; and it is not irrelevant to mention that most of these ladies were opposed to the Government on political grounds.

One can never forecast how an apparently minor matter may blow up into a fierce political storm. The stomach provides a useful political barometer. The decision of the Government to stop the importation of dried egg in order to relieve the balance of payments, caused a domestic revolution, and the resignation of the Minister was called for. The result was that the decision had to be hastily reversed.

World demands on the available food became more pressing

D

and we were confronted with a very ugly situation; there was a shortage of wheat which necessitated our rationing the staple food of the country – bread. It fell to me to wind up the debate on the rationing of bread. The House was packed after a heated discussion following the opening speech by John Strachey, and the early Christians before their consignment to the lions could not have felt more apprehensive than I did that night. The jeers and the counter-jeers drowned my voice time after time, and I emerged feeling that this indeed was the end of my parliamentary career. However, nothing prevented me following a logical argument despite the interruptions and I only hoped that Hansard the next day would prove the adequacy of the case.

Food was a subject of universal interest and I received an invitation from an Oxford society to speak on 'The Technology of Food', a subject concerned with the processing of food. As an example I laboriously explained the method of adding certain vitamins to margarine in order that dietetically it would be equivalent to butter. I was well aware that my audience of students would not for the most part know the difference in taste, but I was equally aware that most housewives would detect it.

My audience was attentive and, except for one student who offered to be subjected to a test, question time did not reveal that they had taken any exception to what I said. It was with profound surprise that I saw next day that the *Daily Express* had made much of this incident.

As a politician I shrugged my shoulders and treated this as just one more outpouring of journalistic spleen. Tomorrow, I thought, another story would intrigue the readers of the *Daily Express* and erase the Butter and Margarine stunt from their minds. For some reason quite obscure to me the butter or margarine story has stuck throughout the years implying I presume that my judgement on other issues is equally faulty. Today the television advertisements repeatedly remind the public that it is impossible to tell the difference between butter and margarine, yet this does nothing to scotch this trivial little story.

From the first day that I entered the Ministry of Food I was resolved to devote some of my energies to ensuring that the milk of the country was made safe for human consumption. Our orthopaedic hospitals were full of children suffering from spinal and joint infections contracted from tubercular-infected milk. And my father's constant reminders of the near-criminal behaviour of those farmers who permitted infected cows to be milked for human consumption were never far from my thoughts, when milk happened to be the subject under discussion.

I was not without support in the Ministry. Strenuous efforts had been made to clean the milk supply by establishing regular inspections of herds and eradicating infected cows, but the regional pasteurization of all milk was strenuously opposed by many farmers. They pooh-pooh the idea that little children could be crippled for life, or even lose their lives, from drinking milk infected with the tubercle bacillus. For years this hopeless battle had been waged against the ignorance and selfishness of certain farmers, and it became clear that only legislation would compel them to raise their standards of milk production. I became obsessed with the subject to such an extent that the poor man who was summoned to my office to report progress became more and more subdued. I recognized that he had decided that the best tactics to adopt were to remain quiet until my barrage of questions on the progress of the work had subsided. I became sorry for him and apologized for my belligerent attitude, justifying it by reminding him of the unnecessary suffering of children in our orthopaedic hospitals. Of course he knew all about bovine tuberculosis, but, as he repeated so often, it was the greed of the farmers that was the stumbling block. The timidity of the Civil Service was partly responsible for the failure to take action against the farmers who were impervious to a little gentle prodding and I had to instil a sense of urgency if we were to make progress. At long last, or so it seemed to me, on 21 February 1949 I stood at the dispatch-box and moved the Second Reading of the 'Milk (Special Designation) Bill'. My only regret was that my father, who had died in 1944, was unable to sit in the public gallery on that afternoon.

I said:

'It is my good fortune today to move the Second Reading of a Bill which at times during the last twenty years I had despaired of ever seeing on the Statute Book.... I am very pleased to see here this afternoon Hon. Members who have played an important part in this campaign in the past particularly my hon. friend the Member for Barking (Dr Somerville Hastings). I think they will all say that today we are here to celebrate a triumph, a triumph over ignorance, prejudice and selfishness. I am indeed very fortunate for it is very seldom that an Hon. Member has the opportunity of moving the Second Reading of a measure of this nature as a Government Bill after having experienced the frustration and disappointment always associated with pleading an unpopular cause.

'I would go so far as to say that this Bill can be regarded as ancillary to the National Health Service Act because when it comes into operation, it will be found to have the effect of reducing the incidence of tuberculosis and disablement. The title alone the 'Milk (Special Designations) Bill' does not seem to herald what I consider to be a reform of great social significance. I shall always think of it as the 'Milk (Save the children) Bill' and I believe that Hon. Members who are also medical colleagues of mine will agree that the majority of the medical profession will do likewise. The history of the Bill covers something like fifty years, but it was not until 1922 that the first milk special designation regulations were introduced under the Milk and Dairies (Amendment) Act 1922. Later still premiums were paid to producers in order to encourage them to produce designated milk. There was a set back in 1938 when proposals for establishing areas in which non-designated milk would require to be pasteurized before sale to the public were included in the Milk Bill, and could not be proceeded with because the Bill had to be withdrawn. I entered the House in 1938 and I was intensely interested in that measure.

'I remember when the Bill was introduced feeling such pleasure and satisfaction that I thought I should like to congratulate the Right Hon. Member for Cirencester and Tewkesbury (Mr W. S. Morrison) who was then Minister of Agriculture. But as a mere back-bencher in 1938, I felt somewhat apprehensive; because the Minister representing the Conservative Government seemed to me inaccessible. However, I waited one day in the Lobby – I remember it very clearly – I am sorry that the Right Hon. Member for Cirencester and Tewkesbury is not here today – and I congratulated him on Part VII of the 1938 Milk Bill. However, I was a little premature. The Bill never had its Second Reading and the Right Hon. Member for Cirencester and Tewkesbury had to resign from the office of the Minister of Agriculture. Once more, prejudice, ignorance and selfishness had triumphed. . . .

'Today I am pleased to say that the consensus of opinion amongst responsible medical people and health authorities is strongly in favour of pasteurization and these authorities are continually expressing concern about the serious consequences that may result unless the Government takes action. I feel that the country owes Professor G. S. Wilson a great debt of gratitude for his work in this field. A recent estimate by him puts the number of deaths that can be attributed to milk infected by the tubercle bacillus at about 1,500 annually and many more thousands are crippled. Our orthopaedic hospitals throughout the country are filled with small children lying in splints sometimes for months, sometimes for years, suffering from surgical tuberculosis which can be attributed to infected milk. So far as the child population is concerned the percentage of deaths is ten times greater in rural areas where of course more milk is drunk raw than in London. This may surprise many Hon. Members who are proud of the milk covered with cream which is obtained straight from the cow in rural areas. Many are ignorant of the fact that in that thick creamy milk lurks the virulent tubercle bacillus. The Cattle Diseases Committee estimates that about 40 per cent of the dairy cows of this country would react to the tuberculosis test, indicating that they were infected with tuberculosis, and that numbers of milk-cows suffer from udder tuberculosis, and excrete active tubercle in their milk. Hon. Members will know that there are other diseases we are anxious to eradicate, but this will take a lot of time and therefore pasteurization is essential. There are contagious abortion and mastitis. Recent estimates of the incidence of these diseases show that probably some 20 per cent of the cows in this country are infected with the former disease, and that 2 per cent are excreting dangerous organisms in their milk which infect human beings with undulant fever. . . .

'The responsibilities of the Government in this matter are made even greater by reason of the official encouragement given to the drinking of milk through our welfare food schemes, milk in schools, and the constant publicity given to encourage people to consume a most valuable food. . . .

'I say, having obtained the best advice possible, that the pasteurization of milk, if carried out efficiently and under proper conditions, destroys all pathogenic organisms in milk. . . .

'Pasteurization does not make poor milk good, and it does not make good milk better, but it makes all milk safe. . . .

'Probably the first area will be specified in a year or eighteen months and the country as a whole may be covered in five or ten years. We must not be too depressed about that. The fight for this measure has been going on to my knowledge for twenty-five years. One of the first speeches I made in my political career was made on this subject.

'Indeed, I may go so far as to say that this is my finest hour.'

A Member anxious to have some regulations rescinded must 'pray' against them and prayers are taken at the end of parliamentary business. As the Ministry of Food was compelled to introduce hundreds of regulations to ensure that our precious food was adequately protected and distributed, we were not unaccustomed to a prayer on the Order Paper to which I had to provide the answer. This necessitated my staying, sometimes, until the early morning hours and it was after one of these long night sessions that I decided to move nearer the House. Within three days an estate agent had sold our Highgate house and we moved to a Kensington flat, and exchanged the 'lung' of Hampstead Heath for that of Hyde Park. We lived to regret the decision and longed to get back to the heights of Highgate, and I experienced an intense relief when my husband later announced that he had found a bomb-damaged house with 'possibilities' not far from our old home.

The day to day parliamentary pressure to which I was subject at the Ministry of Food gave me a form of political immunization against attack which I believed would last as long as my parliamentary life. And so it has proved to be.

In the heat of the battle it is not always possible for the

participants to see the action in its true perspective. One morning after a very noisy and prayerful night the Chief Whip asked me to go to Number 10 Downing Street. I braced myself for dismissal. I had been told by others that the process was short and sharp and characteristic of the Prime Minister. I waited again in the hall and was soon ushered into the Cabinet Room where I found the Prime Minister, with his pipe, emitting great clouds of smoke.

'Sit down, Edith,' he said. 'It seems to me you are doing a pretty good job and keeping our end up against the Tories. I thought of making you a Privy Councillor.'

This was entirely unexpected because it is not usual to make a Junior Minister a Privy Councillor. This honour is conferred automatically when he or she becomes a Minister of Cabinet rank. I replied, 'Thank you very much.'

Then he laughed and said, 'I thought that answer of yours on fish the other day jolly good.

'Well, Edith, thanks very much for your help. Good-bye,' and he shook hands and out I went without another word.

The little ceremony attached to becoming a Privy Councillor is very brief. George VI received me on a day when a Privy Council was being held in a small room on the first floor of Buckingham Palace overlooking the Mall; by comparison with some of the vast apartments in the Palace this room with its charming old furniture seemed almost cosy. I formed the impression that he regarded a woman Privy Councillor as an interesting exhibit, because there had been so very few of us; and no doubt I introduced a little variety after the succession of male Privy Councillors to which he was accustomed. Knowing of his speech defect I had an almost irresistible desire to start the conversation in order to help him. However, it is customary for the King to open the conversation and I held my tongue. He found little difficulty in communicating with me for he was anxious to inform me that he did not wish a woman Privy Councillor to kneel when the oath was taken. George V apparently had held strong views on the subject, for his son told me that under no circumstances would he permit a woman to kneel to him. I should have liked to suggest that, while I welcomed the change in procedure, kneeling to the Sovereign was nothing less than a sycophantic medieval survival not consistent with Cabinet responsibility and should be omitted for all Privy Councillors irrespective of their sex. However, I suspected that the King would not comprehend this constitutional plea for equality for men. After the formalities, the King speaking with little effort, asked if I would mind satisfying his curiosity; he and the Queen often speculated on the private lives of Members of Parliament and, as I was married – in fact the first married woman Privy Councillor and incidentally still the only one, they wondered what my husband did in the evening when I was at the House. I had been told that on these occasions it was customary for the King to indulge in a little informal chat with a new Privy Councillor, but I was totally unprepared for this question. It seemed to reveal unawareness of the close partnership which exists between a man and wife both engaged in professional work and consequently capable of conducting their lives, without complete dependence one on the other. Or did it imply that a woman's place was in the home each night catering to her sire's needs? I felt as though the shade of Queen Victoria, the King's great-grandmother, haunted that room, for despite her own position, she was not prepared to encourage that gallant little band of women who were demanding higher education to fit them for interesting and rewarding work. Victoria made no secret of the fact that she regarded the home as the only place for a woman, and no doubt the very idea of a married woman Member of Parliament attending an all-night sitting of the House, while her husband remained at home, would have scandalized her.

11

Minister of National Insurance:
Some Thoughts on Civil Servants

Another of those laconic conversations took place between the Prime Minister and myself after the 1950 General Election, when he invited me to become the Minister of National Insurance and Industrial Injuries. My predecessor had been Jim Griffiths, the Member of Parliament for Llanelly, my husband's home town; an old miner and pioneer of the Labour Movement in South Wales, he had a special place in the affection of the Labour Movement.

I have never liked figures but I knew that my new Ministry would be well supplied with men and women who would give me detailed briefs on this aspect of my work. The opportunity of helping to provide a measure of security for people during the most hazardous periods of life, in sickness, unemployment and old age, appealed to me; it offered interesting and constructive work and the whole field of industrial illness and injuries seemed right up my street. The Ministry of National Insurance symbolizes the British flair for improvization. In 1947 the comprehensive insurance scheme called for over one thousand office buildings. With the vast reconstruction schemes in progress following the bombing of Britain we could not afford to provide offices especially designed for this purpose; consequently we took what was available and adapted them to our use.

We found Victorian villas, pre-fabricated huts and in Cardiff we used the former Japanese Embassy. They sufficed because we ensured that they were well staffed by people who appreciated the social importance of their work and consequently approached it in a generous-hearted spirit. I have always believed that a building is of secondary importance whatever the institution may be; it is the happy co-operation of human beings and the consequent prevailing atmosphere which makes a success of an enterprise.

On visiting the office in Cardiff I apologized to some of the clerks for the stained glass in the high ceiling windows of the old building which tended to darken the room. They answered brightly, 'Don't worry. We are happy here; our manager is being very kind and helpful.'

The Ministry was situated in Carlton House Gardens, an old mansion previously the home of the American banker Pierpont Morgan. It had elaborately ornamented ceilings and a crinoline staircase; nevertheless, it served its purpose and the staff were remarkably tolerant considering the limitations of the improvised offices.

On arrival I was met by a former woman secretary who asked me whether everything was in order. I looked at the magnificent room with its elaborately painted ceiling and the desk on which were a number of telephones. At the Ministry of Food I had a private telephone. 'Which is my private phone?' I asked. 'There is no special phone; we like to keep a note of all incoming calls,' was the reply. I sensed a resistance to my request. For one moment I envisaged sitting at this desk every day, perhaps until late in the evening, cut off from direct contact with my home. The thought of not speaking to my husband, the children and Nana without the interference of a third party dismayed me. As I stood in that room for the first time as the new Minister I was only conscious of a warm feeling of love for my family flooding my whole being. I knew then that my family took precedence over any worldly aspirations. 'See that a phone is installed,' I said. The telephone arrived the next day.

Undoubtedly women with families can only happily undertake work which carries a high degree of responsibility if they are confident that their family is well cared for in their absence.

A hundred years have passed since the match girls struck for higher wages, and the terrible conditions under which they were condemned to work were revealed to an indifferent public. These girls often contracted a condition known as phossy jaw, attributable to the material which they handled in the processing of matches. Industrial diseases and injuries are not uncommon today, yet there is a curious apathy, even among the workers, regarding the failure to protect them against harmful processes. While certain scheduled diseases, such as lead poisoning, Anthrax, miners' nystagmus and many others, entitle a worker to benefit under the Industrial Injuries Act there are other complaints which it is argued are not related to the use of a certain substance; consequently it is necessary to conduct a ceaseless struggle to prove that the root cause of an industrial disease stems from the process in which the workers are engaged.

Injuries in the pit are accepted as one of the hazards of coal-mining but the more insidious dust diseases, while less spectacular, may have a higher mortality rate. For years the miners' representatives brought to the notice of the employers cases of miners suffering from a chronic cough which gradually worsened while the man's general state deteriorated as he became thinner and weaker. The disease was called pneumoconiosis, and while in the later stages the X-ray revealed a pathological condition of the lung, there was no indication in the early stages that the symptoms differed from any chronic cough attributable, say, to smoking. And so for years the miners' unions and the employers wrangled and the miners continued to contract 'dust disease' and drag out their last painful years of existence as chronic invalids.

The polluted atmosphere of London and my early discussions with my father on dust-borne disease seemed related to the pitiable plight of the miner which had always offended my sense of fair play. At the clinic in Cardiff which had been established for the miners in the Welsh valleys I saw these grim-faced Welshmen and their fatalistic attitude to diseases caused by dust which they regard as an unavoidable industrial hazard; with no alternative work available they are faced with prolonged unemployment if they leave the pit. It was on 25 July 1951 that I introduced the 'Pneumoconiosis and Byssinosis Benefit Bill' and moved the first reading.

Previous schemes to cover those suffering from these diseases were of a very limited character and this Bill made provisions for benefits out of the Industrial Injuries Insurance Fund for those totally disabled, or for the dependants of those dying from these diseases whose workmen's compensation claims have been barred by a time limit. The world of politics is unpredictable and our small majority in the House precipitated a General Election with the result that my successor, Mr Osbert Peake, at the Ministry of National Insurance piloted the Bill through the remaining stages. In explaining the parentage of the Bill, Mr Peake described himself as being in the position of a god-father at the christening, holding the baby and hoping it will not cry.

While this Bill went a long way to help those previously debarred from benefit and enabled totally disabled men and the families of men who had died from these diseases to benefit immediately, nevertheless as I explained to the House, I was not satisfied that we had devised a scheme which would cover all those men showing some early symptoms.

Although pneumoconiosis and byssinosis were comparatively new terms to the House and indeed to the medical profession, for when I was a student we had never heard of them, the symptoms had long been recognized by the miners; yet while the diseases were prescribed under the Workmen's Compensation Act, their diagnosis baffled the medical profession, for an X-ray does not reveal the condition in its early stages.

The Medical Research Council said:

Pneumoconiosis is in general a progressive disease but the rate of progression is very variable. In some cases especially those with complicated pneumoconiosis the progression may be relatively rapid, but in the majority it is slow. An estimate of the likely rate of progression may be made from the X-ray appearance so that the chest X-ray is of importance in prognosis as well as diagnosis.'

I was very anxious to include the partially disabled men in this Bill, but I could not discover how to overcome the administrative and technical difficulties which are of a medical nature.

There are degrees of partial disablement; it is possible for a miner to suffer some distress because of shortness of breath, but to feel that he is capable of undertaking some other job perhaps in the vicinity of the pit. It could be argued that he was suffering in the first or second degree of partial disablement but there is the third and fourth degree, and we must be able to diagnose the degree and assess a man's disability correctly if the men are to be fairly treated. Every miner in my opinion should be given the opportunity of going before a medical board for examination by a chest specialist, but at the time the Boards were overwhelmed with cases and the number of specialists was limited. Therefore to incorporate this provision in an Act of Parliament would be to render the Act unenforceable and thereby instil a new sense of grievance in the men; it was for this reason that we could not embark upon a more comprehensive Bill at that time.

Mr Harold Finch, the Member for Bedwelty, a former miner, said in the course of the debate that the Bill provided for the 'forgotten men' of the mining industry. 'It represents another milestone in the long and weary way we have travelled to secure some measure of security for men from the mining industry who suffer from pneumoconiosis.' The tragedy of these cases, in the South Wales coalfield in particular, is that the men did not know that they were suffering from pneumoconiosis. They felt the effect in the lungs slightly or had a cold or were suffering from what in South Wales is called *diffyg anadl*; and it was not until years after they had left the mining industry that they discovered, after medical examination, that they were disabled as a result of pneumoconiosis.

Debates which concerned miners and their arduous lives always include a contribution from Tom Brown, the Member for Ince, a former miner and the only surviving member of the Committee of Inquiry set up in 1922 to investigate the incidence of dust disease. He reminded the House that when the first scheme covering men disabled from silicosis was introduced, a miner had to prove that he worked in rock strata which contained 50 per cent of free silica compound. As there were only two coal fields where 50 per cent of free silica could be found, in Somerset and the Forest of Dean, the miners of Lancashire,

Cheshire and the North-west areas where the maximum was 43 per cent were not protected by the legislation.

When the regulations were amended they were not made retrospective and consequently the miners who had already contracted this disease received no compensation. Tom Brown told the House that the average time that miners lived after the date of certification from pneumoconiosis was eight weeks.

Occasionally I would appear in the House with a beautiful orchid pinned to my shoulder; it always aroused interest particularly among the wealthier Conservative Members of the House who possessed gardeners expert at growing orchids in luxurious hot-houses. My gorgeous prize blooms were not produced in such exotic surroundings; they came from Tom Brown's little glass-house heated by a coal-fired boiler at a very low cost and cared for with a dedication and devotion which only a miner who had spent years of his life in the darkness and dirt of the pits could lavish on an object of such delicacy and beauty.

I was fortunate in having another ex-miner, Bernard Taylor, the member for Mansfield, as my Parliamentary Secretary. Listening to the stories of the early lives of miners, sons of large families compelled to go down the pit when little more than children, I was always struck by the absence of bitterness in the recital of their early days. The comradeship engendered in the pits from a sense of danger shared was a very precious thing to them and it seemed that they found this lacking in the world at the top of the pit shaft.

'Belly-aching' commonly indulged in by other workers seldom characterizes the miner; I assumed that if one spent many years in the presence of danger the knowledge that one had survived each day's occupational hazards must instil an abiding cheerfulness.

I chose as my Parliamentary Private Secretary a woman, Mrs Dorothy Rees, the Member for Barry. To a busy Minister an efficient P.P.S. is a great blessing. Mrs Rees, a Welsh woman, conscientious, hard-working, with a personal knowledge of the industries of her country and with special knowledge of legislation concerning the Ministry relieved me of the day-to-day inquiries from Members in the lobbies. She subsequently lost her seat. I marvelled at our democratic system which could afford to dispense with the services of one of the most efficient Members of Parliament who had ever served in the House of Commons.

Although a comprehensive insurance scheme should ideally cover every individual in the country there are those who for one reason or the other fall outside it. The National Assistance Board was established to provide for these and to supplement the pension where it was manifestly inadequate.

My father's recollections of his first assistantship often included a description of the old couples who, no longer capable of earning their keep on the farm, were bundled off to the workhouse in a farm cart. While this tragic little scene is no longer enacted in Britain, nevertheless among the old people there is a considerable amount of hidden poverty. The high infantile and maternal mortality rate and the deaths of toddlers and adolescents from preventable disease used to engage the attention of the medical profession, and the problems of the aged were disregarded because in those days you should count yourself fortunate if you survived at all. Now advances in medicine combined with the improved social services enable people to survive the perilous fifties and sixties and live to threescore years and ten and over. Unfortunately their capacity to care for themselves does not show any similar improvement. Eyesight and hearing still fail in the sixties; the arteries thicken, memory suffers and arthritis, a seriously disabling condition, is widespread.

We may, therefore, have conquered pneumonia, 'the old man's friend', but we have not yet discovered how to control the ageing process. This failure on the part of the medical profession accounts for the most pressing social problem today, namely how to house and care for the increasing number of old people in our midst who are unable to manage for themselves. While there is a proportion in every age-group who never fail to demand the maximum attention available, there are very many proud independent old folk who are reluctant to seek assistance. While I was a Minister I sought to publicize in every way the supplementary assistance available, yet we have never fully penetrated those little shabby homes which shelter old people too independent to seek further help.

Not until a Member of Parliament becomes a Minister does she have the opportunity of peeping behind the curtains of the Civil Service which always seemed to me to be discreetly drawn. The scurry which accompanies a question on the Order Paper concerning the department is in part due to the determination to find an answer which, while apparently meeting the question, nevertheless discloses as little as possible. The Permanent Secretary who can successfully handle the Minister by ensuring that his master follows his advice without thinking too much for himself, is highly respected by his colleagues. Tradition and custom play such a large part in the conduct of a department that woe betide the young man, fresh from Oxford or Cambridge, who decides to ventilate the place by introducing a few new ideas.

It seemed very curious to me that, in vast Government departments concerned with matters not unconnected with some branch of science, I never met an administrator with a science degree; indeed it seemed that to introduce a man with such a qualification into the Civil Service was just not done. It would be conceding that a Civil Servant should relinquish his amateur status and possess some expertise which was opposed to all tradition and custom. I knew that until fairly recently a similar attitude had been adopted to the appointment of Ministers. When Dr Addison became Minister of Health, there were those who whispered that it was going against tradition to appoint a man with special knowledge of the subject as the ministerial head of the department.

The only men I met in the Administrative class had been recruited from the Arts graduates of the older universities, and it was accepted that if scientific advice was called for it could be obtained outside the Ministry. There must be a vast amount of time and effort wasted by Arts-trained Civil Servants compelled to pick up some superficial scientific knowledge in a department where a basic training in the sciences would be of considerable value. The hierarchy in the Civil Service privately regard themselves as being superior to any Minister. They quite rightly observe that Governments come and go, but they go on for ever; therefore, while they are scrupulously polite to Ministers, they have no intention, once having made up their minds, of making any concessions unless the Minister proves stronger than themselves.

One day Sir Edward Bridges, the Permanent Secretary to the Treasury, came to see me to ask if I would allow him to transfer my Permanent Secretary to another post. It had already been whispered in my ear what was afoot, and I asked Sir Henry Hancock, the man concerned, if he wished to leave, as the Ministry had suffered from a number of changes which did not make for efficiency and now it was going along very smoothly. Sir Henry Hancock assured me that he was very happy and wanted to stay; in fact he agreed that I should intercede on his behalf. Consequently I decided to refuse to agree to the suggestion that he should be transferred. In my innocence I believed that that would be the end of the matter. Sir Edward Bridges arrived all smiles and suavity and made his suggestion, which I politely rejected. Without further discussion he announced that he was removing Sir Henry Hancock, rose and took his leave. The whole interview was over in a few minutes. When I told Sir Henry he was disappointed but not surprised for he knew the ways of the Civil Service better than I.

The fact that a woman had challenged the Secretary to the Treasury may well have clinched the matter. As women are not encouraged in the Civil Service I assumed that a woman Minister would not find much favour in the eyes of the Head of the Service. Prejudice is so widespread that a woman has to be far superior to her men colleagues of a similar grade to be considered for promotion, otherwise a Permanent Secretary may suffer a lapse of memory in compiling a short list for the Minister's consideration.

I had a short list presented to me on one occasion which did not contain the name of a woman whose knowledge and judgement were quite outstanding among her male colleagues. When I pointed it out, no reason was given for the omission. She was thereupon included and got the job. It seems that there must be three desiderata in choosing a Civil Servant for the Administrative grade. He must have an Arts degree, come from Oxford or Cambridge and belong to the male sex.

With a son and a daughter there I had for some years visited Oxford fairly frequently. I had spoken from the floor at Union debates, notably on the National Health Service with Dr Charles Hill and later to a motion to prohibit professional boxing, which received overwhelming support. Moreover, I had spoken at a number of societies and had been afforded ample opportunity for listening to undergraduates express themselves with a wealth of aphorism and witty allusion, all of which contributed to a humorous and stimulating discussion. In chatting with some of them afterwards I would learn that they hoped to get into the Civil Service.

After having perused numerous Ministerial briefs I decided that if I were a teacher reading essays I would mark most of them, 'Factual but dull.' Where, I thought, were all these bright boys from Oxford and Cambridge who got a First and were immured somewhere in the Civil Service? What had happened to their capacity for producing a pithy comment or a witty phrase? It often seemed that, provided the facts had been given to them, any fifth former in our grammar schools would have been capable of writing some of the briefs handed to me.

I asked Sir Henry Hancock about this. He was generally very helpful but on this point he was a little evasive. No doubt he felt called upon to be loyal to those far lower down the ladder, or he may have thought that my comments were a reflection on the efficiency of the department. However, he must have decided that my criticism was valid and worth passing on because I received an invitation to address an official gathering of young Civil Servants in Whitehall on 'How a Minister regards the Civil Service'.

I told them what a contrast I found between the amusing, witty undergraduate, and the dull outpourings of which he was capable when he had achieved his ambition, and reached the Administrative class of the Civil Service. After my address questions were called for and I was astonished at the apparent dumbness of these young men, in such contrast to their manner at Oxford. However, after the meeting had dispersed one whom I had known at Oxford in his undergraduate days, greatly daring it seemed, told me that the plain answer was that if he wrote a colourful brief every phrase of which might have tickled my fancy would have been deleted as irrelevant by the time it reached me. This seemed to me to be a subtle, but most effective method of subduing the fresh young Civil Servant and teaching him to conform. I presume that he learnt in the process that promotion was dependent upon his capacity to ape his elders. Although there are those in the Civil Service who would welcome change, the dead weight of tradition and custom smothers their cries.

Both my children enjoy a debate, sharing a whimsical humour which they may well have inherited from their father. Shirley, while at Somerville, became an officer of the Oxford University Labour Club, and, denied the opportunity of debating in the Oxford Union, helped to organize a women's debating club. Some years after she had qualified in medicine, she unsuccessfully contested a by-election as the Labour candidate in the Conservative stronghold of Blackpool.

In October 1964 she was returned as the Labour Member of Parliament for the industrial town of Halifax, defeating Maurice Macmillan the son of the former Prime Minister who had held the seat for the Conservatives for ten years. This gave me the considerable satisfaction of being the first mother to sit with a daughter at Westminster although in different Houses. My son-in-law John Ryman also stood for Parliament, contesting Gillingham at this election, but although he did well he was not successful in achieving a Labour victory.

In 1949 my son Michael, who was reading Law at Merton, and was a fairly frequent speaker at the Oxford Union, put a motion down on the Paper asking that Rule 11 should be amended in such a manner that members of the women's colleges should be admitted to the Oxford Union Society.

I was a Member of the Government, and on that night there was a two-line Whip which Ministers had been asked to observe; for this reason I knew that I should find it difficult to obtain a pair. I explained to the Chief Whip, not too successfully, that this was an occasion which I could not miss. At that moment Captain Crookshank, the Conservative Member for Gainsborough and later Lord Crookshank, happened to be passing; he heard my *cri de coeur* and he, a bachelor, a little remote, and not particularly well disposed to women Members, offered his services as my pair. I never knew what prompted him to do this; it was very gallant, but not in character. That night I sat with my husband in the Public Gallery and listened to Michael expounding a case, which a few years later was accepted as a natural development of co-education; the interruptions and howls of dissent suggested that he was making a proposal opposed to all the decencies of life. The suggestion that intellectual ability was not confined to one sex unleashed yells of fury. The reminder that the result of the examinations proved beyond doubt women's eligibility for membership caused a tumult. Any statement which might be interpreted as favourable to women was drowned in a din. The motion was lost by a large majority, but that did not to my mind affect the resounding moral victory.

A few years later, John Ryman, who was reading Law at Pembroke, moved a similar motion. He had a much quieter reception and lost by a much smaller majority. A very pleasant little incident marked the opening of that debate. A few months earlier, I had spoken from the floor and was subjected to constant interruptions from an undergraduate; his curious sense of humour prompted him to indulge in physical contortions which combined with his unkempt appearance served to distract the audience. I suffered this patiently and then I was compelled to deal with him a little unkindly. I was in the public gallery with Shirley, who was reading Medicine at Somerville, for the debate on the admission of women to the Union, when the President rose and said that before the debate opened a member of the House would like to make a presentation to a visitor in the Gallery. The House was packed and all eyes seemed to be focused on Shirley and me. Shirley looked apprehensive; she anticipated some kind of practical joke. Disengaging himself from a crowded bench, a pleasant-looking young man holding some flowers advanced towards that part of the gallery where we were sitting; then standing on a chair he held a spray of carnations up to me. I realized that it was my interrupter, well-groomed, immaculate, completely transformed. I bent over the gallery and took his delightful offering, which he accompanied with a little speech of apology for his behaviour on my last visit; his return to his seat was accompanied by tumultuous applause.

This astonishing incident seemed to me to be absolutely out of character with the Oxford Union; it served to prove to me, not for the first time, the unwisdom of arriving at hasty conclusions.

12

The Ignoble Art

Invitations to open bazaars, judge baby shows, give school prizes and attend events of various kinds came my way as they do to all candidates and Members of Parliament; I probably received more than my share because of my medical qualifications.

It was in the thirties on a very hot afternoon, in a hugh marquee in a Midlands town that I vowed never again to judge a baby show. The howls of the poor infants preceding the judging had distressed the mothers, but when the whole business was over and the prizes announced the heat and general discomfort were not conducive to a display of good manners.

Every woman should have had a prize for being a good mother, who does her best for her baby, and it was utterly wrong within the space of a few hours to pick certain babies out of a good bunch. One mother would have little difficulty in feeding a child herself; another would strive to do what she knew was best despite the advice of friends to give it a bottle. I decided that afternoon, that it was not the baby who should be judged but the mother, and her efforts to achieve a high standard of motherhood.

Boxing contests often play a part in the various social activities of boys' clubs. According to one well-intentioned but not highly intelligent social worker these clubs could not be kept going were it not for the boxing. 'The boys like fighting each other,' she said.

Of course boys like fighting each other and they continue to like it when they are grown men. The aggressive instinct is a powerful one and like other instincts leads to trouble unless checked.

As I watched these displays, I noted that crooked legs among our children were a thing of the past, yet while the medical profession had applied its energies to this aspect of preventive medicine it permitted, in the name of sport, small boys to deliver punches to the most sensitive part of the human body – the brain. Certain headmasters permit this because they believe that the male of the species should be prepared to fight with his fists if provoked; and in some schools it is the rule that other boys must watch the process. It would seem that the male code of behaviour in this respect has not changed since primitive man settled his disputes.

Today fighting is glamorized on the television screen and brought into the living-rooms of the people, where youngsters form a large part of this captive audience. Prize-fighting is still accepted as a display worthy of a civilized people despite the fact that all those connected with it are fully aware that it caters to the latent sadistic instincts.

The man who protests that this is a natural form of behaviour might protest equally loudly if he were commanded to take a second wife, just because his natural procreative instinct was sufficiently strong to warrant it.

Those who watch bullfighting, or boxing bouts, resent being told that the infliction of pain gives pleasure to some people. Nevertheless, cock-fighting was prohibited in this country not primarily for the sake of the cock, but for the protection of the public from a degrading display.

Supporters of boxing assert that Rugby football is equally dangerous. This argument cannot survive examination. The primary objective in football is to score goals and not to knock your opponent insensible; I have never heard of a 'punch-drunk' Rugby football player.

I find it difficult to distinguish between amateur and professional boxing. The rules are almost the same and the objective is the same, namely, to knock your opponent out in the shortest possible time. The fist cannot distinguish between a professional and an amateur brain.

The amateur wears a vest and is permitted to box for a canteen of cutlery, or a gold watch, but not for the equivalent in terms of cash. Nevertheless, he is subject to the same injuries as the professional and many cases have been reported of death in the ring, or shortly after a fatal blow has been struck.

If a school 'tradition' demands that boys should learn to punch each other then some higher authority should intervene; for violence in all forms is harmful, physically, mentally and socially, and should not be countenanced in any school. I have always sought the advice of surgeons and doctors who are fully competent to express an opinion. Mr J. H. Doggart, M.D., F.R.C.S. an ophthalmic surgeon in an address to the British Ophthalmological Society said, 'In spite of all assertions to the contrary by gladiatorially minded sentimentalists facts will out. Medical literature abounds with records of havoc wrought by boxing and it seems clear that sight, sanity and life itself are endangered when a man pursues this sport over a period of years especially in the professional ring.'

The President of the Society said that at one time or another he had had a number of pugilists as patients. One he had seen at Moorfields curiously enough had the name of Bill Softly. Bill had on one occasion suffered an injury to the superior oblique muscle. When trouble had recurred following subsequent injury, he had pointed out to Bill that seeing double must be rather awkward for him, whereupon Bill had replied, 'Yes, I see two chaps in the ring and I hit the one that isn't there and the one that is there hits me.'

Investigations have been conducted at Guy's Hospital and the Manchester Royal Infirmary into the condition of men who have been engaged in boxing for some years. Dr Ian Isherwood, Dr C. Mawdsley and Dr F. R. Ferguson of Manchester, at an international medical conference in New York in September 1964, reported that in carrying out X-ray studies of the brain in sixteen former boxers, they learned that only three were normal, while the other thirteen had a variety of pathological features. They reported that the origin of brain tissue damage in neurologically diseased ex-boxers suggested that previous injury presumably caused by blows to the head was responsible.

The *Lancet* reported that the same doctors from the Manchester Royal Infirmary had arrived at the conclusion that, 'It seems certain that boxing can cause progressive mental disease.'

Undoubtedly more doctors are evincing an interest in the possible effects of boxing on the brain and the British Association of Sport and Medicine held a Conference in November 1963 at the University of London Goldsmiths College on the Medical Aspects of Boxing.

Even the *Lancet*, in June 1959, urged all doctors to fight for the abolition of boxing; it described boxing as an evil which could lead to 'brain injury, imbecility, blindness, or death.' In a leading article it warned doctors that any move to stop boxing would have to contend with the very large financial interests concerned, with the public appetite for violence and bloodshed, and with plain indifference. It said that, 'The individual doctors can help by warning boxers, headmasters, parents, and the sports enthusiasts who run boys clubs about the danger of delayed brain injury.' It reminded its readers that in four years there have been sixty-four boxing deaths including twenty-two amateurs. That, it says, is surely a prohibitive price to pay for a sport which makes the brain and its exquisitely sensitive extensions such as the eye, legitimate – in fact main – targets. Not only is nothing done to end the evil, says the *Lancet* but 'official' bodies such as the B.B.C. extend the spectacle to ever-widening audiences, including children'. This article brought protests from the Boxing Board of Control whose secretary, Mr Teddy Waltham said, 'There is an element of risk in anything. No one goes into boxing with a pistol held to his head. Are all the young men so dull and stupid that they are going to walk into a hell of danger?' At least the secretary of the Boxing Board of Control admitted that the conditions described by the *Lancet* were in fact 'a hell of danger'. Unfortunately the physically fit boys and young men who enter the ring know nothing of the anatomy of the brain and its functioning so they are completely ignorant of the 'hell of danger they are walking into'.

A South African Member of Parliament who practised surgery in Durban for thirty-seven years has drafted a Private Members' Bill to ban boxing.

He said in an interview on 3 October 1963, 'If you hit a man on the head with a club you are jailed and if he dies you are hanged. But you can go into a small roped enclosure and in the presence of thousands by skilfully using your fists you can maim, mentally cripple, or kill a less skilful person. It is important to remember that careful medical examination and care and vigilant refereeing can't prevent the first injury – and the first injury may be fatal.'

He is right. A few skilled experts may escape but after about thirty to sixty professional fights the boxer begins to soften up; mental and emotional changes manifest themselves which are obvious to his relations. His memory deteriorates and his mood alternates between euphoria and deep depression. His lot is certainly a grim one for this is the only sport in which wounds inflicted and blood drawn give colour, zest and a sadistic thrill to the display. Professional boxing is the only sport in which to confess injury and retire is to risk a hostile demonstration from the spectators.

The sports commentators always express surprise when a champion fails to deliver his punches correctly. Are these experienced men, who have seen this happen again and again genuinely surprised? Or are they compelled, for economic reasons, to try to divert the attention of the public and other aspirants to ring fame, from the tragic end of yet another young boxer?

There are some correspondents shocked by the ringside scenes who have the courage to denounce the business in no uncertain way. Richard Starnes writing in the *New York World Telegram* on 26 March 1964 said:

'Senator Philip A. Hart's anti-trust and monopoly sub-committee is conducting hearings on the Liston–Clay pushing match. "Time," Hart warned at the start of the hearings, "is running out for the boxing business unless something is done."

'Just by calling it the boxing business, the Senator from Michigan did a lot more for the rowdy old racket than it deserves. It is a nasty, degrading enterprise and enriches hoodlums at the expense of the broken bodies and shattered minds of the poor slobs who work at it. It maims and it murders, and any decent society would have outlawed it at about the time bear-baiting was prohibited. . . . Prize-fighting is not manly, it is not an art, and it has nothing to do with self-defence. What should be engaging the attention of the good, if not quite bright, Senators is a law abolishing it forthwith. That is the only means available to dry up a seething cesspool that is an affront to decent people.'

Alistair Cooke in September 1963 writing for the *Manchester Guardian* in New York under the title 'Burlesque of the manly art' described the Liston–Floyd Patterson fight in Las Vegas, Nevada, the night before, when 'Sonny' Liston knocked out Floyd Patterson in 130 seconds. In Chicago in September 1962 he did it in 126 seconds. 'The only dispute,' wrote Cooke, 'among the experts swirls around the mystery of this four-second delay. . . . Liston walked over to Patterson and hit him with a right and a left and knocked him down. Patterson got his statutory eight seconds breath. Then he fell in a drowning embrace on Liston who pummelled him on the chin, the chest and the neck. He fell down again and took another breather. Then he stood with his gloves down around his hipbones and Liston clouted him with a straight left and hooked him with a right.

He flopped down and threw his arms out, panted awhile, got on one knee, waited respectfully for the count of ten, and went back to his dressing-room to collect £110,000 to clap on his famous moustache and beard and get out of town before he was spotted.'

In November 1962 I received a card from a restaurant on 49th and 50th Street, New York, autographed, 'Good Luck. Jack Dempsey.'

I hope this means that one of the fortunate men who can still earn his livelihood has had second thoughts about the wisdom of encouraging young men to be exploited by the boxing business. Undoubtedly, public opinion is changing in favour of controlling prize-fights if not altogether banning them.

In 1953, the Hardwicke Club, a debating society for lawyers to which all barristers and students are eligible asked me to propose the motion 'That this House wishes professional boxing could be banned.' The meeting was held at Niblett Hall, King's

Bench Walk, Temple. I found it difficult to find any man willing
to second the motion; although men often told me, out of ear-
shot of their men friends that they supported my point of view,
it was impossible to persuade them to speak publicly on the
subject. I therefore invited one of the young barristers present
to support me. Mr Jack Solomons, the boxing promoter,
opposed the motion, supported by Mr Peter Wilson, the sports
writer, and the late Mr Freddie Mills, a former boxer.

We were given twenty minutes each to put the case. I was
armed with a skull, which I had borrowed from my daughter,
then a medical student, and I carefully described the effect of
the impact of the soft brain on the sharp sphenoidal ridge,
following a blow to the point of the jaw, and how comparatively
light blows caused the brain to bounce about in its hard case.

Then Mr Solomons spoke, and after a few minutes resumed
his seat. He said that he knew of prize-fighters who, on retirement, had bought public houses, others who had proposed to
rich women, and one had acquired a vast sum of dollars.
'What's wrong with the business if they can do that?' he
asked.

When the vote was taken I had a narrow majority.

In 1958 I debated a similar motion at the Oxford Union
Society. The House was packed, students were sitting on the
floor and I suspected that I was to be the subject of an uproari-
ous rag. On the contrary I was heard in an attentive silence,
and to my surprise and gratification secured an overwhelming
majority.

The motion before the House was – 'That boxing is nasty and
brutish and ought not to be regarded as a sport.' The copy of
the *Oxford Magazine* of 13 November 1958 which reached me
containing an article by Mr Kevin Garry was very welcome.
He wrote:

'I wonder that we could have been so grotesquely betrayed
by the popular Press into thinking of Dr Summerskill as some
sort of nineteenth-century governess, thin-lipped and humour-
less, for ever forcing margarine with inexorable zeal down the
throats of her butter-craving charges. With charm and humour
enough to captivate a hostile coalition of Lord Lonsdale and

John Knox, she took arguments and illustrations from every quarter to build a case that remained unshakable. The voting is a just reflection of the superiority of her arguments. Mr Denzil Batchelor (Worcester) the sporting journalist, is clearly a nice man, but, alas! niceness is not enough without hard argument. Commendably he faced squarely the charges Dr Summerskill had made, but his rebuttals were all too often merely trivial. Worse, towards the end of his speech he unveiled a bewildering series of monuments to jingo of a sort that is persuasive in Cambridge but is only embarrassing here. It was, for example, a lethal miscalculation to think to rally the House by referring to boxing as one of the forces that had 'made our race glorious once upon a time'. The House voted against his side by 511 to 184, which gave a majority even more decisive than that against women.' [The reference here to women concerned the vote given against the admission of women to the Union.]

I am well aware that I fail to leaven most of my speeches with humour. In their preparation I get carried away with the serious import of the subject and forget that a laugh provides some little respite from a weighty theme, besides the physiological fact that it also increases the oxygen supply. This report therefore gave me considerable comfort.

However, I have not always enjoyed such a respectful hearing. In 1953, speaking in the House in opposition to an amendment to the Budget, the purpose of which was to reduce Entertainment Duty on boxing, such was my reception that I found it difficult to make myself heard.

In 1954 I rose again on a similar amendment to the Budget anticipating the same kind of treatment and I was agreeably surprised to find that the House was prepared to listen to me without interruption. I was so relieved that I said 'You will recall, Mr Hoy [the Chairman] that last year a similar amendment was moved and that I opposed it. It was late at night and my speech was accompanied by jeers, cheers, and interjections of all kinds. I must confess that it is very pleasant this afternoon to rise in this peaceful and, I hope, slightly more sympathetic atmosphere. I wish to present a rational case. . . . I think that it is clear that public opinion is changing, and I believe that even since last year, a volume of public opinion has been created in this country of such a degree that there are many people who will read my speech tomorrow with much greater sympathy than that with which they read my speech last year. . . .'

Anticipating the amendment, I arranged in March 1954 for a deputation of men representing medicine, sport, education and the Church to put the case to the Treasury. I had heard that deputations led by the most vocal advocates of prize-fighting made a rule of seeking an interview with the Chancellor or his representative before the Budget.

As a former Minister who had received many deputations, I formed the opinion that the deputation, consisting of Mr J. H. Doggart the ophthalmic surgeon, Mr Ralph, Organizer of Physical Education in Gloucestershire, Mr Fred Roberts, Headmaster of Willesden Grammar School and the late Mr Llewellyn Williams, a Nonconformist Minister and Member of Parliament, which I led, made an excellent impression. They received their reward when the Chancellor of the Exchequer in the Budget which he presented the following month did *not* reduce the Entertainment Tax on prize-fighting.

I do not believe that men will stop playing football or cricket if profits are removed altogether. These are genuine sports which men enjoy solely for the game, but I suspect that prize-fights would stop immediately substantial profits for the middle man disappeared.

I have always been a little disappointed to find that a woman Member of Parliament, Mrs Bessie Braddock, has opposed my attitude to boxing. However, I can quite understand how Liverpool, a boisterous cosmopolitan community with a large Irish element in the population, came to regard fighting both inside and outside the ring as a means of dissipating superfluous energy. Furthermore, Mrs Braddock's late husband had been a boxer and apart from other considerations loyalty alone could determine her attitude.

When for the second time I was defeated in the House of Commons by 120 votes to 17 in my attempt to introduce a Bill to prohibit boxing Mrs Bessie Braddock joined Colonel Bromley Davenport the Conservative, a heavyweight boxer in his Army days, to 'tell' for the 'Noes' in the division lobby.

The picture was accurately presented by Norman Shrapnel the Correspondent of Parliament to the *Manchester Guardian* when he wrote:

'In point of fact, even the soundly defeated Dr Summerskill could claim some success in this attempt to introduce a bill prohibiting professional boxing, for when she tried to do the same thing ten years ago there was such a row that she could not make herself heard at all. This time the House was a shade more gentlemanly though not much. Members who disagreed with her allowed her to have her say, but greeted almost every sentence of her speech with derisive laughter.

'Some of this had an effect more in the line of Hogarth than of Pickwick. After a certain number of fights, Dr Summerskill said, "the ordinary boxer begins to show obvious signs of deterioration" – a remark that greatly amused a number of backbenchers. "His great tragedy," she went on, "is that he loses his mental health and his capacity to concentrate, to co-ordinate his movements, and to hold down a responsible job."

'They found this excruciatingly funny. Perhaps they were thinking how undeteriorated and mentally healthy the ex-boxing colonel looks. But, as the doctor went on to describe the cumulative effects of a long series of small haemorrhages and torn brain fibres, leading to punch drunkenness, the amusement gradually faded. When she said that "these injuries do not heal and the disturbance to the brain cells is permanent" nobody laughed at all. . . .

'Mrs Braddock tried hard to get in a few anti-Summerskill blows but the doctor managed to keep her political ally out of the ring. . . .

'It was soon over, but Dr Summerskill remained strictly perpendicular in defeat.'

On 10 May 1962 in the House of Lords I moved the Second Reading of a Bill to prohibit boxing.
It read:

Be it enacted by the Queen's most Excellent Majesty by and

with the advice and consent of the Lords Spiritual and Temporal and Commons in the present Parliament assembled, and by the authority of the same as follows:

1. Any person who organizes for profit a boxing match shall be guilty of an offence under this Act, and shall be liable, on conviction on indictment, to a fine not exceeding two hundred pounds, or to imprisonment for a term not exceeding three months, or to both.
2. This Act may be cited as the Boxing Act, 1962.

I had formed the opinion that the Lords were always prepared to listen to a case and I considered that the time had come when I might test the feeling of the House. Fourteen speakers put their names on the paper for the second reading of the Bill but I knew the House would be reluctant to commit itself without a full examination of every aspect of the business. Therefore in my opening remarks I said that in the event of my securing a Second Reading I proposed to move that the Bill be referred to a Select Committee.

I had a fairly full House and people listened attentively. I supported my case by quoting Billy Walker, the 'Blond Bomber from West Ham', who on 26 March in an interview with a *Daily Herald* reporter concerning his decision to become a professional fighter said: 'I'm no longer a sportsman. How can you call professional boxing a sport with all the villains and rogues who are part and parcel of the game? It's a business. A hard business all the time, a cruel business some of the time. I've no illusions about the noble art of self-defence or any of that kid stuff. That's all right for the amateurs. But from now on I'm paid to hurt. The more I hurt, the more I'm paid.'

I was followed by Lord Brain, the neurologist, who said that the President of the Royal College of Physicians had told him that the College had the matter under consideration and was prepared to set up a committee to go into it from every medical point of view. He said that as far as he knew the human brain has no way of distinguishing a blow delivered by a professional from a blow delivered by an amateur.

Those who opposed me jumped at the opportunity offered by Lord Brain to delay matters, particularly Viscount Scarsdale, Vice-President of the Boxing Board of Control. Lord Hailsham clearly anxious to avoid, by some procedural means, coming to a decision, sought to divert the attention of the House by a discussion on whether it was proper for the House to vote for the Second Reading in order that the Bill should be sent to a Select Committee.

However, as I had received some heartening support I insisted that it should go to a division. Their Lordships divided: Contents 23; Not Contents 29.

With my usual optimism I had anticipated a victory, this time; but as I only lost by seven votes, I was assured by my supporters that the result was very satisfactory having regard to the large number of abstentions which augured well for my next attempt.

Once more arguments on the merits and demerits of boxing began in the Press and elsewhere, and I was encouraged on receiving a much higher proportion of letters in my favour than I had on other occasions. Opponents always stress the importance of morale. Can it be argued that British morale would suffer if every boxing promoter was taxed out of existence? That British youth would deteriorate physically and morally if it were denied the opportunity of watching two men, either in the flesh or on television, fighting each other until one is overcome?

In an atomic age, when wars will be directed by scientists who have never been near the ringside can it be argued that the boxing promoter and his hangers on are indispensable to Britain? Furthermore is there any evidence that boys who do not learn boxing or attend prize-fights are of an inferior calibre to those who do? The courage displayed by men and women in heavily bombed Fulham, my constituency in the last war, was not acquired in the boxing-ring.

Of all the religious denominations, I found the Methodist Church the most forthright in their support of my attitude. I was very pleased when the secretary, the Rev. Kenneth G. Greet, informed me on 15 July 1963 that a resolution in the following terms was passed by the Methodist Conference by an overwhelming majority:

'Because Professional Boxing involves the deliberate infliction of injury, often permanent and sometimes fatal, on the

E

contestants, and also thereby incites an unhealthy audience reaction, the Conference holds that it is an undesirable sport. The Conference directs that this expression of opinion shall be brought to the attention of our people.'

There has been a change in the attitude of schools in the course of the last few years, and while Grammar Schools and Secondary Modern Schools, if they are presided over by an enlightened headmaster ban boxing without attracting publicity, the attitude of the public school is still regarded as being indicative of a trend.

The *Daily Express* of 29 July 1963 reported:

'Boxing has taken the full count at Bradfield College, the £152 a term public school near Reading. The physical training master Mr Robert Hartigan said: "The decision to ban it has hurt me more than any punch." Mr Hartigan, known to the boys as "Sergeant" went on: "Many of the boys will be sorry to see boxing go. I have been teaching it for twenty years and I never thought a school like this would ban it. I am sure many parents will disagree with the decision. Boxing builds up the strength and teaches smaller boys how to look after themselves!"

'The sports programme of Bradfield will continue to offer fencing, cricket, physical training, football, hockey, sailing, tennis and most forms of athletics.

'The headmaster, Mr Anthony Chevenix-Trench, who was soon afterwards appointed headmaster at Eton, answered a question at the time on his attitude in the future, "I cannot say yet what decision I would make about boxing when I take over at Eton. But it is a matter which I would have to seriously consider, and I would discuss a possible ban with my medical officer. I am told there have been at least two or three occasions when the deaths of young boys have been traced back to boxing injuries.

'"All my boys apparently agree with the decision. . . ."'

Prince Charles's headmaster at Gordonstoun, Mr Robert Chew, said of the ban: 'I think it sounds a sensible decision. We don't teach boxing at Gordonstoun. You have to be very careful teaching older boys boxing.'

Charterhouse dropped boxing two years ago. The Headmaster Mr B. W. M. Young said, 'There has been a growing tendency to leave boxing out of a school curriculum. For one reason there is great difficulty in matching boys in fights.'

Coal miners, particularly in South Wales, have always shown a keen interest in boxing and always followed closely the careers of their local champions. But it would seem that there is a change of attitude in the pits for in 1964 the National Coal Board decided to discontinue the miners' amateur boxing championship because of falling support and lack of entries. In peak years there were 650 entries, but in 1964 there were only 103.

The special significance of this amateur reluctance to join a boxing club lies in the fact that the professional boxer is recruited from the amateurs. A boy who shows promise is encouraged by managers in the commercial world of boxing to become professional with the dazzling prospect of a sudden accumulation of wealth. This falling off of amateur boxers therefore accounts in part for the spectacular drop in the number of registered professional boxers.

In 1955, I wrote *The Ignoble Art*, The Case against Boxing, and I have been encouraged by the number of Library Committees that have placed the book on their shelves. It is not unusual for schools and universities to debate the subject; and apparently, if I am to judge from the letters I receive asking for further information there is no difficulty today in obtaining a proposer for a motion to ban boxing.

All the media of propaganda are used when the prospect of war is imminent, because the aggressive instincts of a disciplined people in peace time are not easily aroused. Men who have been taught to believe that fighting in any form is commendable need little encouragement. Hitler glamorized violence and fostered the aggressive instincts of the German youth by every means in his power and with such success that when the time came for them to sacrifice themselves they gave their lives unquestionably, singing songs glorifying Hitler.

When countries are locked in warfare the chance for people to think rationally may be lost. It is in peace-time that we should consider whether the community has fulfilled its responsibilities to our young people by teaching them to hate violence and to control their aggressive instincts.

Women can no longer regard war as a man's pastime. Modern warfare threatens the whole family from the oldest to the youngest. The conception of gallantry of medieval times which limited warfare to the physically fit has now been abandoned.

If we do not call a halt to the production of nuclear weapons, the armament manufacturers will seek to develop others with an increased capacity to inflict harm. The atomic bomb does not necessarily represent the last word in armaments. It seems that no threat of war, however destructive, deters those who profit from the glamorization of violence. The captive audience in most homes is indoctrinated through its TV sets to regard fighting in one form or another as an inescapable part of civilized behaviour. We appear to be making no deliberate effort by education to control the aggressive instincts of people. If the supreme folly of nuclear war encompasses the world, I might derive some small but morbid satisfaction from the knowledge that it will destroy the blameworthy politicians and armament manufacturers equally with the millions of innocent victims.

The United Nations has done its best to pacify its members and eliminate jealousies and suspicions, but its representatives in every country should concern themselves more closely with the cult of violence which seems to be a constituent part of the education of the people.

On 20 June 1956 Christina Foyle gave one of her Literary Luncheons at the Dorchester Hotel, with the author Mr Louis Golding, in the chair to mark the publication of *The Ignoble Art.*

Despite the subject of my book, among the two hundred or so guests at the lunch there were approximately nine times more women than men except at the top table where the sexes were evenly balanced. Mr Golding, in introducing me, told the audience that he did not agree with me and that he 'would like to have a go' at me. He had come to the conclusion that it must be the masochist in him because once he had had a go at Bernard Shaw in the Y.M.C.A. and 'he chewed me round with his equine teeth and I loved it'. Mr Golding did not think boxing was an ignoble art. Boxers, he said, were gentler than lady politicians. My husband, Shirley, Michael and Alexander Frere, the Chairman of Heinemann, my publishers, provided me with all the moral support, if I had needed it.

I told the audience that since my book had appeared my post bag had been full; one gentleman from Manchester, writing in support of the noble art, said, 'If I could have ten minutes with you, I would bash your brains in.' I was delighted to welcome Mr Len Harvey, a former champion in the boxing world, as one of the guests of honour. He bore me no ill-will for having written a book condemning prize-fighting, both on medical and social grounds. Indeed, it seemed to me that in retirement he had been able to view the whole scene more objectively, attaching less importance to the size of the purse for which a young man was fighting, and more to the probable outcome of successive fights on his health. Among the other guests was Eartha Kitt, the popular cabaret singer from the United States. I wondered what could possibly have induced her to accept an invitation to the lunch, and in answer to my forthright question she gave me the astounding reply, 'Of course I accepted, I am a feminist.' I confess that I had always regarded Eartha Kitt as being possessed of all the feminine powers of seduction, but I had never expected her to expound the feminine philosophy with which she delighted me in the course of our short chat. A little later I was not surprised to hear her engaged in animated conversation with Sir Gerald Kelly, R.A., on Chinese philosophy and the difference between physical and mental beauty. 'He thinks that where there is physical beauty, mental beauty naturally follows,' commented Miss Kitt, 'I think he is quite wrong.' Further down the top table Shirley – a medical student – chatted to Len Harvey. Afterwards Shirley told me that they discussed Italy, Cornwall, and women's hats – Shirley being hatless – but boxing was never mentioned. Mr Uffa Fox, the Duke of Edinburgh's yachtsman, who told me that he had flown from Paris for the luncheon, sat next to Sir Beverley Baxter, the Member of Parliament and journalist. As both seemed to enjoy the function and were extremely pleasant, I gathered, I hope correctly – that neither were violently opposed to the views which I had expressed in *The Ignoble Art*.

There are those who believe that my condemnation of boxing stems from either a feminine aversion to physical violence or an unfavourable medical assessment of the occupational hazards of a boxer's career. While both these considerations may affect my approach to the pastime, I am more deeply concerned with the effect on the audience of the spectacle of two men battering each other, accompanied by a commentary which emphasizes the pain and the extent of the bleeding suffered by the contestants.

A youngster is allowed to watch prize-fighting on television and listen to the uninhibited yells of the crowd in the presence of a father who clearly favours this kind of behaviour. The boy not blessed with a high intelligence is influenced by the official approval of these displays in the shape of his father and the broadcasting authorities.

Fighting in boxing-rings and wars has been glamorized to the extent that most boys believe that there is some special virtue in fighting even though he or his opponent may be killed in the process. Some people find it difficult to accept that the infliction of pain can give pleasure; no normal individual would consciously inflict physical pain unless he had criminal tendencies, but a sadistic streak is found in most people despite their protestations to the contrary. While there may be some conscious element in our social and sex lives, for the most part this impulse is hidden in our subconscious minds; this accounts for the repudiation of the suggestion that a boxing contest in which blood flows freely can provide a satisfying form of entertainment. It cannot be denied, however, that the hysterical yells of the onlookers increase in direct ratio to the bloody signs of wear and tear which mark the active participants in the proceedings.

It is argued that the ordinary citizen should enjoy his leisure as he thinks fit. If a spectacle is calculated to degrade and brutalize the onlooker, should the community absolve itself from all responsibility for these exhibitions? Devotees of prize-fighting hint darkly at what might happen if this powerful subconscious impulse is repressed. It is even suggested that to return to a more primitive standard of behaviour would free the modern world or its army of neurotics.

This theory dismisses the fact that civilized man is slowly evolving and each new social advance affords him considerable satisfaction. His greatest triumph is undoubtedly the emergence of a moral self which is concerned with the control of his instincts. The contention that to reject what it has taken him many ages to acquire would afford contentment and yield an integrated personality is to ignore the long and painful journey in which man has been engaged. Impulses are sublimated by directing them into other channels. As fighting in the ring involves premeditated violence, the energies of the physically fit youth would be more beneficially employed in other games and sports.

If instinct alone is to determine an action on the grounds that it is natural, then polygamy should be equally approved. In the days of Mohammed, tribal wars may have determined the pronouncements of the Prophet, but in our modern society we accept the monogamous state and reject polygamy as being socially undesirable and against the best interests of family unity. Those who declare that fighting with the fists is natural and therefore not to be discouraged should be equally vocal in favour of an Act of Parliament which compels a man to take more than one wife.

The schoolboy code ordains that to show fear is unmanly and to be prepared to fight on the slightest provocation is deserving of admiration. No doubt the aggressive boy likes fighting and there may be lots of other things he would like to do unchecked. This background cannot be discounted in considering the root causes of war. The United Nations' concept of universal peace is supported by all right-thinking people, but the propositions that law not war should determine the approach to international problems is not accepted by some Statesmen reared, one suspects, in the belief that force alone can ensure the successful outcome of an argument.

The commercial interests in boxing like to assert that the Welfare State has sapped many would-be pugilists of the spirit to fight. Before the war there were 4,000 licensed boxers; after the war the figure fell to 2,000 and has now shrunk to 500, and of these probably only 350 are active boxers. There is no doubt that the boxers' lot has changed considerably from the days when hunger drove him to accept a few pounds or any offer of a fight. In the old days a fighter going six three-minute rounds would earn £1; for fifteen two-minute rounds the pay would rise to £7 10s. 0d. At least one welcome result of the present shrinking number of professionals is that a man need now fight relatively few matches to reach a title and his exposure to brain damage is thereby reduced.

Most fighters want to win by a knockout for this builds up a fighter's reputation, making it possible for him to earn more money and advance in division ratings. Most knock-out blows are delivered to the head and, even when a fighter directs his attack to other parts of the body, it is usually a diversionary measure to get an opening to the head. Boxers know that if they are to inflict injury to the brain, then the facial and chin blows prove more effective than any others and consequently they concentrate on these.

According to the old hands, public taste has changed. Whereas years ago the science of evasion was stressed, nowadays the demand is for offensive action. If one is to judge from the newspapers, the public is not interested in the scientific approach to boxing; it wants gossip about the fighters before the event and a bloodthirsty description of the fight afterwards. Of course there are newspapers which still attach great importance to moral values, and during the last few years certain editors both in this country and the United States of America have had the moral courage to denounce prize-fighting, but a boxer does not look to these to give him publicity.

The manifestations of injury to the brain are colloquially referred to by such terms as 'grogginess' and 'punch-drunk', and it is not sufficiently recognized that these conditions indicate the presence of serious cerebral disorders. Occasionally similar injuries occur in sports other than boxing but here they are accidents rather than sequences of intentional acts. Professional boxing is the only sport in which a participant seeks to knock his opponent out in the shortest possible time. It is the only sport in which wounds inflicted and blood drawn gives colour, zest and a sadistic thrill to the exhibition. It is a business in which the fighter himself may not realize that he has been damaged and that his mental processes are gradually deteriorating. If he does, he may not admit it, for fear of being barred from further fights.

The gradual changes which take place in the boxer who becomes an obvious punch-drunk are familiar to the managers and promoters. The skilful amateur boxer who may be spotted in a boys' club will master the finer points of pugilism by training in a gymnasium. He is heralded as a future champion and, desperately anxious to fulfil the predictions of his supporters, tends to fight rather than to box, and so receives some degree of injury in each of say thirty or forty short amateur matches. Later as a professional he meets stiff opposition and engages in longer fights, but he is young, strong, enthusiastic, and making money. After a period of approximately four years as a professional boxer, during which he is engaged in about thirty to sixty bouts, he begins to soften up. A blow to the jaw now shakes him badly and he remains dazed for a longer period than formerly, while his legs will feel weak and numb. His timing begins to fail; his defence deteriorates and the pugilist who had been skilful enough to avoid disfigurement now develops a flat nose and cauliflower ears. Later his knees begin to give way after a blow to the head and a slight dragging of the feet may be noticed. The fighter assures his associates that he is feeling fit but he loses contests which in his early days he could have won with ease. The knock-out blow which so often takes the crowd by surprise (and even the man who delivers it as well) is often decisive because a boxer has been so dazed by previous blows that he leaves himself exposed to the final punch.

Those with a monetary interest in the business argue that the referee is there to see fair play and to protect the fighters from sustaining serious injuries. There is of course no effective protection for the fighters; the crowd sees to that. If a fighter shows that he has had enough and drags his feet or retires prematurely then he is the target for abuse. The same treatment is meted out to the referee who may in all good faith stop a fight, because he thinks that enough damage has been inflicted on one of the contestants. Time and again the referee's ruling has been challenged by a hostile crowd afraid of being deprived of a sordid entertainment.

There was the well-known case of Eugene Henderson, the referee who stopped the first Freddie Mills v. Gus Lesnevich contest for the world cruiser-weight title in 1946. He stopped this fight in Lesnevich's favour in the closing seconds of the tenth round when Mills had reached what was in his opinion the utmost state of physical exhaustion to which a boxer should be allowed to go. Mills's manager, Ted Broadribb, fully concurred in this action and subsequently Mills in writing of the incident expressed approval of Eugene Henderson's decision. Nevertheless the wisdom of his action was called in question and subsequently Eugene Henderson resigned from refereeing for a period. The boxer generally tries to please the customers. If he fails to do so or ignores them and concentrates on style then he risks ridicule and boos.

Randolph Turpin in his last appearance at the Harringay Stadium was the victim of a running commentary of taunts from those who had come to see him batter his opponent into insensibility and were disappointed. Although Turpin was the winner he was stung into retaliation and shouted as he left the ring, 'You don't want boxing; you want murder.' We are told by the promoters that the object of the contest is to provide the spectators with an exhibition of boxing regulated by rules framed to protect the contestants and to ensure the maximum enjoyment of boxing technique. Yet these bouts are accompanied in the newspapers and on the radio by a commentary which is deliberately phrased to emphasize the brutish element. We are familiar with the radio commentator who gives a graphic description of freshly opened cuts, particularly those over an eye which bleeds profusely and so blurs the vision of the fighter. Blows over the heart and kidneys are mentioned with special relish and the words 'savage', 'slaughter' and 'smashing' represent the verbal currency of those whose duty it is to give an accurate picture to the listening public of the 'noble art'.

Would anybody seriously suggest that the screaming crowd round a boxing-ring is having implanted in it the fine qualities of pluck, endurance, and restraint? If these qualities are inculcated in the boxing-ring why do we not see boxing promoters putting their young sons in the ring for, say thirty to forty fights, just to toughen them up and strengthen their moral fibre so that they can face life as better and finer men? The sharp eye of the manager accustomed to the sequence of events is quick to observe those changes which indicate that the mental health of his charge is deteriorating. The boxer finds it difficult to concentrate and his memory deteriorates; in the middle of a conversation he may suddenly change the subject; euphoria alternates with depression and he may resemble a person who is a little drunk.

The pugilist's family suffer from his drunken bouts and fits of violence, and a wrecked marriage may well be the sequel to years of unhappiness. When the symptoms have developed they may progress for a year or so, when they will usually become stationary.

The fist gloved and ungloved is not the only instrument responsible for the injuries sustained by the boxer; the boxers' heads colliding with each other can inflict injury as well as the hard floor coming into contact with the man's temple. Multiple blows to the head lead to small haemorrhages in the brain and these are followed by patches of cerebral atrophy. The old boxer who excitedly, illogically and incoherently, with defective enunciation, seeks to defend prize-fighting is manifesting punch-drunk symptoms. Commitment to a mental hospital may be the last act in this tragedy.

The degree of damage to the brain cannot be measured solely by a few heavy punches but must be assessed in relation to the minor head blows received over the years. A few skilled experts may escape but the ordinary fighter, after about fifty fights, in a few years begins to show the unmistakable signs of deterioration. He fails to time his blows properly because the damage to his brain has caused cerebral atrophy, his defence is inadequate and soon he is a back number; his promoters have quite deserted him and with them his good-time friends. He is forgotten by the public and he finds himself a bitter and disillusioned man. His great tragedy is that he has lost his mental health, his capacity to concentrate, very often to co-ordinate his movements and to hold down a responsible job.

A death in the ring hits the headlines, but the injuries inflicted on a man's brain over the years, reducing him to a subhuman mental condition without necessarily making him certifiable, are only fully appreciated by those in direct contact with the unfortunate individual. When the structure of the brain is considered, it must be obvious that this sensitive organ cannot fail to be damaged following the impact of a succession of blows over the years. The brain weighs about three pounds; it is of the soft consistency of cold porridge; it is not tied down and rests in a fluid in the bony skull. A blow causes it to wobble from side to side; even a moderate blow will cause it to bang against the side of the skull, and a more severe blow may cause such a sudden forceful movement against the bony parts of the skull as to bring on bleeding or bruises.

In part the brain rests on the sharp, bony sphenoidal ridge. A severe blow which jolts the frontal lobes of the brain against the ridge will destroy the tissue, tearing through the fine membrane which covers the brain and the brain substance and inducing bleeding. These injuries do not heal and the destruction of the brain cells is permanent. The frontal lobes which are damaged in this way are those parts which control man's highest functions, namely the power to co-ordinate his movements, to restrain his impulses, and to exercise his power of self-control. Another injury to the brain can be caused by small haemorrhages in the *pons* and *medulla*. These haemorrhages are apt to occur during a severe beating in which the boxer continues to fight although he is only partially conscious, a condition called 'out on his feet'. This condition generally precedes the knock out. These small haemorrhages are not revealed in an X-ray and therefore any medical examination in this respect is useless; they are only revealed on post-mortem examination.

There is agreement among the experts as to the causes and effects of head injuries. There have been experiments upon animals and model human brains and these together with post-mortem findings support the view that boxing in which the head is subjected to severe blows involves serious permanent damage. Those in the boxing business apprehensive as to the future of their vested interest seek to brush aside the opinions of the experts and even attempt to ridicule them.

The more intelligent boxer recognizes the danger, and Gene Tunney, one of the most famous heavyweight champions of his day, tells in his autobiography how, after sparring with two of his partners, he suffered from concussion and became semiconscious for a period. He said that after returning to normal he decided that any sport in which such accidents could occur was dangerous and the first seed of retirement was sown then. The possibility of becoming 'punch-drunk', he said, haunted him for weeks.

Despite the hazards to health and life itself it is possible to find medical men prepared to encourage youths to enter the ring. Professional men in this category are to be found attached to the various Boxing Boards of Control which in this and other countries are concerned with ensuring that the regulations which govern boxing are observed. There are others who despite the most damning medical evidence are reluctant to condemn boxing. Here I suggest is a clear case of emotion defying reason. The aggressive boy is encouraged by his school and his father to regard fighting with the fists as a manifestation of the finest male attributes. Later in University and Medical School the same code of behaviour is encouraged. So powerful · is the effect of public opinion that even the certain knowledge that blows to the head are injurious would not persuade some young men to reject a pastime which might imply that they were lacking in courage. With this background it would be remarkable if male doctors could completely re-educate themselves emotionally and allow only their reason to dictate their attitude towards boxing. While many of the athletic activities of young men are associated with risk of injury and, rarely, of death, their value in developing physical fitness and character more than justifies the risk involved. Boxing is unique among the sports of civilized communities in that the object of the boxer is not only to hurt his opponent, but if possible to render him unconscious. The conditions in the boxing world here are only a pale reflection of what happens in the United States of America. In 1955 the National Boxing Association of America asked Congress to use its powers as the Association was unable to put its own house in order.

Heavy gambling on fights cause frequent scandals which are

exposed in the papers. The bookmaker seems to be an indispensable part of this business and his activities both before and during the fight contribute to the rather squalid atmosphere. The excitement of a fight whether viewed from the arena or on television can certainly be intensified if the viewer also has a financial interest in the result, however small. In America, boxing has tended to symbolize the American way of life; it has emphasized the importance of aggressive qualities, of strength, endurance and the ability to receive heavy blows. During the last few years a noticeable change has taken place in the attitudes of many responsible people. Scientists, doctors and physical instructors who have studied the effects of these bouts on the contestants and the public are now opposing these exhibitions. A few boxers also have expressed adverse opinions based on their own personal experience.

The amateur boxer generally condemns prize-fighting unequivocally. He has the utmost contempt for the sordid business interests which surround the professional ring.

However the sheer humbug of the professional versus the amateur distinction in sport, whether it be in boxing, ice skating, or lawn tennis, is revealed when an individual who has been a stickler for all the proper forms of etiquette being observed in relation to the amateur turns professional overnight. This transformation is invariably accompanied by a contract carrying some little compensation for the rapid metamorphosis.

It is undoubtedly true today that professional boxing carries a social stigma. Lord Knebworth in *The Lonsdale Library* gives this explanation:

'When there entered the professional ring a number of ill-made, ugly, unworthy men who could no more box than they could appreciate fresh air, but who understood the subtle arts of finance and showmanship and "boost" the degradation of the professional ring began. . . . As the love of money took the place of pride in victory, as clean fighting was superceded by clever manipulation, so the mad lunacy of twentieth-century sport burst upon a bewildered and little-understanding world. . . . The public which attended boxing contests was no longer either interested, well-informed or enthusiastic so much as a great herd of ignorant and befuzzled people. Potential ticket buyers were fooled by the Press, fooled by the boxers and fooled by every bookmaker who troubled to relieve them of their cash.'

In my condemnation of prize-fighting I confess that I have never become quite so offensive as this authority on the business.

13

Winston Churchill and Others

In 1950 I found an unexpected ally. Mr Attlee had arranged a dinner-party at Number 10 Downing Street to which I, as Minister of National Insurance was invited. Sitting just opposite me was Winston Churchill. He was unusually quiet and uncommunicative and the expression of his mobile face seemed to indicate that he was sunk in deep thought. I speculated on this and found no difficulty in coming to my own conclusions concerning the cause of his reverie; for after the most triumphant years of his political life at Number 10, when he had every reason to expect that he would be returned for many more years to preside over the shaping of the peace, he had been rejected by the people in 1945 in a most decisive manner. Any visit to Number 10 must revive this bitter disappointment.

Suddenly, my reflections were interrupted; apparently they were very wide of the mark, for Winston Churchill lent over and said in his rather slurred speech, 'You are quite right; boxing is a horrible business; they've invited me to their fights on many occasions but I always refuse to go. You carry on, you're sure to win.' I thanked him for his support but said that I had never expected to receive it from him. He frowned, 'Why?' he asked. I told him that those who opposed me argued that boxing implanted courage and endurance, qualities which are called for in a soldier, and I thought that this argument would appeal to him. 'Absolute nonsense,' he snapped. 'Discipline and the cause make a good soldier and I can't see much of either in the

squalid fights described in the newspapers.' This little interchange was unexpected because I never imagined that Winston
Churchill was concerned with social problems of this nature.
Moreover, I was astonished to learn that it was his rule never
to accept invitations to fights. What interested me more was
that he had been prepared to congratulate a woman Member
of Parliament on any activity in which she had been engaged.
He had bitterly opposed those who had struggled to secure the
franchise for women, and had aroused such hostility that Hugh
Franklin, a redoubtable suffragist, had threatened to horse-
whip him. Having listened to Nancy Astor's description of the
boycott she endured during her first years in the House, I
questioned whether he had mentally registered me as a Member
of Parliament much less a Minister in Her Majesty's Government.

It was after the same dinner that Lady Spencer Churchill –
Mrs Churchill as she then was – and I had a long chat on
domestic matters. The contribution which she made to her
husband's comfort reminded me of Ellen Wilkinson coming
into the Women Members' Room during my early days in the
House, with a brief-case in one hand and a dozen letters which
she had just collected at the House Post Office, sighing, 'Oh!
for a wife.' I looked puzzled. She added, 'If I had a wife, she
might have collected these, drafted answers and finally typed
them. She would help with the women's section, give a hand
with the bazaar and, when I get home fagged out, have a
delicious meal ready for me.'

I told Mrs Churchill this little story after she had described
how she managed to feed her husband's six secretaries when
they arrived at different times of the day and night and still
keep the cook in good humour. Her secret was to secure the
co-operation of a little hostelry close by; her evident dedication
to the job of looking after her husband and oiling the wheels of
that complicated machine which regulated his various activities
could have left little time in her life for creative activities of her
own.

But social occasions with mixed political company were not
always as amicable as this one.

As a feminist I find it very difficult to score a point at the expense of a woman, and I can only recall doing it publicly on one occasion. It was at a Foyle's luncheon in honour of the 83-year-old Duchess of Atholl on the publication of her book *Working Partnership*; I was asked to move a vote of thanks to the speakers most of whom had known the Duchess in her earlier days in the House of Commons, and, having reminisced about the Duchess, who had been a Member when I arrived in the House of Commons in 1938, I said casually – too casually perhaps – as I cast my eye along the table, 'I suppose I should say something nice about the speakers.' At this Dame Florence Horsbrugh, the Conservative Member of Parliament for Moss Side, Manchester, as she then was, who had made a contribution not unmixed with political party points, positively bristled.

'You needn't bother,' she snapped. I said gently, 'I'm sorry a few political barbs should be introduced into the lunch. Dame Florence said that the best Conservatives are women. I should like to add that the best women are not always Conservatives.' Although the audience appeared to enjoy this little sally, the next day when I saw this exchange reported in the *Daily Herald* I was sorry that I had allowed myself to retort in kind, and I always feel that Baroness Horsbrugh has never forgiven me.

14

The Married Women's Association

Debates on economic and social problems never failed to
remind me that though they have secured the franchise,
women were still denied full economic emancipation. In the
last century women were kept in subjection by more legal,
economic and social restrictions than ever before in history.
The industrial revolution meant for women the disappearance
of some of their traditional activities, leaving the wealthy with
unlimited leisure and limited interests and the poor too long
hours of drudgery.

As I had early seen in the case of my father's sister, the chief
occupation of the daughters in families where the father could
afford to keep them at home was concerned with preparation
for marriage; the only employment open to women of some
education and of inadequate means was that of governess or
companion; while the women working in the new textile mills,
factories and workshops were kept at the unskilled and lowest-
paid work.

The Sex Disqualification (Removal) Act 1919 permitted
women to earn their living in all the professions with the
exception of the Church of England; it did not stipulate that
the women should be paid at an equal rate with the men for
work of equal value. In medicine, law, journalism and architecture this was accepted but it was not until many years later
that the principle was approved in the Civil Service and teaching.

In industry women had been welcomed as cheap labour,

provided the employment situation was healthy. When unemployment threatened irrespective of other considerations, home was regarded as the only proper place for women. The First World War gave women greater opportunities to demonstrate their ability, and in industry of half a million who entered the metal trade 90 per cent were engaged in work normally done by men; this, however, made no difference to the custom of paying women less than the rate for the job.

After the Second World War, although Ernest Bevin, as Minister of Labour, had given fulsome praise to the women workers, equal pay was still withheld. Although the trade unions have always exercised the greatest vigilance to ensure that no man is paid less than the rate for the job, they appeared on the whole indifferent to the exploitation of women's labour by employers. Successive Governments when pressed on the subject have always sought to evade the issue by maintaining that it was a matter for the employers and the trade unions.

In 1964 when the economic situation of the Government was critical and a demand was made to call a halt to any increase of wages over 3 per cent per annum it seemed to me that, while this might be acceptable to the better-paid workers, it would be grossly unjust to the women who were still denied the rate for the job.

As this matter had now become one of national interest I said on the address in reply to Her Majesty's speech on 10 November 1964, '. . . While a great deal has been said about productivity keeping in step with wage increases – in fact, every time we open our newspapers we read an addition to this theme – little is heard of the millions of women workers whose productivity outstrips their meagre wages. And while the economists and the statisticians and technologists argue among themselves, industry in this country is being kept going in a great measure by the exploited labour of the women who are denied the rate for the job. During the Election it gave me considerable satisfaction in the industrial towns of the North, where there are very many women workers, to point out that Labour's Manifesto alone promised equal pay. I would say that, if accumulated unpaid wages of women denied the rate for the job were calculated they would assume a colossal sum, which would represent the amount by which the employers of women's labour in industry have been subsidized over the years. Women workers, I feel, will particularly welcome the promise to establish an incomes policy based on a close relationship between the increase in productivity and the growth of income. However, in this case equal pay must be basic to any arrangement arrived at by the two sides of industry.'

While economic equality has eluded women outside the home, the changes which have taken place in personal relationships inside the home have not been accompanied by any improvement in the financial status of the wife. While a married woman has the right to her own property since the Married Women's Property Act of 1882 and she can enter into a contract independently of her husband, the woman who has no money in her own right is entirely dependent on her husband. She is deemed to be his agent even in respect of the housekeeping allowance.

In 1964 rather more than half the women between the ages of sixteen and sixty were housewives occupied solely in the care of their homes and families. A few wealthy families can afford staffs but the majority of women either do all the housework themselves, or if they can secure one, have an occasional daily help. Although vacuum cleaners, refrigerators and washing-machines have changed the character of domestic work, nevertheless, few of these appliances work themselves. The housewife is still the cleaner, cook, laundry-maid and nurse for the average family and as such is not legally entitled to a share of the family income.

The Married Women's Association founded in 1938 by Juanita Frances, of which I was President for some years, to be succeeded by Miss Vera Brittain, the authoress, was formed for the purpose of focussing attention on the inequitable economic position of the wife in the home, with a view to securing legislation to establish an equal financial partnership in marriage. The dependent position of the wife cannot be conducive to marital harmony, and, according to the reports of the Marriage Guidance Council, trouble between husband and wife very often flows from a trivial quarrel over money.

It would seem that while my Aunt Eleanor, had she been

born in the twentieth century, would have enjoyed an education commensurate with her abilities and been enabled to earn her living in a variety of ways; yet had she married without private means of her own, her position would be similar to that of a wife a century or more ago.

The case of Mrs Blackwell, with which the Married Women's Association closely concerned itself, illustrates the economic position of the married woman in the mid-twentieth century.

Mrs Blackwell, was a hard-working housewife, who by taking in lodgers strove to help her husband to pay off the mortgage of their house. She was a thrifty woman; she shopped at the Co-op and left her dividends to accumulate; and over sixteen years of married life they totalled £103. Then the marriage broke up and Mrs Blackwell left the home taking her savings: subsequently Mr Blackwell applied to the County Court for the savings to be transferred to him and the application was successful.

The Married Women's Association financed an appeal and the case was heard on 28 October 1943. We briefed a woman barrister, who in the course of the case, brought to the notice of the three learned Appeal Judges, the contributions in terms of service which Mrs Blackwell had made to the family. Should she not receive some financial return in recognition of sixteen years of service given to running the home economically and taking in lodgers, thereby helping to reduce the mortgage?

The Judges ruled that this could not be admitted, for Mrs Blackwell had been using her husband's beds for the lodgers and therefore she was not entitled to claim a penny.

Finally, pleaded our Portia, here was a thrifty woman who had given her services to the home unstintingly in a manner most profitable to her husband; should she not be entitled to some portion of the £103 which are in fact savings out of the housekeeping allowance?

This proposition apparently shocked their lordships. 'If we permitted a woman to save out of the housekeeping allowance, and keep the proceeds, then women would be tempted to give their husbands tinned meat rather than roast meat,' commented one of the learned Judges. Lord Justice Goddard said, when agreeing to the decision of the court:

'In my view there is no legal right for a wife to retain savings made out of housekeeping money. Even if there had been an arrangement between the husband and wife with regard to these savings, I am far from saying that this sort of domestic arrangement can necessarily result in a legal contract.'

And so Mrs Blackwell after sixteen years of unremitting toil on behalf of her family was not entitled to a penny for her services. She was a pathetic little figure in her basement room when I visited her in London, where she worked as a waitress in a restaurant. She was helpless and hopeless, a victim of a legal system which still in the twentieth century treats the wife as a chattel of her husband.

Some years later, although the Married Women's Association, as a comparatively new organization with limited resources, had been unable to undertake a great deal of propaganda I considered that an attempt might be made by introducing a Bill in Parliament to remedy the injustice suffered by women in the position of Mrs Blackwell. The Married Women's Association had concerned itself not only with the case of the married woman harassed through lack of means, but with the plight of the separated and divorced wife and the unmarried mother, where the maintenance and affiliation orders had not been observed.

It was decided that a Bill of a comprehensive character would therefore render the best service to all these unfortunate women, and on 25 April 1952 I moved the second reading of the Women's Disabilities Bill. I reminded the House that we had opened our proceedings with a Prayer in which we asked that our deliberations should be 'free from all prejudice and partial affections'; accordingly I asked those members who did not belong to my sex to try to free their minds of all prejudices and to consider my proposals in a rational manner.

The first clause sought to protect the woman where the man defaults in payment of a maintenance order, or an affiliation order. I proposed that in these circumstances, if a man is in regular employment, an order should be made by the Court requiring the man's employer to pay to the Court certain sums in respect of the arrears and current payments which are due to the applicant. This arrangement operated well in Scotland and I saw no reason why it should not be equally effective in England and Wales.

Clause Two made some further provision for the wife where marriage is terminated in the Courts and I illustrated my point with the Blackwell case, reminding the House of the services which Mrs Blackwell had given to the home. I said:

'Here we see a premium placed on thriftlessness. If this woman had spent on herself the £103 over the sixteen years of her married life the husband could not have demanded the surrender of these savings. But she was a thrifty wife; she looked after him well; and she was an energetic woman, otherwise she would not have taken in lodgers; she saved £103 believing no doubt, in her ignorance – as women do all over the country today – that the money in the Co-operative Society, represented a little nest egg of her own. However, the Appeal Court ruled that it belonged to her husband, because she was only acting as his agent. . . .

'It may be that an over-generous husband keeps a proportionally small share of the family income for himself – although that happens, I think only in very exceptional cases; by so doing he affords his wife an opportunity of making a substantial saving. In the event of the marriage breaking up it would be unjust if this man were to be deprived of a share; on the other hand, a thrifty wife may enable a less thrifty husband to make savings, and to deny her a share would be unfair, having regard to the joint effort involved in running the home.

'I believe that both husband and wife make a contribution to the home and that this should be recognized. While the husband provides the money, the wife makes her contribution in the form of services, and the sooner this partnership is given its proper place in the pattern of home life, the sooner will the institution of marriage command greater respect, especially amongst our young people.

'In this clause both husband and wife are safeguarded against the profligate partner, for while a direction is given that savings may be divided equally, they may also be divided in any proportion which may seem just to the Court.'

The Bill also made provision for the wife who is forced to leave her home on the termination of her marriage. Although all women are not angels and not for one moment would I suggest it, nevertheless, a woman may be an exemplary wife and mother and yet, as the law stands today, a man can compel his wife to leave his home, which by her industry and thrift she may have helped to create, in order to make room for another woman. Time after time magistrates have commented on the hardship endured by women and children in this position.

I proposed that the wife in these circumstances should have for her use certain furniture and household goods, while the court is empowered to give her the tenancy of the flat, or house, where that may seem to the court to be just and reasonable.

Throughout the Bill the husband and wife were both safeguarded. When I came to Clause Three I knew it was necessary to anticipate opposition, for here a man's self-interest was closely involved, and I was speaking to a House in which men predominated.

I said that most marriages are successful and that the success of these marriages is in some measure due to the recognition by a husband that a wife is entitled to a housekeeping allowance proportionate to his means. Nevertheless, the law needs to be adapted not to the good but to the bad husband. There are plenty of men, stupid men, who do not disclose their wages to their wives. There is no more certain way of alienating a woman's affections than by adopting this practice and the man who deliberately alienates the affection of his wife is, indeed, a stupid man.

The legal right of a wife to an adequate allowance to cover household expenses and personal needs has never been properly established. Who can deny the justice of this claim, from a woman who cooks, cleans, mends, irons and washes from one year's end to another?

There are those who delight in proclaiming the sanctity of the home and the importance of the family unit in society, but who deliberately blind themselves to the needs of the one who is the very pivot of the home, and without whom the home loses all its meaning – the wife and the mother. Clause Three gave her the right to apply to the Court for protection and help against a man who exploits her labour, and her love of her home and children, by refusing to give her a reasonable allowance to meet expenses which she must incur.

In those cases, where a man failed to comply with an order that he should pay his wife what appeared to be just and reasonable, the money might be deducted from his wages at the source. If he still evaded payment the proceeds of his property, in whatever form, may be vested in the wife to meet the terms of the order.

Summing up I said: 'Bills designed to protect minorities offer a target to those opponents who argue that the measure is superfluous because the majority are content. No doubt during the passage of this Bill all the old familiar arguments against any form of emancipation of women in the home will be advanced, carefully disguised, of course, by legal arguments designed to prove the impracticability of these proposals. No doubt we shall be told today that far from removing frictions this Bill will introduce an element of ill-will into the family circle.'

Mr Cyril W. Black (Conservative Member for Wimbledon): 'Hear Hear.'

I have found nothing more calculated to catch a prejudiced man off his guard than a speech advocating the further emancipation of women.

Later on this member elaborated his objections to the Bill. Mr, now Sir, Cyril Black is a family man with one son and two daughters, a temperance advocate, pillar of the Nonconformist Churches and among his recreations in the 1962 *Who's Who* is listed public work.

The argument that the emancipation of the housewife might cause dissension in the home is an old one. When legislation to protect the wife from a brutal husband was introduced in the last century, Members of Parliament asserted that to withdraw the husband's right to assault his wife would cause more trouble, not less.

The Married Women's Act, the forerunner of the Married Women's Property Act 1882, which sought to give women some legal rights over her own property, and consequent protection against a profligate husband, was introduced in 1857. Sir John

Buller, M.P. moved, 'That the Bill be read this day three months.' History repeated itself for the amendment on the Order Paper framed to oppose the 'Women's Disabilities Bill 1952' was, 'That the Bill be read this day six months', and the motives of the members who put the amendment down in 1952 were similar to those of their predecessors a hundred years ago.

When the Married Women's Property Act was introduced in 1882, to secure for women who inherited, or acquired, a small amount of property the same protection as their more wealthy sisters could secure through marriage settlements, a Member for a Scottish division was so outraged at this measure, which threatened to undermine the privileges of men, that he said it was a Bill of 'enormous importance'. He assured the House that it was 'as important as all the other Bills that had passed since the Parliament began; and he declared that the women 'righters' had been exceedingly energetic, whilst the friends of the poor married man were indolent; in consequence his case was hopeless. Another Member, Mr Walton said that the Bill would change the position of the sexes and make the woman, instead of a kind and loving wife, a domestic tyrant.

I expressed the view that men who had put their names to an amendment opposing the 1952 Bill might choose their words more carefully than had Mr Walton and Sir John Buller, having regard to the political power exercised by women today. Furthermore, I anticipated that they would adopt the practice, not unknown in this House, of erecting all kinds of legalistic barriers; as there were at least five M.P.s with legal qualifications who had attached their names to the amendment, this seemed to me to be an obvious deduction.

With one exception, that of Sir Edward Boyle, the Member for Handsworth, I was not surprised to see the names of the men opposing the Bill but I had formed the opinion that this plump, smiling, softly-spoken bachelor was one of the more radical of the Tory Members.

A few days before the debate I had heard him on the radio make a contribution to a discussion on marriage; he said that in the event of his marrying he would never under any circumstances make use of the divorce laws. Sir Edward's confidence in his capacity to make a success of his marriage even before a trial run, was surprising; therefore I was astonished to see his name on the Order Paper opposing a Bill calculated to establish equity in the home. Had he added his name, because completely ignorant of the married state and all its trials, he is opposed to mending marriage as well as ending it?

By a coincidence a book, *Women's Life and Labour* by Dr F. Zweig, a Simon Research Fellow of Manchester University, was published at about the same time as the Second Reading Debate of my Bill. In order to demonstrate that I was not without support outside the House I read a relevant extract:

'A woman regards herself primarily as a helpmate to man, but that conception may in practice be carried too far and her status of a helpmate deteriorate to that of a servant or a little slave; . . . a real equality of status could be attained only if a woman who is staying at home could also become at least partly independent in economic terms. . . .'

I was soon aware that the anti-feminists had gathered in force against me; nevertheless, I had the wholehearted, if silent, support of the public gallery which consisted almost entirely of members of the Married Women's Association. And sitting below the gallery was my husband giving me an encouraging smile whenever I caught his eye.

My last word on the Bill was to remind the House that this was a non-Party measure; it benefited Conservative, Labour and Liberal women alike; it represented a charter for the housewife and, by endorsing it, the House would be earning the gratitude of many thousands of women, unorganized and inarticulate who serve the nation in the homes of Britain.

To my astonishment Lieutenant-Colonel Sir Thomas Moore, the Conservative Member for Ayr, who had the reputation of holding views to the right of centre in the Conservative Party, rose and gave me warm and unequivocal support. He warmed my heart in his opening remarks when he said:

'I should like to preface my support of Dr Summerskill by congratulating the husband to whom she has referred on the privilege he has had in listening to a case presented so convincingly, so persuasively and so intelligently. As the Right Hon. Lady has told us, this Bill is long overdue. Indeed I am confident that when it is passed, as I hope and believe it will be, there will be thousands of women throughout this country who will be willing to forget the Right Hon. Lady's politics and rise up and call her blessed.'

Although a few lawyers had indicated their opposition, I had support from some of the most eminent men whose forensic ability and stature in the legal world was undisputed. Sir Lionel Heald the Attorney General, who after a strenuous week paid me the compliment of being in his seat on a Friday afternoon, while not giving me his whole-hearted support on every aspect of the Bill particularly Clause Three, nevertheless carefully analysed its provisions, and expressed the view that the law called for amendment in the interests of the housewife. He reminded the House of the Hoddinott case, where the husband and wife used their joint savings on housekeeping money to invest in football pools. The forecasting was a joint business and the Court of Appeal held that furniture purchased with prizes won by that method belong to the husband; as there was no gift to the wife of the winnings nor a contract that she should have them. The Attorney General added, 'That was one of those cases where someone might make a rude remark about the law.'

He recalled another case Newgrosh *v.* Newgrosh in which Lord Justice Denning had made observations about the rigidity of the law at the present time. He said, with regard to the transfer of the matrimonial home in Clause Two, that in order to cover cases of hardship of that kind it would be a hollow benefit for the wife if she could not rely on all her husband's rights under the Rent Restriction Acts; because the transfer of the title to the house would not avail her in circumstances where a landlord was suing for possession.

Speakers who were opposed to the Bill reminded the House that the Royal Commission on Marriage and Divorce was sitting and that they would undoubtedly consider proposals similar to those embodied in the Bill; therefore it would be wiser to delay coming to any conclusion before we had their recommendations before us. This time-honoured device has been used on innumerable occasions to obstruct progress.

Mr Barnett Janner, Labour M.P. for Leicester North West, a very able solicitor and the father of a solicitor daughter, in supporting the Bill spoke from his wide experience of the courts. Before he rose Mr Hay, a Conservative Member, tried to bring the debate to an end by calling for a count.

Mr Janner said: 'It is a shocking thing, when we are considering a Bill of such tremendous importance as this, whether it be right or wrong, that there should be an attempt made to stifle its discussion.'

Mr Clement Davies, the Member for Montgomery, and Leader of the Liberal Party, in supporting the Bill reminded the House that in 1847 a Member, Mr William Barclay, was venturesome enough to suggest that women might be permitted to hear the debates. There were Members so horrified at the thought that their wives and daughters might come to hear what was being said that they had no hesitation in throwing out the Bill.

Dr Horace King, the Labour member for the Test Division of Southampton who in 1965 was to become the Speaker of the House of Commons speaking in support of the Bill, challenged the lawyer, who said that hard cases make bad laws. 'But,' said Dr King, 'like all adages there is some truth in that, but I found it is hard cases which often call the attention of people to the necessity for making a new law. . . .' He went on: 'The hardships and injustice caused by the present state of the law of marriage is much in excess of the number of cases that find their way to the magistrates' courts. Through sheer fear of the destitution that the Bill seeks to prevent, many women endure untold hardships.'

On Fridays, when Private Members Bills are taken, one often hears Members at their best. The heat and burden of Party wrangling is over for the week and the atmosphere is less inhibiting and more conducive to quiet logical argument, than when the benches are crowded. In this debate there were several splendid examples.

Mr. J. E. S. Simon, the Conservative Member for Middlesbrough West, later Solicitor General and now Sir Jocelyn Simon and President of the Probate, Divorce and Admiralty Division of the High Court, has throughout his legal and political career never failed to champion the wife and mother faced with problems stemming from the break-up of her marriage. He gave me the most powerful support by replying in their own language to those lawyers who sought to destroy the Bill. He said:

'There is nothing extraordinary in the machinery of this Bill. It is not really extraordinary that the employer should be asked to co-operate in seeing that his employee's families are maintained. . . . If the wife saves money out of her houskeeping allowance, or out of her separation allowance given by the services while her husband is away, that belongs in law to her husband; but that surely cannot be supported in equity. If it cannot be supported in equity, it should not be supported in law, and the law should be amended in that respect.'

He had some misgivings about Clause Three; but he thought that the purpose I had in mind could be achieved by devising machinery less formal in atmosphere than the ordinary court of common law, to adjudicate between husband and wife, and to ensure that a reasonable proportion of the man's salary, or wages, went to the support of the wife.

The Married Women's Disabilities Bill was debated on a Friday, when the Whips were off, and therefore only a social conscience or a genuine intellectual interest in the subject brought members to the House. It is customary on a Private Member's Bill for the promoter to move 'That the Question be now put' before four o'clock, otherwise the opponents of the Bill might attempt, as happened on this occasion, to talk it out. The House divided on this motion with the result that the Ayes had 54 and the Noes 20.

As a hundred members had not voted with the 'Ayes' I was not permitted by the rules of the House to move the Second Reading of the 'Women's Disabilities Bill'. While I felt this setback keenly, and the faces of the members of the Married Women's Association in the public gallery registered their own great disappointment, I had the satisfaction of knowing that fifty-four Members had indicated their sympathy; and that this augered well for the future.

Among those who remained in the House that afternoon to vote were Edward Heath, Harold Wilson and Ian Mikardo. Edward Heath, a bachelor, indicated by his vote sympathy for the Bill, while Sir Edward Boyle, also a bachelor went into the opposite lobby.

Harold Wilson I should have thought would have been too preoccupied with other matters, and the same also applied to Ian Mikardo, then Labour Member for Reading, whose persistent and consistent opposition to certain aspects of Labour Policy irked me. However, he certainly redeemed himself in my eyes that afternoon.

In a debate concerned solely with the welfare of women it is not easy to predict how a man will vote. I have known apparently kindly men representing industrial seats, aware of the difficulties of the working housewife, assume an entirely different expression when I have suggested that a man should disclose the amount of his wages to his wife. The smile has faded from his face, his eyes have hardened and he has charged me with interfering in a man's business. And even in my Fulham constituency I was asked by a member of the Labour Party General Management Committee, the father of eleven children, not to speak or write articles on the emancipation of the housewife.

There was a sequel to this debate eleven years later in the House of Lords when I initiated a debate in the Lords on the position of women in industry, with regard to their pay and conditions, and the economic position of the wife who worked solely in the home. In the course of my speech I quoted from the 'Report of the Royal Commission on Marriage and Divorce' published in 1956, which unanimously recommended in Paragraph 701 that, 'Savings made from money contributed by either the husband or the wife or by both for the purpose of meeting housekeeping expenses (and any investments or purchases made from such savings) should be deemed to belong to husband and wife in equal shares unless they have otherwise agreed.'

In the Commons, many years before the publication, I had incorporated a similar provision in my 'Women's Disabilities Bill' but had achieved little success. It was therefore with considerable satisfaction that I heard Lord Dundee, in his winding-up speech tell me that this might be a suitable subject for a Private Member's Bill and that the Government would be prepared to accept the recommendation of the Royal Commission.

I had observed Lord Dundee leave the Chamber in the course of my speech, no doubt, as it transpired, to consult with the Lord Chancellor Lord Dilhorne. He could have adopted the indifferent attitude with which I was very familiar; indulged in a few light-hearted comments on women's activities and, without any reference to their economic welfare, resumed his seat fully satisfied with a contribution devoid of any constructive suggestion. I was expecting with some resignation this exasperating reply to my speech and I was a little incredulous when Lord Dundee made his proposal.

With the help of Mr Perceval, a Clerk at the Table I lost no time in drafting a Bill, one of the shortest on record consisting of twenty-five words, but words of such significance that they could change the economic basis of marriage.

The Married Women's Savings Bill read:

'Be it enacted by the Queen's most Excellent Majesty, by and with the advice and consent of the Lords Spiritual and Temporal, and Commons, in this present Parliament assembled and by the authority of the same, as follows:

1. If a wife makes savings out of what her husband gives her for housekeeping, half of any money so saved shall belong to her absolutely.'

In moving the Second Reading I reminded the House of the Report of the Royal Commission on Marriage and Divorce with regard to the position of the housewife, which read, 'She has no way of ensuring that she gets a sufficient allowance on which to run the home. . . . She has no legal right to any allowance for her own personal spending. Any money she manages to save from the housekeeping allowance is in law her husband's. She can lay no claim to a share in the home and the furniture except to the extent that she can prove that she has contributed out of her own separate income. The profits of her husband's business are his own, although she may work with him in it without taking any wages.'

Both sides of the House gave me a sympathetic hearing and I was particularly impressed by the Lord Bishop of Manchester's commendation of the Bill. 'Some people are of the opinion,' he said, 'that if passed into law it may be a difficult measure to enforce.' But he asked whether it might not be comparable in some sense to what is being done by the United Nations in the Charter of Human Rights. This is something which cannot always be enforced, but something which holds up an ideal to which all can strive. 'I believe,' he added, 'although I have no right to speak for it – that informed Christian opinion in this country would be solidly behind the provision of this Bill.'

Apart from a light-hearted intervention from Lord Boothby concerning the possibility of the housewife saving at the expense of her husband's food there was no opposition.

To my infinite satisfaction the Earl of Dundee wound up the debate and then gave me some further advice.

As I had moved the Second Reading at the end of the session and consequently there would be insufficient time for it to go through the Commons before prorogation it would be necessary for me to reintroduce the Bill in the following session; Lord Dundee advised me therefore that the drafting might be re-examined in the meantime. The Bill stated that half of the money should belong to the wife absolutely, whereas the recommendation of the Royal Commission was that it should be deemed that the whole of it should belong to the husband and wife in equal shares. Having had the principle accepted I was only too happy to let the experts examine the wording, even if it resulted in a Bill somewhat longer than twenty-five words. The title was changed for administrative reasons to 'The Married Women's Property Bill, 1964'.

At the beginning of the next session the redrafted Bill was approved by the Lords without any opposition.

Now my real difficulties faced me, for it had to go to the House of Commons and I had to find somebody as dedicated as myself to pilot it through. The procedure of the Commons permits any member of the House to obstruct a Private Member's Bill by simply saying 'Object' on the Second Reading. An opposed measure can, however, be moved again on a subsequent Friday. This process can be repeated for the rest of the session until the proud parent of the Bill loses heart and confesses defeat. Nevertheless the same machinery can be put into motion the following session, if the Member possesses sufficient moral courage and determination to face the possibility of obstruction on successive Fridays.

Although my Bill had received the blessing of the Lord Chancellor, the head of the Judiciary, no power could prevent some man with a private grudge against women in general or against this Bill in particular from shouting 'Object'. Indeed, there was a well-authenticated case of one bachelor, having been rejected by his fiancée shortly before marriage, finding solace in sitting in the House every Friday afternoon and shouting 'Object' to any Bill designed to benefit women.

The curious aspect of this piece of parliamentary procedure is that the objector need not identify himself and in fact can disguise his identity by practising the ventriloquist's art. This is precisely what happened when the Second Reading of the 'Married Women's Property Bill' was moved for me by Douglas Houghton the Member for Sowerby, who never failed to use his influence and authority on behalf of those women, who he thought were not getting a square deal. I sat in the Peers' Gallery gazing anxiously at the various Members waiting to take action on some Private Member's Bill.

I was an old hand at this: I knew my men and I spotted a number of anti-feminists who had opposed the 'Women's Disabilities Bill'. Was it possible, I asked myself, after the lapse of some years and since the unanimous recommendation of the Royal Commission on Marriage and Divorce, that they would continue to obstruct a measure designed to help the housewife? As I was musing on this the Speaker called out 'The Married Women's Property Bill' and 'Mr Douglas Houghton'.

Then suddenly in muffled tones some member shouted 'Object'. My eyes had not left the faces of the men opposite Douglas Houghton and I failed to observe any movement of the lips of any one of them; at least the member responsible had some sense of shame for he was not prepared to reveal to the House that it was he who had obstructed a Bill designed to help the housewife; and equally he was determined that the Press were denied the opportunity of informing his women constituents that they were represented by a mean, ungenerous individual.

I was deeply disappointed.

Then Mr Charles Pannel, Labour Member for West Leeds an acknowledged authority on parliamentary procedure rose and challenged the right of an individual to keep his identity secret in circumstances where a piece of legislation was acceptable to many members, including the Government. To my astonishment the Speaker, Sir Harry Hylton-Foster, instead of mildly reprimanding Charles Pannel for questioning a time-honoured custom, agreed that it might be abused and therefore he proposed to ask the Committee on Procedure to examine the matter.

Although this provided me with a crumb of comfort I was well aware that this would be a long-term process and even if the Committee recommended that the objector must in future identify himself, a near paranoid anti-feminist would not allow himself to be thwarted in his designs. The time factor, also, could prevent me from getting the Bill through both Houses in the same session, and consequently I should have to start all over again in the Lords the following session with the chance of once more having it obstructed in the Commons.

The following Friday found me alone in the Peer's Gallery watching an identical scene. One after another the Private Member Bills were called, and again and again rose the cry of 'Object'.

I braced myself waiting for the fatal word like some poor unfortunate creature waiting for the executioner's axe, with an iron determination not to wince when the blow fell. I heard the words 'The Married Women's Property Bill' and then, could it possibly be – silence. The objector of last week was in all probability on the benches but last week's outcry culminating in the Speaker's proposal had effectually silenced him. No doubt he was well aware that the House was evincing a special interest in the ventriloquist powers of Members that afternoon.

I sat there, all alone, because I had warned the officers of the Married Women's Association of a possible defeat and I wished to save them further disappointment.

The announcement of the next Bill was an indication that the silence which succeeded the calling of my Bill was complete, I smiled broadly with relief and happiness, and those in the House who had supported me looked up and smiled with equal satisfaction. Then I went down to the Members' lobby to meet them all as they streamed out of the Chamber and where I must confess to establishing a precedent in that holy of holies by kissing Douglas Houghton soundly on the cheek; and he reciprocated. As I had been at Westminster for twenty-five years I felt that all the officers and messengers who witnessed this unusual demonstration to mark the final outcome of this struggle on behalf of married women, would view it with some sympathy and understanding.

My pleasant partnership with Douglas Houghton on this occasion symbolized the growing co-operation between men and women and their mutual desire to remove those obstacles which prejudice and custom had erected. Douglas Houghton possesses moral courage and a tenacity of purpose: unmindful of the mocking asides of some of his fellow-men, he identifies himself with those seeking to destroy the surviving discriminations against women.

For many years he has been the Secretary of the Inland Revenue Staff Federation and believes that, when it comes to income tax, husbands and wives both have grievances. The statutory duty of making a return of a wife's income falls upon her husband; he has the distasteful obligation of asking his wife to declare her income to him. Some wives find this invidious and there are some who have saved money out of the house-keeping unknown to their husbands. Afraid to admit it to their husbands, they innocently put 'None' in the space for 'Wife's Income' on the tax form.

In 1951, banks, including the Post Office, were called upon to disclose the names and addresses of those having accounts credited with more than £15 interest in any tax year. Wives with secret savings were found out all over the country and husbands received queries from the tax inspector about bank accounts they never knew existed.

While there is still further room for reform, the Married Women's Property Act 1964, will save women from the necessity of adopting methods such as these in order to outwit a mean husband, and enable them to save in their own right.

15

Egypt and National Insurance: Arabs and Jews

Home affairs and particularly women's affairs, occupied my mind and my energies in these and other ways. But I found myself also involved abroad and notably in the Middle East, almost by chance. In 1950 Ernest Bevin, Britain's Foreign Secretary visited Egypt to discuss various matters of mutual concern, thus providing the opportunity of establishing more harmonious relationships between the two countries.

On his return he had a chat with me about the social conditions in Egypt. He asked me to assist the Egyptian Minister of Social Affairs, Mr Ahmed Hussein, whom he had invited to this country, in any way in which I thought fit to help to establish a limited form of national insurance in his country.

Mr Ahmed Hussein arrived shortly afterwards and called to see me at the Ministry of National Insurance. He had been attached to the Cairo University as Professor of Agriculture before being invited to join the W.A.F.D. Government as an Independent Member. I arranged for him to visit clinics, National Insurance offices, schools and hospitals and any other institutions which he considered held some special interest for him.

About six months later I received an invitation to visit Egypt for the purpose of opening an Insurance Office designed to administer an insurance scheme for widows. This was my first visit to Egypt and the Middle East and I was accorded the traditional Arab hospitality. And apart from the interest aroused by the visit of a British Minister, Ahmed Hussein told me later with some amusement that the fact that I was a woman Minister, married, travelling with two male Civil Servants, without my husband, invested my journey with special significance in a Muslim country.

Madame Hussein, his wife, was a beautiful and highly intelligent woman, and I formed the opinion that they both welcomed a visit from a woman Minister as some encouragement to the tiny feminist movement in its struggle to emancipate the Egyptian women.

Following my visit I was invited to address Arab societies, in this country and elsewhere, who were always anxious to learn what stimulated my interest in their part of the world. I did not seek to hide from them my distress at finding the Middle East, a comparatively short flight from London, still condemned to such dreadful misery, which I attributed to poverty and preventable disease.

One could say that it was the water of the Nile which brought me into the politics of the Middle East for it determines the future of Egypt. The rapidly growing population of Egypt is dependent on the Nile, the Canal and a limited amount of industry chiefly concerned with the manufacture of cotton. The Egyptian is poor because he is land hungry, and he is subject to certain diseases because he lives to some extent in the water. He is passive, slow and generally undemonstrative because for a thousand years his country has been dominated by successive occupying powers which have sought to keep him in mental and physical bondage.

A hundred years ago it is said the Egyptian was stronger and healthier than his descendants today, and it is generally believed that the southerner is more robust than the Egyptian of the Delta. The all-the-year-round system of irrigation carried out by a network of canals is to blame for his ill-health, for he is compelled to clean out the canals and ditches standing in the ooze which he uses for his fields. All the processes of cultivation are carried out in the same unhealthy conditions and, when the very hot weather arrives then the whole family with the exception of the mother, bathe in the canal to free themselves from the dust. And half of them drink the polluted water. The ditches and canals and even the Nile shallows are infested with a parasite, the bilharzia, the larvae of which enter the body through the skin. This parasite attacks various parts of the body, particularly the bladder and the kidneys, causing ulcers and fistulas and a chronic intestinal condition. Then the faeces are deposited in the canal and so the cycle of infection is completed.

Bilharziasis is not associated with a great deal of pain, but the infected person becomes pale, apathetic and loses flesh very rapidly. This horrible disease affected about 80 per cent of the population before sustained efforts were made fairly recently to combat the cause of the infection.

While the water parasite takes a fearful toll, Ankylostomiasis, an even more serious condition, is contracted from an earth parasite which multiplies in the soil and human faeces, and penetrating the fellah's naked feet attacks the intestines. Victims of these two diseases, and many suffer from them simultaneously, may survive for twenty years in a chronic condition of exhaustion and anaemia. In one factory I visited I was shown a jar containing worms which a worker had passed that morning.

Malaria still occurs in the Delta rice fields. And diseases of the eye, particularly trachoma, which is attributable to a combination of dust and strong sun and flies which carry the infection, account for the tragic plight of the blind, who are to be seen everywhere led by a child or a partially-sighted friend or relation. Added to this are the nutritional diseases, the most acute being pellagra, which stem from a diet deficient in most of the important nutriments and vitamins. It is not surprising that the people adopt a fatalistic attitude when disease seems to be the common lot.

When I visited Egypt for the first time, about 75 per cent of the people were illiterate, but increasing efforts have been made to remedy this, and in 1950 Taha Husain, the Minister of Education, a remarkably able and dedicated man, himself blind, introduced a measure designed to make education compulsory. This was the signal for a great improvement, yet how is it possible to insist on this when child labour is used in the fields? Although the children love school the family cannot manage without their wages, and even when the boys are sent to school, the girls are kept at home or on the land. A Muslim society finds it difficult to accept the dictum that when you educate a mother you educate the family.

When I was taken into the countryside my companion pointed out a village. I looked in vain for what, to me, resembled a village. I saw a collection of grey mud huts without a tree to relieve the monotony. These one- or two-room huts are made from crude bricks of mud and straw and shaped as they have been for thousands of years; indeed since the days when Moses complained about the way the slaves mixed their mud and straw.

The fellah with his naked feet treads the mud together with chopped straw which is so valuable that the cattle are allowed it only for food, and not for litter; then the bricks are set out to dry in the sun. Should the Nile flood then the whole village is washed away and has to be rebuilt. The little houses are crowded together round narrow alleyways without gardens, and the flat roofs are used for stalks of maize or cotton or piles of 'cakes' of manure and straw, all of which help to provide fuel.

Animals roam around and in and out of the little houses; the camel and she-buffalo particularly are treated well as befits their value. The floor of the house is of beaten earth, the windows are tiny because of the heat and sometimes a fellah who has made the pilgrimage to Mecca will decorate the outside of his house with simple drawings which tell the story of his journey. If the village has no tap water laid on, the women go down to the river and carry the water back on their heads.

Efforts were being made to establish a way of life in keeping with the times and accordingly the Government proposed to establish a modern rural unit for the purpose of demonstrating to the people how they should conduct their lives. The Liberation Province was the Egyptian version of our New Town; with small whitewashed houses equipped with all sanitary conveniences. The inhabitants were specially chosen for families must not exceed three children and polygamy, divorce and mothers-in-law are forbidden. When I returned some years later the Province, regarded quite rightly as an important social experiment, was well established and I was shyly welcomed into the homes of some of the new tenants, who were delighted with their new quarters. With the advent of President Nasser renewed efforts were made to raise the standards of the people and industrialization helped by foreign loans proceeded apace; but at the same time the improved health and the reduction in the infantile mortality rate increased the population.

The consequent pressure on the economy now made the great project of the Aswan Dam a matter of tremendous urgency for, apart from irrigation, it would supply power for the new industries especially the fertilizer factory. Some of the best civil engineers in the world chose the site for building the most powerful hydraulic station in existence and there is no doubt that this is where the Suez crisis originated. The refusal of the Loan, so desperately needed by the Cairo Government, was tantamount to condemning the millions who live crowded in the Nile valley to starvation. In a century the population has increased fivefold while little land has been added, and in the two years, 1954–5, the population rose by a million and a half.

In striking contrast to my visits to the huts of the agricultural workers I visited, at his request, King Farouk. No doubt the king had interviewed many women in his time but for reasons other than those which prompted him to ask our Ambassador to arrange for me to see him. I drove up the long drive to his luxurious palace outside Cairo, walked through a long, richly decorated hall between two lines of motionless guards and was ushered into a luxuriously furnished but dimly lit room where the king, wearing dark glasses, sat. Then a very curious conversation took place. He recited my insertion in *Who's Who* to indicate his detailed knowledge of my career, which, far from flattering me, only led me to the conclusion that he was a rather stupid man. This was confirmed by his subsequent observations; with few preliminaries he told me that like his father before him he had lucky numbers, seven and thirteen I believe they were, and that he was always secure because he made certain arrangements in which these numbers played some part. It was apparent that, despite his 'luck', he had good cause to be nervous for he gave me details of restaurants, night-clubs and places entirely unknown to me where his secret agents were stationed; he assured me that everything that went on in Cairo concerning the activities of certain individuals and organizations was reported to him.

Despite this efficient secret force and his repeated assurances that all was well in the country he asked me if I could obtain an invitation for him to visit England. Farouk had not been *persona grata* in Britain for some years and I did not think that the Prime Minister would be very anxious to oblige the most notorious royal playboy. At no time did he ask me for my views on the pressing social problems of his country, or indicate that he was concerned with the poverty and misery of the Egyptian masses confined in the narrow Nile valley.

I remembered all this six years later when suddenly, without warning, in November 1956, Egypt was the victim of an unprovoked attack by Israel, France and Britain. With the knowledge which I had acquired of the poverty and social problems which beset Egypt, I was appalled at the wanton destruction inflicted on her. The National Executive of the Labour Party of which I was the previous Chairman arranged an emergency meeting. We decided that the matter was of such vital importance that we would hold a mass meeting in Trafalgar Square on the afternoon of Sunday, 4 November to demonstrate against this aggression. Ray Gunter, a popular trade union member, to become in 1964 Minister of Labour, was to take the chair and Aneurin Bevan, Anthony Greenwood and I were to speak.

When my husband and I arrived at the Square we were glad to have the help of a crowd of strong young Labour supporters to get us through the dense crowd and up on to the plinth at the base of the Nelson column. I have spoken in Trafalgar Square on many occasions and we always considered that to half-fill the Square represented a reasonably successful meeting, but never before had I seen such a colossal crowd as that which assembled as a protest against the 'Suez' act of aggression. The crowds overflowed into Whitehall, up the Strand and Cockspur Street.

I devoted most of my speech to describing the economic conditions of Egypt and the lot of the ordinary agricultural worker. I gave them details of the poverty, hunger and disease responsible for the weak and debilitated condition of the people and how the High Dam, the cost of which was the basic cause of this attack, was vital to raising the standards of the people.

Aneurin Bevan rose to tremendous heights of oratory on that occasion, no doubt conscious of the fact that he, too, belonged to a small country, and the audience listened with the quiet intensity of people who have made a spontaneous gesture against an action which they consider morally wrong.

When the meeting was over a crowd estimated at 10,000, carrying banners inscribed 'Law not War', surged down White-hall to deliver a resolution to Number 10 Downing Street, demanding a cease-fire. A line of mounted police charged the crowd, knocking men and women to the ground, and one policeman was dragged from his saddle. Ambulances shuttled to and fro taking the injured away and more than twenty-five arrests were made and eight policemen injured. A meeting of Ministers was in progress at Number 10, so the police banned the way of the surging crowd, but the marchers in front could not turn back because of the pressure from the masses behind. Then, according to the *Daily Herald* reports, 'Suddenly the police moved in, they formed a line across the road and rode stirrup to stirrup towards the crowd. A stampede started. Women screamed as they tried to retreat . . . in vain.

'The police line kept moving on, determined not only to bar entry to Downing Street, but to clear the whole of Whitehall. Men and women fell, trampled by the hooves of the horses. The police retreated, formed up and went on again to widen the ragged space their first charge had made. The crowd was furious. There were cries of 'Police State' and deafening boos. Angry men, trying to protect their wives, began to shout and shake their fists at the horsemen. Fathers held their terrified children above their heads to save them from the crush. Again the police charged. A couple was hurled down. Both were squirming and screaming under the hooves of a prancing horse. The woman was snatched away but the man lay groaning in the roadway as the police pressed on. Banner-bearers used their poles to protect themselves. They struck out at the horses. The police then rode again into the throng. Two men stopped one mounted policeman's charge by holding a banner across his path. The horse reared and several women were thrown to the ground in the rush to escape. Youths hurled fireworks, terrifying the horses.

'Meanwhile a call for reinforcements had gone out. Constables were picked up off their beat and rushed by the vanload to Whitehall. They formed a cordon across the road and pressed slowly forward. Finally, as more and more foot police reinforced the horsemen, the crowd slowly dispersed.'

That night Hugh Gaitskell broadcast to the nation; in his peroration he said, 'Only one thing now can save the reputation and the honour of our country. Parliament must repudiate the Government's policy. The Prime Minister must resign.'

I was invited to visit the Lebanon in January 1957 and continued my journey to Port Said to visit the hospital where those severely injured in the bombing of the Suez incident were still being nursed; for I had formed the opinion that Parliament was being deceived over the casualties in the Port Said fighting.

In Port Said I saw streets and buildings which closely resembled an area after a series of heavy air attacks. I walked round bombed schools, and everywhere were great heaps of rubble which had not been explored.

I had a long talk with Dr Hofney who was in charge of the general Government hospital which normally has 275 beds. As a result of the first effective air raid water pipes were damaged and electricity cut off. Surgeons operated by hurricane lamps and there was no refrigeration so blood plasma deteriorated and became unusable. During those two days, the 5th and 6th of November, about 550 casualties were admitted and about 800 brought in dead; most of the casualties were civilian, the majority men, but there were a great number of women and children. At another hospital, the Mabassa, there was a direct hit on the operating theatre and there was also damage to the Eye Hospital, the Fever Hospital and many schools. The Government statement that only the Arab shanty town had suffered was completely inaccurate.

I visited many wards in the General Hospital accompanied by the Medical Officer and as we entered each ward he said: 'This is a lady doctor; she has a white face but she is our friend.'

I saw men, women and children who had lost limbs or were otherwise severely incapacitated; they looked at me with their great dark eyes, unsmiling and silent. There were children who had been blinded or seriously wounded, who had their mother or some other relative sitting by the bed. As I said good-bye to the Medical Superintendent I felt that words were quite inadequate to express my indignation at the brutal and senseless attack on innocent civilians.

I visited Cairo and, as I was strolling along, a guide spoke to me and asked if he could show me round. I thanked him, declined his offer and said that I was leaving shortly. He looked at my 5 ft. 9 in. curiously and asked, 'What country do you come from?'

My ancestors seemed to have distributed themselves between Norway and Yorkshire and I possess a volume recently sent to me by Dr Henrik Sommerschield, a surgeon in Oslo describing the various ramifications of the family. When the Egyptian guide put his question my mind was still full of the tragic little patients I had so recently seen in Port Said, the innocent victims of an aggression which Hugh Gaitskell said had tarnished the honour of our country. In my anxiety to dissociate myself from this horror I answered 'Norwegian'.

Colonel Nasser invited me to discuss some of the social problems of Egypt with him and I recalled my meeting with King Farouk six years before. There was a striking difference between the fantastic extravagance of the royal palace and the low white house where the President of Egypt lives with his family; with a sentry posted outside and a secretary to receive callers and take them to the President. I was agreeably surprised with the informality which surrounded my visit. I was ushered into a modest book-lined study where I found Colonel Nasser dressed in an open-necked white shirt and cardigan. He made no attempt to minimize the social and economic problems which confronted him or to hide the worst features of his country, the low standard of living and the need for partial industrialization. However, these things cost money in a country which has only a river and a canal as producers of revenue.

The freezing of the payments by other countries for the use of the Suez Canal must reduce the number of schools and clinics and other services being provided for the people. Those who hoped that this would undermine Colonel Nasser's position were quite unrealistic, for the Suez attack has considerably strengthened his position among the people.

The Egyptians have been dominated by foreigners for hundreds of years and they are determined to establish their independence. Colonel Nasser said that he had been blamed for anti-British broadcasts from Cairo; he asked me if I had heard the violent anti-Nasser attacks broadcast by us to the Egyptian people. He had been blamed for getting arms from East European countries, but did I think that after the Suez attack he could tell his people that arms were unnecessary?

I was left with the impression that I had heard a frank statement from a man dedicated to help the Egyptian people and to try to repair the neglect of centuries. It is a pity so much energy is directed to castigating the leader of the Egyptian people instead of directing our attention to the needs of those people without tying it up with military aid as President Eisenhower seemed prepared to do.

The religion and traditions of the Muslim people reject Communism which is illegal in Egypt and most Arab countries, nevertheless the social conditions offer a fertile ground for Communist propaganda.

On my return to London, the Editor of the *Star* asked me to write an article describing the conditions in Port Said.

I made no secret of the fact that, having witnessed the effects of the cruelty inflicted on the civilian population by a barbaric attack by three countries acting in collusion, I was ashamed to admit identification with the perpetrators. I can only describe the result of this article as explosive. I received a volume of correspondence, some of it in sympathy with me, but most of it couched in terms of such a character that the postman felt obliged to apologize for having to deliver some of the postcards on which filthy words were inscribed.

I formed the opinion that Jingoism is more common in this country than we suspect and that there was a considerable number of people who believed that Anthony Eden's only mistake had been *not* to mount a greater attack on the Egyptians and thus annihilate them completely.

Undaunted by this vicious attack I visited other countries in the Middle East, and in the course of this I learned at first hand of the bitterness engendered by the creation of Modern Israel.

One stifling hot day, I visited the refugee camp at Jericho, hundreds of feet below sea level. I was thankful that I had shoes and my naked feet were not exposed to the sharp stones and the dirty sand which infected the cuts and abrasions which I saw on the feet of the children. A tiny casualty room provided first aid for these children who stood or squatted on the ground patiently waiting to have their feet treated.

I was shocked to find on visiting the Eye Clinic a queue of men, women and children standing in the scorching sun waiting for treatment. My guide introduced me to the doctor who deftly everted the eyelid of each patient and applied the treatment for incipient trachoma. When I saw the length of the queue I asked if I might help him; he brusquely informed me in English, without stopping his work, that he did not need any help from me. This hurt; but I knew that as a doctor in these appalling conditions he felt he needed to show no consideration for a tall woman with a white face who obviously belonged to a Western civilization which had permitted this inhuman situation to exist.

I visited the huts which accommodated whole families at night packed tightly like sardines, on the hard mud floors. I was told in answer to my questions about sanitation that early in the morning a cart went round to collect the excreta. Ration cards were given, but food was in such short supply that it was not unusual for a family at night to secretly convey the corpse of a member into the hills in order to retain the ration card. Babies had supplementary rations but the small girls who took their baby brothers and sisters to receive this extra food all looked as though they were in need of similar treatment; I did not see one person that I considered carried one pound in excess weight. Unemployed men mooched around, demoralized and feeding on their hate.

The Israeli Government invited me to visit their country and I accepted on the condition that I could continue my journey through to other Arab countries. I was accorded the unusual privilege by the Arab countries of using one passport for both journeys.

I found in Israel in the field of health exactly what I had expected. Highly qualified doctors from Europe were doing good work in the preventive and curative branches of medicine and surgery, and well equipped laboratories were available for those anxious to undertake research work.

I found it difficult to understand how these intelligent men and women, having experienced the misery and degradation of being treated as second-class citizens in Germany, were prepared in their own country to impose the same treatment on the Arabs.

With Jim Griffiths I visited Ben Gurion in the Negev where he had retired to contemplate from a distance the political scene. Although Jim Griffiths has the eloquent and tireless tongue of the Welsh and my own is fairly mobile, it was difficult to get a word in edgeways. I was disappointed to find a garrulous politician talking of past and future political battles rather than an elder statesman, experienced and mellow, prepared to give of his wisdom to a younger generation.

Israel in its formative years has made tremendous strides in increasing its agricultural output, in reafforestation, irrigation and the reclamation of land. Establishing new industries and expanding the old has been more difficult. However, Israel possesses invaluable assets in the form of men and women with vision, energy and determination, consequently she stands as good a chance of surviving as any other small country.

The conception of Theodor Herzl, the Austrian journalist who propagated the Zionist faith, was not simply that of a State run by Jews on an economically sound basis. He envisaged a National Home which the Jewish people, persecuted, harried, driven from one country to another by pogroms and the ghetto could at last call their own.

Yet while refugees from the Yemen seek a home in Israel the $5\frac{1}{2}$ million Jews in the USA show little inclination to settle there. I met a few from Britain; some of them told me that they returned for some months every year, and I thought that I detected a little nostalgia in their questions about London.

The older Zionists must not despair if their children do not show that enthusiasm for the cause which inspired their parents;

recitals of horror of the bad old days have never been known to make a lasting impression on young people, or greatly to influence their actions.

Jewry has a wonderful opportunity to command the respect of the world; the Semitic peoples include the Arabs and I believe that the destinies of the Arabs and Jews are closely intertwined. Jewry must aim at something bigger than the Zionist State and plan to build a Welfare State for their kinsmen, the Semitic people and the Middle East where poverty and disease have for generations condemned millions to a life of misery.

I had an opportunity to say something of this when in July 1955, as Chairman of the Labour Party, I was invited to address the Socialist International Congress meeting in the Caxton Hall. It seemed to me that, while world attention was focused on the Arab–Israeli dispute, yet it was allowed to fester year after year, while the victims, in the refugee camps, powerless and inarticulate, were left in their misery to subsist on an allowance from the United Nations Organization.

I felt that a Socialist Conference composed of men and women who had devoted their lives to the promotion of a creed which embraces all races and colours would respond to an appeal made by the Chairman of the British Labour Party.

After speaking about some of the wider problems of Africa and Asia and of my recent visit to China I said:

'I have a more localized problem which I now want to deal with as shortly as possible, and, I want to emphasize that I speak in an individual capacity. A few months ago the Foreign Secretary told the House of Commons that he believed that the most serious problem confronting him was that presented by the Arab–Israeli dispute.

'Every now and then we read in our newspapers that some "incident" has occurred in the Middle East. The euphemistically called "incident" means an attack by the Israelis on the Arabs or the Arabs on the Israelis resulting in some loss of life. An inquiry takes place and then there is a lull until another incident occurs. There is fortunately a lull now, and therefore I can approach this question as objectively as the circumstances will permit. Early this year I was invited, simultaneously by the Israeli and Jordan Governments, to visit their countries, this was a privilege and an honour, which I appreciated.

'I am neither Jewish nor an Arab; I went there as a Socialist well aware that there might be two sides to a question. I know that there is here today a powerful delegation from Israel and from the International Jewish Bund, yet the Arab countries have no delegate to speak for them.

'As a Socialist I hold no brief for any reactionary Arab government; but as a Socialist I am concerned with the conditions of the ordinary people, whoever they are, and whatever their language, colour or creed. I recognize that the Israeli Government, despite the most tremendous handicaps, has established a welfare state within its borders which must command the respect and admiration of the world.

'Yet I felt as I met those wonderful technicians, the professional people and all those who are devoting their energies, their enthusiasm and their vision to building a Welfare State in the Middle East, that they could have shared it more widely among the Arab population.

'The misery and hopelessness of the Arab refugees in their camps is in striking contrast to the life of the Israelis just across the border. The bitterness of losing their country is accentuated by the fact that so many of them have also lost the only thing that they have in the world, their home. Perhaps only somebody like myself, a stranger without bias, could feel the bitter hatred and hostility which has been engendered; this is profound and there can be no easing of the situation until some restitution is made. I think that the Israeli Government should be told this sooner or later, preferably sooner, as I am telling you now, for I believe that they are surrounded by friends reluctant to tell them the real truth. The hostility has not lessened. The Arab has a timeless approach to life; a few years means nothing to him. His memory is as green today as it was a few years ago. He is bitter and he is almost nourishing himself on his own sickness.

'There are two steps which should be taken immediately, not only for the sake of Israel but for the sake of the whole world. Those Arabs with property in Israel who wish to return should be allowed to do so. Many of them don't wish to, then in those cases they should receive compensation for losing their homes.

'Let me illustrate this point by telling you a little story. I rode on a bus a few hundred yards from the Israeli border and the driver stopped in order that some women on it could stand up, look over the Israeli border, to see their homes. The bus driver told me that he did this whenever these particular women were with him. Their little homes were expropriated with every bit of furniture that these women possessed. A home is a woman's life in whatever country she may live. Can you not understand why these people are bitter, and this bitterness may eventually become a threat to the peace of the whole world.

'The other thing that should be done concerns the demarcation line. I believe that the demarcation line between Israel and the Arab countries was drawn hastily and insufficient consideration was given to it. This line must be revised immediately. May I again illustrate this quite incredible position?

'I went along the demarcation line with one of the men whose duty it is to try to maintain order between the Israelis and the Arabs. To my astonishment I found it marked in some parts, only with a piece of barbed wire, which went right through the garden of one man's house. He was allowed to develop his garden on his side but not on the other.

'In one village the line went right through the village cutting off the mosque from the Arabs, and leaving it on the Israeli side. This line was drawn hurriedly, and inaccurately without prior consideration and I am quite sure that both sides at this stage would welcome a revision.

'Now the way to prepare for peace talks, I would say to my Israeli friends, for I have been assured that Israel wants peace, is to settle these legitimate grievances. People will not come round the peace table until they feel that their outstanding grievances are settled.

'Again I say that I hold no brief for any reactionary Arab government. I know that the policy of such a government is to blame a foreign power for the poverty and misery of the masses. We British ought to know that. Every colony, rightly or wrongly, has blamed the British for any trouble that may occur. Today

I say to Israel, "You are giving a reactionary Arab government the very weapons it needs against their people." When a government shows no concern for the social conditions of the people and fails to remedy them it can turn to them and say "This is the doing of Israel. Look to them for the solution of your problems."

'Israel should take every opportunity to weaken the hands of reaction not to strengthen them by failing to take immediate action. I say this in all friendliness, knowing that many of my Jewish friends agree with my point of view and I know, if I may say so, that this is the voice of common sense.

'We make speeches here proclaiming the international brotherhood of man. We debate world Socialism, the case for world disarmament; and for securing the security and happiness of the world family. Yet this must all be regarded as pure rhetoric unless we apply answers to the immediate problems that are now within our power to resolve.

Socialism generally begins at home, because the grievances of those nearest to us are the most clamorous and insistent. Similarly in the Middle East. I would ask the Israeli Government in all friendliness to look beyond their borders, not with fear and apprehension of the future but with understanding, tolerance and magnanimity.'

Although I had one interruption I was not prepared for the the violence of the attack which followed from the Israeli delegate who denounced me for daring to use my position as Chairman of the British Labour Party for the purpose of promoting the Arab cause.

Although this distasteful little episode was entirely unexpected, I was not so ignorant of the strength of feeling in the Jewish Community to be entirely unprepared for some expression of disagreement. However, the Jewish youth and the women's organization asked me to speak at their meetings and they showed some sympathy and understanding for my point of view; but the men were entirely unmoved.

On the other hand, the Jews attached to the Bund organization wrote and thanked me for what I said and a few asked if they could come and see me at my home.

There is a tendency for minorities to believe that, if you are not always with them and you reserve your right to criticize them then you must be against them.

As a woman, being one of a minority on many occasions, I was very conscious from the first day that I entered Parliament that minorities must be protected and given every opportunity to ventilate their grievances and consequently I was always vigilant on their behalf. And it so happened that one of my early questions concerned Jew-baiting in the East End.

I asked the Home Secretary whether his attention had been drawn to the case of a boy Leslie Silverberg aged fourteen of Wapping who was beaten with an iron bar by youths professing Fascist sympathies; and whether he would consider augmenting the police in the East End with special instructions to detect and punish Jew-baiting.

Not wholly satisfied with the answer I followed with supplementary questions: 'Is the Right Hon. Gentleman aware that Jewish people in the East End are terrorized by these gangs, and in view of the frequency of unprovoked incidents of this kind has not the time come when he should take stronger action?'

While in New York in 1938 I visited a large hospital in Brooklyn. The Medical Superintendent was Jewish and in discussing the administration he mentioned his deputy, a woman doctor. I expressed surprise that a woman should hold such an important post having regard to the prejudice against women doctors.

The Medical Superintendent who had been responsible for the appointment looked at me and remarked, 'Don't you think that we should stand together?'

16

China, Japan and the Return Journey

In the last chapter I referred briefly to a visit to China. This was in the spring of 1954 when the National Executive of the Labour Party received an invitation from the Chinese Government to visit China. We had waited hopefully for this invitation because we knew that the whole Labour movement was anxious for us to make a good-will visit to the Far East in an attempt to establish more cordial relationships. Clem Attlee, Aneurin Bevan, Morgan Phillips, the Secretary of the Party, and I were among those chosen to represent the Party. The announcement of our visit caused something of a stir because this was the first occasion that an official invitation from the Chinese Government had been received by any political party.

The Press, very anxious to accompany us, chartered a plane and followed as best they could; the result, although the journalists had been informed of our itinerary, was not altogether satisfactory. One hot afternoon I was relaxing in a bathing-pool in central China when suddenly a head popped up by my side, and a voice said, 'How do you do.' Said I, speaking slowly: 'You speak English very well.' The head with some asperity said, 'I ought to. I'm *The Times* correspondent. This is the first time that I have caught up with you.' On another occasion (this time in the Soviet Union) we were having a meal, when Clem Attlee observed in a low voice: 'You see that man on your other side, Edith? I would say he comes from Georgia. You can generally tell them from the shape of the head and the long hair.' I glanced to my left and answered: 'That is George

Gale, a newspaper correspondent; he has been following us since we left London.'

The news that we were going to China had quickly spread and the Swedish Prime Minister had invited us to stay the first night of our journey in Stockholm. We accepted, and our first 'hop' was marked by a delightful dinner as the guests of the Swedish Cabinet at an old inn on the outskirts of the capital. In the course of the dinner a cabaret performer sang two suggestive songs in 'English'. The company were slightly embarrassed and Aneurin, at his best, commented: 'We understand the sentiments if not the words.' The Foreign Minister, greatly concerned, assured me that the singer had been chosen by the restaurant and not by the Government.

Before we left England we had received an invitation from Mr Malenkov, the Prime Minister of the Soviet Union, to break the journey at Moscow and to be the guests of his Government for a few days. At Helsinki Airport we found a shining sage green plane emblazoned with a red star awaiting us. The interior of the plane had been especially equipped with two divans upholstered in brown poplin, a plum-coloured carpet and brown table covers all trimmed with fringe to match the carpet. The charming little air hostess gave us a shy smile, but as she had no English and we had only a few words of Russian, communication was a little difficult until she mentioned 'choi', then we all nodded vigorously and with glasses of tea all round the atmosphere became warm and friendly and we exchanged smiles and nods all the way to Moscow.

There was no lack of spontaneity shown in our welcome in Moscow. Our hosts made every effort to ensure our comfort. We stayed at the Sovietski Hotel and I wondered, on looking round my sumptuous, yet garishly furnished suite, whether the interior decorator had a place in the Soviet economy. How could one reconcile, I asked myself, the ugly vases and the mats and table-covers with the exquisite decor of the Russian ballet?

The delightful, highly intelligent young woman deputed to look after me was married to a Civil Servant and was the mother of two young children; she told me that the nurse-help arrived at her home at 8.30 and left at 6 p.m. when she usually returned home. She did not guess how many professional women with children in Britain would envy her that precious domestic help.

That lovely, warm summer evening we drove about twenty miles outside Moscow to Maxim Gorki's old home. It is the dream house of every woman; a long, low, white building nestling in the lovely mature countryside. We were taken through the house and there, standing in a group at the end of the garden, looking towards us, was the Inner Cabinet of the Soviet Union. They were gazing at us with a curiosity equal to our own. Never before had I wished with such intensity that I had brought a really outstandingly beautiful frock with me; for I felt, as our group strolled down the garden, closely watched by our hosts, that it was of profound importance that we make the right impression for the sake of establishing a more harmonious relationship. In retrospect it was a little curious that, at that moment, I, as a politician, did not concern myself solely with the subject matter of an ensuing conversation. However, my woman's instinct and not my political sense had taken over. I regretted that I had listened to all those people who warned me not to take any clothes with me other than those which would merge with a rather dreary sartorial landscape. I was assured that in China the women would wear linen trousers or dark skirts and blouses. So, heeding those who should know, and anxious not to appear ostentatious I had complied; and there I was on that warm, balmy evening in Maxim Gorki's lovely house in a grey and white faintly patterned silk afternoon frock, bearing the scrutiny of a group of interesting men, many of whom, I was told, had never met an English woman before.

With Mr Malenkov were Mr Molotov, Mr Mikoyan, Mr Kruschev, Secretary of the Party, Mr Vishensky, Mr Troyanosky, Madame Papova, and Mr Shvemik, Chairman of the Trade Unions. I was surprised to find Mr Malenkov much shorter and plumper than I had expected, yet his eyes were humorous and it was clear that he was determined to extend to us a very friendly welcome.

He was dressed in a high-necked tunic and trousers of cream-coloured material of ample proportions.

There were no women present except Madame Papova. This did not surprise me. I have yet to find any Government of any political colour which does not feel that it has satisfied its obligations to women by appointing *one* woman only of the highest rank.

Sir William Hayter, our Ambassador, and his wife accompanied us. Within a few minutes we were chatting together with the aid of the most skilled interpreters I have encountered. We dined on the terrace which commanded a view of a lovely green, gently sloping countryside, reminiscent of Surrey; and we sat down at a long table covered with a variety of delicious *hors d'oeuvres*. An interpreter sat just behind each Minister so that his voice carried over the shoulder with such good effect that afterwards I was a little uncertain as to which of our hosts could or could not speak English. These poor men sat without eating a morsel or drinking a glass of wine throughout a meal of many courses of tempting food. Clem Attlee sat on one side of Malenkov and the Ambassador on the other. I sat immediately opposite the Prime Minister next to Molotov and the table was not too wide to prevent an easy exchange of conversation. Aneurin Bevan sat on the other side of Molotov and farther down on the opposite side was Mr Kruschev. If one could judge from his placing at the table it would seem as though Mr Kruschev was not regarded as being a member of the innermost circle. As the dinner progressed Malenkov and I managed to exchange views very easily and he laughed at some of my exchanges with Aneurin; these were sometimes of an admonitory kind because, while I understood Aneurin's more boisterous type of humour and his running commentary on all he saw, I was afraid lest he be misunderstood by the Russians.

One delicious course succeeded another, interrupted with increasing frequency by toasts. We toasted everything and everybody until, lost for a new toast, we drank to Mr Mikoyan's recently born grandchild; I believe it was his thirteenth. The toast having been drunk the glass is turned upside-down, 'bottoms up', to indicate that the drinker is a real 'he man' who knows how to take his share.

I am not a 'he man' and, after a short time, I came to the conclusion that it would not further Anglo–Soviet friendship if, under the effects of Vodka, the only woman in our party slipped quietly beneath the table. In discussing the 'bottoms up' custom with friends in England, I had been warned that if I did not consume the wine of the country it would be regarded as an unfriendly gesture. However, I had to make up my mind whether the cause of international friendship would gain more from my remaining sober or otherwise. Mr Mikoyan who spoke excellent English had been chatting about his family to me and after about the fourth toast, encouraged by his easy manner, I explained my dilemma. He laughed heartily and in rapid Russian told Mr Malenkov of my fears. He replied equally rapidly and Mr Mikoyan translated: 'The Prime Minister says that it is a pity there are not more men who feel equally nervous.' Then Mr Mikoyan called a waiter and ordered a light red wine for me. 'Take as much or as little of it as you like,' he said. I sipped it, then I took a little more. After I had tasted it, Clem said, 'What do they call that? That would suit me.' I kept my secret for it was a raspberry fruit non-alcoholic cordial. I smiled gratefully at Mr Mikoyan who slightly closed one eye in response. Then with gay abandon I toasted all and sundry.

As the evening wore on hosts and guests became less inhibited. The question of China's representation on the Security Council was raised. Aneurin suggested that the best tactic was to get her put on the Assembly of the United Nations first. At this, Kruschev leapt to his feet and roared his disapproval, whether because that would be an insult to China, or for some other reason I was at a loss to understand. I reacted sharply against the Secretary of the Party; 'this man is a loud-mouthed tough', I thought, who must have bullied and shouted down thousands in the course of his career. However, I have learned that there are so many imponderables in politics that it is impossible to make sound judgements concerning political events and personalities in any country other than one's own.

Some time later, when we were entertaining Mr Kruschev to dinner in the House of Commons, George Brown who was sitting next to me, loudly interrupted Mr Kruschev's speech and my sympathies on that occasion were all with our Soviet guest.

During the interchanges between Kruschev and Aneurin, Mr Malenkov sat silently observing the scene. I thought that this attitude indicated extreme displeasure and I wondered what fate lay in store for the Secretary of the Party. Would he be demoted or expelled to Siberia? I did not then guess that the Soviet Prime Minister might be experiencing a sense of political insecurity and that Kruschev's confidence was born of the knowledge that he commanded powerful support. History was to prove that the latter was the case.

About midnight the feast ended and a charming young woman came into the room carrying a bouquet which Mr Malenkov presented to me. Then he invited me to see the flower-garden and we strolled out into the still warm evening air and he tried to teach me the Russian for the stone deer at the entrance. I told him that I had been slightly apprehensive at the beginning of the meal but now I was reluctant to leave. He replied: 'We shall be seeing you again soon; tomorrow at your Embassy.' He then strolled over to a bed of phlox and picked a bunch; his colleagues were standing in a group laughing and apparently encouraging him. He ignored them, came over and presented me with a second bouquet. I interpreted this little courtesy as a means of showing that I had not lost face in his eyes by refusing to conform to a time-honoured custom.

Sometime afterwards when I poured tea for him in the Harcourt Room at Westminster I reminded him of the incident. He remembered it very clearly and remarked: 'After picking those flowers I thought that it might be said that I had succumbed to the blandishments of the West.'

When I told Sir William Hayter that the following night Mr Malenkov with the rest of the party were coming to the Embassy he was a little incredulous, because although he had invited them he had not received an acknowledgement. Indeed this would be the first time that the Prime Minister had been prepared to accept our hospitality.

When I arrived at the Embassy for our party I went to the dining-room to see how the table looked just as any woman likes to survey the scene before the guests arrive. The silver and cut glass sparkled and old paintings gave a dignity and charm to the room. While the British may not be the best cooks in the world they know how to set a table well and make a dining-room extremely attractive.

When our guests entered they stood and stared and looked around at this little piece of British territory with an absorbed interest. Lady Hayter sat at one end of the table and I at the other. We did not try to compete with the lavish entertainment we had enjoyed the previous night. Four courses of well-cooked English dishes were served and it was a tribute to our hospitality that our guests were still with us discussing world affairs at one o'clock in the morning. Malenkov could not understand why we had allowed Australia and New Zealand to join in a regional defence pact with the USA. I explained the constitutional position: we could not control the actions of the Governments of the Dominions and, moreover, I reminded him of the powerful geographical factor. Morgan Phillips urged Molotov to negotiate trade agreements through the British Federation of Industries and the recognized trade channels in the USSR. He explained that the *ad hoc* political organization in Britain alienated Labour opinion; this impressed them.

Aneurin enjoyed himself by coining aphorisms which dumbfounded the interpreter and confused the listener.

There had been tremendous progress in some respects since my first visit to the Soviet Union in 1931, when, believing that certain parts of the country were experiencing a chronic food shortage, I ate large quantities of bread and increased my weight by half a stone. I visited a Maternity Clinic and Hospital with the Chief Medical Officer of Health of Moscow and found that there was no change in the treatment of women at childbirth since my last visit. They were given the 'suggestion' treatment and denied anaesthetics. As I watched three moaning women in labour dutifully massaging their powdered tummies I seemed to be back in those days before I wrote *Babies Without Tears*.

Malenkov had discussed feminism with me and declared himself a champion of women. He said that the fault lay in the fact that they were too modest in their demands. The picture presented to me in the Maternity Hospital certainly served to prove his case. I asked the Medical Officer whether she had had children; she smiled without answering. I said that I had experienced two confinements and on each occasion arranged to have an anaesthetic. Furthermore, I did not know of any woman doctor who insisted on the 'suggestion treatment' for her own confinement.

Our stay in the Soviet Union seemed all too short, but as the object of our journey was to visit China we could not delay longer and we took to the sky once more. The Soviet authorities lent the Chinese Government a plane, and our air hostess, a tall, blonde English-speaking girl, showed an interest equal to our own in the journey, for this was her first visit to China. Clem had a pain in the tummy soon after we were airborne and I gave him a dose of a mixture I had brought from England in anticipation of such an event. It had a miraculous effect.

However, descending at 3 a.m. at Sverdlovsk and finding the Chairman of the Executive of the town waiting to greet us with a lavish meal consisting of salmon, egg in aspic, tomato salad, hot chicken and rice, potatoes, fruit and ice cream, with vodka, wines, champagne and cognac, felt this threatened to cancel out my therapeutic dose.

This generous hospitality was repeated at 8 a.m. in Novosibirsk, the capital of Siberia where I was surprised to find lush green pastures and flowers similar to those grown in England. While the menu was the same in most respects as that of Sverdlovsk they had added, for the sake of variety, cold pork chops, cold fish in all varieties and cream cake soaked in wine.

That evening we arrived at Irkutsk ready for a night on firm ground. The little hotel provided for our accommodation looked most inviting and as we were taken to our rooms the manager with a bow ushered Clem Attlee and me into a most charming double bedroom under the impression that we were husband and wife.

The meal here surpassed all the others for caviar, chops, steaks, soup heaped with cream supplemented all the delicious things with which we had been tempted in the course of the previous night. So when we landed at Ulan Bator the capital of the Independent Mongolian Republic I felt a little guilty at not being able to respond to the magnificent repast which the Mayor had prepared for us.

Over the Gobi desert we flew and the great cultivated, fertile plains of China; a most impressive example of the industry and patience of the Chinese. The land gives the appearance of some vast geometrical exercise so symmetrical is the planning of the myriad agricultural projects.

Then the vista changes abruptly to a series of mountain ranges, eroded as though cut with some sharp instrument to form giant steps down the mountain side. The water courses are dry, but wherever a fertile patch appears it is carefully cultivated. Across one of the ranges curls the great Wall of China, crumbling in places and intersected with small round towers. We cross more cultivated plains and then begins the descent to Peking.

The air hostess and I with noses pressed to the window anxious to miss nothing were both enthralled by the panoramic view and we exclaimed almost simultaneously as some fresh and exciting glimpse of the Chinese countryside came into view. In that aeroplane, high above the earth, with its warring elements and its national jealousies, we seemed very close as though we belonged to the same people; far removed from those who would seek to separate us into West and East. Shortly, we would part, probably never to meet again.

There was not much time in which to indulge in such philosophical reflections. Ready to greet us were eight little children each clasping a bouquet of gladioli and night-scented blossom which they presented with bright smiles; my little girl clasped my hand with both of hers as though I were a long-lost relative. Then we moved down a line of about forty of the City's dignitaries, among whom I observed were only three women, before being claimed by our interpreters. Mine was a young woman named Chang Tsung Ann, aged about twenty-four, married with two children.

The most detailed plans had been made for our comfort and entertainment and the Prime Minister, Chou En-lai, was one of the first to welcome us at an introductory party arranged by Government organizations and the professions. There was no attempt to create an aura of mystery around his activities. He presented himself in the middle of a clamorous party and told us, without any reservations, that he was entirely at our disposal. Whenever we wished to see him he would be available. He was as good as his word and attended many functions, particularly lunches and dinners, where he was a captive audience prepared to hear our comments and answer questions. As the only woman in our party I was always placed by his side. He could speak a little English but it was clear that he understood all that was said, from the way he corrected the ubiquitous interpreter whose voice carried over our shoulders during every meal.

There was not the slightest suggestion of the inscrutable Chinese about Chou En-lai. After we had established a friendly relationship I told him that the Chinese character and personality bore no resemblance to the mysterious Chinaman that writers were fond of depicting in the Western world. Chou En-lai laughed and told me that it was a pose of the old diplomats, who liked to establish a reputation for learning by talking in abstractions. 'Mind you,' he said, 'it is not difficult in a country where the great majority are illiterate to establish with only a rudimentary knowledge of literature the reputation of a great scholar and poet. They found it very pleasant,' he added, 'to live, waited on hand and foot by near slaves who regarded their commands as having some spiritual significance, and, therefore, requiring unquestioning obedience.'

Chou En-lai was very anxious to obtain my opinion on a matter which he said was of paramount importance to China. On arriving I had found placed in my room a small book in English on *The Marriage Law of the People's Republic of China* and I had thereupon read it through before going to sleep. The Prime Minister explained to me that the Law was one of the first to be enacted in China after the Liberation. 'You may think,' he said, with a smile, 'that this is an illustration of a new feminist approach, but I am not going to lay claim to virtues that we may not possess. We knew that the Chinese youth, brought up in a home where he was prized above his sisters and consequently spoilt and subsequently making his wife a slave whom he could discard, was not the material with which a new China could be built. We considered it essential therefore to establish firm foundations for our new state by ensuring that the character of its men was moulded in the finest possible way.' The new marriage law gave women an equal right with their husbands to divorce, and child marriage was prohibited; furthermore, Conciliation Courts were established for hearing both sides before a divorce was granted.

In my journeyings I met a young woman engaged in a

secretarial capacity and I asked casually: 'Are you married?' She hesitated and then said: 'I hope that you will not think any the worse of me when I tell you that I have taken advantage of Chou En-lai's new law and divorced my husband. He was unfaithful and beat me unmercifully.' I assured her that, on the contrary, I was pleased to find a social reform not only promulgated in Acts of Parliament but also enjoyed by the people for whom it was intended. The girl was very relieved to hear this and became more communicative. She told me that her mother had first met her husband on the day that they were married; she was much younger than he and her whole life was spent in fear of his violence.

Chou En-lai welcomed my questions on social problems to which he had clearly given a great deal of thought. The tiny feet of the very old women appalled me. I envisaged the cramped bones of the little feet which had been deliberately crippled in childhood. I asked for an explanation and Chou En-Lai told me that there were two theories. The wealthy men of China admired women who swayed slightly as they walked, and undoubtedly it was impossible to walk with a deliberate and confident gait on crippled feet. On the other hand, it was the custom for farmers to choose young wives to help in the fields and in order to ensure hard work and obedience to beat them systematically. It was more difficult for a girl to run away if her feet had been bound and, consequently, this cruel practice obtained support from influential quarters, both in the wealthy and poor sections of society.

At meals the menus which contained the names of seeds and roots processed for human consumption never failed to remind us of the widespread poverty and hunger of pre-revolutionary China and the desperate attempts made by an agricultural population to survive. Brought up to eat everything that was put before me and under no circumstances to leave food on my plate, I was accustomed in my travels to observe the same rules. In China a guest is helped to food by the host from a central bowl and my first experience of this proved a little embarrassing. I murmured 'thank you' and proceeded to eat every morsel placed in my bowl and even to accept a second helping. After this had been repeated with two or three courses and it appeared

G

that more were to follow I felt that I really must call a halt although I assured my hosts I had found the food delicious. I had not been warned that to empty one's bowl was the signal for it to be refilled and, therefore, the polite guest, unwilling to deplete a host's larder, would leave a little food to indicate that he had had more than enough.

Although circumstances did not necessitate their use, the menu of the Government banquet included traditional dishes:

Hors d'Oeuvres

—

Consommé of Chicken with Slices of Liver

—

Shark's Fin in Brown Sauce

—

Loquat of Chicken

—

Peking Duck in Lotus

—

Roots in Fair Colours

—

Mushroom and Sprout of Bamboo Sautés

—

Stuffed White Gourd Vegetarian

—

Macédoine of Fruits in Water Melon

—

Steamed Cakes

The overwhelming hospitality which we received on our journeyings from Moscow was in marked contrast to the widespread poverty of Asia; nevertheless, it was this very misery of the common lot which established the custom; providing generous hospitality and so ensuring a visitor of his welcome. Similarly, in Arab countries the hazards of the desert demand that a stranger must be given sustenance.

Our political discussions would often range around the status of Formosa. Clem Attlee favoured a compromise; he said that for a period of years Formosa should be governed by an independent authority and then given the opportunity to choose for herself whether to remain independent or align herself with another state.

Chou En-lai asked what we could do to further good relations between our two countries and then proceeded to criticize our voting at the United Nations Organization. He was inclined to disregard the fact that there were two main political parties in Britain and so was charging us with the political misdeeds of the Conservative Government.

I was taken to the Ministry of Health which is housed in the former palace of the Dowager Empress; the buildings roofed with green, highly glazed tiles, were grouped round a square court-yard and the entrance guarded by two stone Chinese lions.

The Minister, a woman, Madame Li Te-ch'uan received me very cordially. She conducted me to a red plush settee complete with antimacassar, and invited me to sit on her left, the position of honour for a guest, while a doctor interpreter sat on a red chair similarly upholstered. Sitting at a long table covered with a white cloth and laden with fruit and sweets at right angles to us were about twenty men and women, the doctors, officers and directors of hospitals and medical schools; having welcomed me, the Minister moved to the table where we could converse easily with her advisers. The story of the epic struggle against disease and the preventive measures employed was gripping in its awful detail. Cholera was rampant before Liberation but was now well under control; while Plague, which was endemic in Manchuria, chiefly where rats breed with wild rodents, had shown a spectacular decrease and there had been no single case in the south for a few years. Widespread propaganda was conducted to enlist the help of the villagers; the agricultural workers were warned that rats eat their grain and that if a man contracts a disease he will be disabled for a period and consequently unable to work in his field, a dire penalty. I saw in the windows of the chemist shops in Peking models of rats accompanied by a simple story of how disease can be spread by vermin. And there was widespread use of D.D.T. with excellent results.

Advice on preventive medicine flows from a provincial committee down to the District and so to the family; a street committee is convened to conduct propaganda and, as I was told about the work of the leader of the group, I was reminded of our wartime street wardens. When a people are faced with the threat of extermination, whether from war or disease, they are capable of organizing their resources in the most effective and economical manner.

The number of qualified doctors in our sense was very limited and the medical work of this vast country was undertaken in the main by 'old-style doctors'; men who had felt a call to the practice of medicine and had acquired most of their knowledge through their own experience. Vital statistics were difficult to collate as under the old régime nobody troubled about registering the births or deaths of those living in the country districts, or indeed of the poor living in the towns.

Illiteracy was widespread; and, the new Government of China deputed some individual in the village who had a smattering of education to attend the dying and to record a description of the symptoms which accompanied the death. These were collated by an official in the chief town of the region preparatory to compiling some national records.

The dedication of the Government officers combined with the co-operation of the people had undoubtedly effected the most marked improvements. I visited the Peking market with the intention of discovering how effective were the means employed to protect the perishable goods from contamination. The market is a vast place selling all kinds of foods and articles for use in the home and at work. As I strolled about I thought of my father's first local election campaign in which he declared war on flies, the cause of so many gastro-intestinal complaints. The whole place was singularly clean and I did not see one fly; this was a tremendous triumph for the public health authorities of Peking because it indicated the success of the educational crusade among the people.

On my return to England I found in certain circles that it was considered a good joke to denigrate the work of the Chinese people and to point to the successful eradication of the fly as the sum total of their achievements. Even if I had found nothing else to praise I would have regarded as of paramount importance the destruction and prevention of pests which undermine and finally destroy the health of a people. Some days after my visit to the market, at a dinner of doctors in Peking, one fly was perceived. All conversation stopped, the enemy was in our midst and I found myself as enthusiastic in swotting that fly as any professor of public health in the gathering.

The modesty and courtesy of the Chinese was illustrated at a dinner of doctors in Hangchow. I discovered on my arrival that while I was accompanied by Chang Tsung Ann there was no other interpreter present. It seemed to me that the silence was a little oppressive as we sat down; I anticipated a difficult meal ahead with my professional colleagues apparently unable to speak a word of English and with my Chinese limited to the few words I had mastered since my arrival. After the first course interrupted only by the united efforts of Chang Tsung Ann and myself to conduct a conversation, a very pleasant-looking man sitting opposite informed me in a perfect English accent that he had qualified in a London medical school. He then proceeded in idiomatic English to describe the delights of our capital city. This acted as a signal, one doctor after another told me in quiet modest tones that they also knew England well, because they had pursued their studies in one of our medical schools. I was dumbfounded. Then, laughing, I told them that I had feared that the dinner would not have been a success because of our inability to communicate with each other. The bond which binds doctors of all countries ensured that, on the contrary, the dinner was outstandingly successful.

The extreme modesty of these men forbade them to reveal that they were bilingual until we had settled down to our meal and I had been afforded the opportunity of speaking on some general topic; then a bold spirit, having broken the ice, each made his own, but highly intelligent contribution to the general conversation. Those of us in England who are bilingual are only too anxious to show off our prowess when occasion demands.

In Peking, Mukden, Anshan, Tangshan, Shanghai, Hangchow, Canton and everywhere I went I commented on the number of babies to be seen. I was told that it was calculated that the average family consisted of five children. Recognizing the undeveloped condition of the country and the inevitable pressures of a rapidly increasing population on the food supply, I expressed the opinion that family planning should be encouraged. On other matters when I had proffered a suggestion, the pros and cons of the case were eagerly discussed. But on birth control the country seemed to be united in their opposition. The reply was without exception 'Mother China needs more children'.

A few years later it gave me great pleasure to entertain the Medical Officer of Health, Madame Li Te-ch'uan, in my home when, in her turn, she sat by my side on a settee and I was able to perform the British tea ceremony for her. She told me that she recalled my advice and that new China had decided to include family planning in its social services.

I took the Minister to our famous Children's Hospital in Great Ormond Street where she inspected every new device installed to facilitate the work and provide the maximum benefit for both the children and the staff. With the modesty characteristic of her race she thanked the Matron and said: 'One day we hope we shall have an equally wonderful place for our children.'

I could not fail to notice the remarkable good temper of Chinese children. Those who are fond of decrying the way of life in a Communist country are apt to assert that any good impression which a visitor might receive was in consequence of some careful prearrangement. At least nobody could arrange for the hundreds and hundreds of Chinese children I saw to be on their best behaviour. Chang Tsung Ann could not give me the answer; her own manners were so pleasant that she accepted the fact that her own and other people's children should be equally equable. I asked a much-travelled Civil Servant for an explanation. He said that he attributed it to the Confucian philosophy, the principles of which were inculcated at a very early age although it was considered by many to be incompatible with Communism.

While we can justifiably pride ourselves on our health services, nevertheless the medical problems of our population of approximately 50 millions living in a temperate climate in a comparatively small geographical area cannot compare with the difficulties which confront the Chinese. With a population of 600 millions, in a tropical country covering a vast area with only the most primitive forms of transport available, they are faced with formidable obstacles to the establishment of a comprehensive health service.

In order to tackle some of the diseases which call for specialist care, short courses are devised to train men and women to learn to diagnose and treat those conditions responsible for a high morbidity and mortality rate. I lunched in the little home of a father of four children who was being taught to detect and treat diseases of the heart and lungs. And I took this opportunity to learn from his wife in the little lean-to kitchen how the delicious concoctions of beans, tomatoes and eggs were made. It all seemed very simple as I watched her put oil in an iron basin, heat it until a haze appeared and then, one by one add the ingredients according to the time each needed cooking. Then she, her husband, the four smiling children and I with the baby of nine months in a high chair chuckling at the curious pheno-menon who had suddenly descended upon them, sat down to our little bowls while mother helped us from the large bowl in the centre of the table. This simple meal with its delightful setting remains fresh in my memory while some of the most sumptuous banquets which I have attended in the rest of the world have long since faded from my recollection.

Tuberculosis was a common complaint in villages where the cramped living conditions were often responsible for the trans-mission of the disease from one member of the family to another. The 'Chest' doctor became so expert with his stethoscope that he could make a diagnosis more quickly than a fully trained doctor with a full knowledge of the anatomy and physiology and the diseases peculiar to a tropical climate.

Similarly, it was found necessary to provide treatment for those whose mental health had deteriorated whether to a minor or a major degree.

In Peking the most famous 'Old Chinese Doctor' called and invited me to visit his clinic. He was seventy-three with a perfect command of English and in a lined brown face his eyes twinkled mischievously as he recounted his experiences. He told me that at the age of thirteen, on account of his mother's illness, he decided to become apprenticed to the Village 'Doctor'. Among other things he learned about herbal medicine and psychosomatic diseases. While he recognized that his experience supplemented by the various courses he had taken had given him a vast knowledge of the human body and the diseases to which it was subject, he regretted that he was not twenty years younger when he would have asked to be enrolled for a full medical course at the Peking University. Not for one moment did he decry modern medicine; he was a keen admirer of the tremendous progress he had seen achieved in the course of the last few years. At his clinic I found old 'Chinese Doctors' like himself having refresher courses in modern methods of diagnosis and, in pathology and bacteriology. I watched three men being treated for neuroses by acupuncture; by the side of each stood a student who occasionally twiddled three large pins stuck into the skin over various parts of the patient's shoulder-blades.

I asked the patients to tell me the nature of their complaints. There seemed to be a striking similarity for they all complained of 'a feeling of insecurity, fear of unemployment, failure of their wives to understand them and sleeplessness'. I looked at the head of the Clinic whose eyes twinkled knowingly. I said I was under the impression that a Communist society had resolved all these problems and that they were regarded as being identified with a Western civilization. The wise old man said: 'Human nature is the same, West or East, and it takes more than Government policy to change it.' I asked the patients whether their symptoms had responded to the treatment. The three of them had been visiting the Clinic for four weeks and they were highly appreciative; they assured me that the symptoms of which they had complained had been relieved.

The old doctor told me that he had read all about our psychiatric clinics in Britain and the USA and the highly specialized equipment used in them; but so far as he could apprehend on reading the medical journals of these countries, his results were equally good. And I was not disposed to disbelieve him.

It is not easy for a visitor to discover how a country manages to discipline its population, or to inculcate a social sense; one can only comment on what one sees and is told by reliable people. In Shanghai which had, before Liberation, a notorious underworld and a high rate of crime, we were told by an English manager of a British factory, that before Liberation the company lost between 3 and 4 per cent of its production from pilferage; whereas today they rarely lose anything.

A business man who was not feeling very well disposed towards the Chinese Government because he was unable to send his earnings out of the country, told us that before Liberation his wife was attacked in the street and afterwards was afraid to go out. Now she was quite unafraid to go out at any time of the night and visit friends in different parts of the city, confident that she would not be robbed or molested.

The previous international character of Shanghai was apparent from the architectural style of its buildings. The former exclusive French club with its superb swimming-pool which, in pre-Liberation days, excluded the Chinese, was now used by Chinese officials and their friends. Chang Tsung Ann and I spent many happy hours there and, with chuckles of delight Ann received her first swimming lessons from me. In the evening on a tiled patio outside, an excellent dance band played modern Chinese and Western tunes and I danced with our hosts until I was completely exhausted. The fun, the laughter and the general gaiety were infectious.

I visited a cotton mill where 600 workers were employed, the great majority women; it was equipped with a nursery, a primary school and a nursing room for mothers who were given regular time off to suckle their babies. It seemed to me that almost every other woman was pregnant, many in an advanced condition and I expressed to a welfare officer my concern regarding the effect of the long hours of standing on these women. She sought to reassure me by showing me a hostel attached to the factory where women who are ill could be accommodated. I visited a woman who was receiving treatment at dinner-time and peeped into her feeding bowl; it contained bean soup with eggs and tomatoes and smelt delicious. I was slightly mollified in consequence, but it failed to erase from my mind the picture of those docile inarticulate expectant mothers standing at the machines.

Our visit to the Forbidden City in Peking included our first meeting with the Chairman of the State, Mao Tse-tung. He rarely appeared in public but never failed to greet the people at May Day and Liberation Day celebrations. I had expected to find some wizened, inscrutable elderly man whose calculated silences might hamper our efforts to establish a harmonious relationship. On the contrary Mao Tse-tung, much darker in complexion than his Prime Minister, was a plump, jovial man, apparently in very good health. We discussed world affairs very frankly. Mao made no secret of the fact that he was determined to carry out all the undertakings he had made to the Chinese people on the day he assumed power. He turned to me and asked if I had read the new Marriage Law and whether I thought that it could be improved upon. I congratulated him, although I had reservations about divorce by consent because a woman's attitude towards marriage and the children were not identical with those of the man. I told him that the law in one respect was in advance of ours for the Chinese women were given an equal share of the family possessions, whereas in England a married woman had no legal right to a share of the family income.

I discovered that a simple pattern of Chinese life was not necessarily the rule everywhere. I visited a hairdresser's shop owned by a White Russian and his wife who had settled in Peking after the Russian Revolution; I observed that they were very discreet in their comments on the activities of the Soviet Union.

I met a Catholic priest and a Nonconformist clergyman who assured me that despite the atheistic context of Communism they were not debarred from holding services; the priest told me that he had held three well-attended masses that morning.

I was reminded of the conditions of life in old China when I was invited to tea by the European technical manager of a factory. We were waited on by Chung a manservant of fifty-four who had been with the family for twenty years. His wife lived 300 miles away with their six sons. He told me that he sent his family a regular allowance and visited them once or twice a year; habit being so strong he expressed himself as well satisfied with the arrangement. During his absence his wife and sons had cultivated a patch of land, and Chung dreamed of the day when he would return in his old age to live, happily for ever after in his own home. I envied him his philosophy; but it seemed to me that a lifetime of toil in a foreigner's home, 300 miles from your family, seemed a high price to pay for an unpredictable period of leisure when the capacity to enjoy life to the full had faded.

There is an old Chinese saying, 'Above is heaven, below is Hangchow'. We stayed in Hangchow at a Government guest house on the banks of the Three Lakes and although I could not vouch for the absolute truth of the saying I can understand the sentiments which prompted it. Our visit had been a little strenuous and our hosts had planned a rest at this lovely place just when we were longing for the peace and quiet of the countryside. At dusk I lay on a long cushion on a boat on the lake, paddled by a strong young woman: I then partook of a delicious dinner and retired to a room with a temperature of 90 degrees and a bed covered with a smooth, cool canvas on which I enjoyed the best night's rest of our journey.

The Chinese saying would certainly not apply to Canton where the water-borne homes made one reflect on the state of the public health. The faces of the people were thinner than those of the North; the eyes were wider and less slit-like, and the children at first glance seemed less well nourished. Women, bare-footed, many of them past middle age, dressed in black blouses and trousers, provided much of the transport. They sweated and strained pulling carts piled high with produce, and at the wharves on the river they stood silent, cowed, like ill-treated animals waiting to be loaded with heavy sacks of grain. The sampans in which vast numbers of families lived on the river swarmed with children with faces which seemed prematurely aged, and many of them were suffering from prickly heat accompanied by the inevitable sores.

The memorial figure of Sun Yat Sen, dressed in European frock coat, high collar and watch chain struck me as incongruous in this floating city of the poor.

I dined that night with the Chief Medical Officers of Canton and some of the town's doctors. I could not fail to tell them of my profound disappointment at the condition of the women and children whom I had seen in the streets and on the river. They assured me, and no doubt they were right, that the infantile mortality rate had been reduced in a spectacular way.

Nevertheless no statistics could erase from my mind the picture of the old women I had seen bent nearly double beneath their heavy loads.

Our visit to China had been planned and executed, to the smallest detail, in a manner which enabled all of us to examine certain aspects of life with which we were familiar at home; and therefore on which we were able to exercise some valid judgement. We were not dragooned, or kept under surveillance; when I occasionally disappeared without warning to roam the neighbourhood Chang Tsung Ann's only reaction was one of concern lest I might get lost and be unable to make myself understood.

While some of the men of our party, former miners, went down a coal mine, others, who had taken a special interest in penal reform, visited the courts and prisons. I concentrated on the whole range of social services, hospitals, clinics, factories and agricultural communities which enabled me to see a cross-section of Chinese life.

The Government made a final gesture of friendly co-operation by providing us with a private train to take us on the first stage of our journey to Hong Kong; this was the first occasion, since the revolution, on which a train from Canton had been allowed to cross the frontier.

The journey through the paddy fields, flanked by banana trees and irrigated by tread mills, sometimes operated by a woman with a baby on her back, or a water buffalo, presented the picture of the East which Miss Collins used to describe in my childhood. I gazed at the ambling water buffalo with a warm regard having after years of waiting at last made his acquaintance. We disembarked all too soon and said farewell to our little group of Chinese friends who had cared for us so assiduously. I kissed Chang Tsung Ann and then, greatly daring, offered her some earrings as a parting gift. No Chinese woman wore jewellery; but I hoped that the good manners of the Chinese would not allow her to refuse a small gift which was a token of my friendship and gratitude for her never-failing care and good humour. Chang Tsung knew this, and shyly thanked me. I thought that I detected in her expression a pleasurable anticipation similar to that which one would expect to see in any woman looking forward to trying on a pretty trinket. We were on British territory now and were welcomed officially by the British representatives from Hong Kong. I was suddenly transported home on learning that one of them had been up at Oxford with Michael and one of the wives had been at St Paul's school with Shirley.

Of all the magnificent views that I have known nothing transfixes the attention so completely as the first glimpse of Hong Kong, an amazing product of nature's freakishness and man's ingenuity. The massive rocky island rises steeply from the sea; from the base to the apex, well designed multistoreyed offices and attractive houses in white and pastel shades shimmer in the brilliant sunlight. The harbour is alive with boats of all sizes from the Chinese junk to a turreted, long grey warship, sinister in its stillness. Every six minutes an elegant little white painted ferry boat darts across from the mainland to the island with a kind of impudent abandon.

Clem Attlee had decided to accept a long-standing invitation to Australia and New Zealand and so we parted at Hong Kong. Aneurin Bevan and I were invited to stay at Government House, a long white attractive building looking out on the Bay. I was looked after by an elderly over-attentive Amah who appeared to view my persistent questioning about herself, her family and the social conditions in Hong Kong with some suspicion. Her slave-like attention to my simple needs led me to the conclusion that a lifetime of being seen and not heard made it virtually impossible for her to communicate freely with me; she presented an inscrutable front which it would have taken longer than we could afford to spend in Hong Kong to penetrate. One is very conscious in Hong Kong of the sharp contrast between luxurious mansions and offices and the shanty town where the poverty and wretchedness of the growing army of refugees presents a constant challenge to the municipality; for their housing and social welfare calls for ceaseless planning and supervision by experienced officials.

Our next destination was Japan where we had been invited to address some Socialist Party meetings and to meet the Prime Minister and members of the Government. In the course of our flight we touched down at Okinawa to refuel. The air-conditioned restaurant was crowded with American Service men whose round faces and thick necks presented such a striking contrast to the slender Chinese men that I felt momentarily as though we had arrived on another planet. The tables were covered with plates filled with substantial meals, or with food which had been left half finished; even the American Service men's capacity has its limits, and he is not taught that food should not be wasted. These substantial repasts were washed down with Coca Cola.

The most exquisite little Japanese waitresses, dressed in elegant European style, flitted about the room; they all wore the same demure expression and I gathered that their work was strictly limited to satisfying the gastronomic appetites of the troops.

We arrived in Tokyo in a violent rainstorm which served to control the crowd who gave us a tumultuous welcome. The Vice Speaker of the House of Representatives entertained us at our first luncheon in Japanese fashion; but when I saw the low table and realized that I was expected to squat on my heels, or sit on a cushion and put my legs under the table I quickly decided on the latter. Even European men in trousers find this something of an acrobatic feat but for a tall woman in a skirt to descend gracefully to the floor and tuck her legs under the table is not so easy. While I accomplished it, I was concerned as to how I should extricate myself without exposing an undue expanse of leg and possibly even lingerie. Aneurin sat next to me and I confided to him my fears; we agreed that he would struggle up first and present himself as a screen while I effected my escape.

That night, the Speaker invited us to dinner and I was relieved to find that it was in European fashion and I could sit at ease on an upright chair.

Our first public meeting was in the Hibiya auditorium which held three thousand, and on that occasion, we were told even the standing room was filled to capacity. Aneurin Bevan and I were asked to speak and as I gazed over that vast auditorium of shining black heads I could identify only a dozen women. I opened my address by asking whether we had arrived in a country of one sex. This was greeted with shouts of laughter and applause from which I gathered that the Japanese male felt no sense of loss, or failure, certainly not shame, at having his political life represented by only half the population.

Without giving any notice of my intention I asked to visit a cotton mill. I found nearly a thousand girls employed, and sleeping four to a room in an adjoining building. They received about £2 a week part of which was deducted for board and lodging. The dust in some of the work rooms resembled a light London fog, and I raised the matter with the male manager and male trade union representative. I was assured that Japanese dust when inhaled, unlike Western dust, did not affect the lungs. In an adjacent small room I pointed to two X-ray machines: 'Then why has someone thought fit to instal those machines if not for the purpose of X-raying the girls chests? This suggests that the danger is present.'

The reply was a shrug of the shoulders.

I was looked after by a Member of the House of Councillors, Mrs Cato, formerly Baroness Ishimoto and Mrs Satoko Togano, a Member of the House of Representatives, both of whom spoke excellent English. Mrs Cato was imprisoned in 1963 for some weeks for promoting birth control.

One question only dominated our political discussions. What was our attitude to the Atomic Bomb?

Although the social conditions of the rapidly growing industrial population of Japan presented many problems no interest was manifested in the domestic policy of our Party or how we tackled some of our more pressing social questions. There was a totally different approach when I addressed about five hundred women trade unionists, professional women and housewives; they freely expressed the sense of frustration they experienced in a society where men were concerned only with their own standard of values. They listened with intense eagerness to my description of women's struggle for emancipation in Britain; when I sat down well phrased, intelligent questions, chiefly concerned with how to establish a society based on equity and social justice, were fired at me from every part of the hall.

At a university dinner I found myself seated next to Dr

Katsuo Takenaka, a Member of the House of Councillors, a Professor of Sociology in Wassada University and author of a survey *Prostitution after the War*. I asked him how prostitution differed in Japan from other countries, for I was under the impression that the factors conducive to prostitution were the same all over the world.

He said, 'Have you never heard of the eighteen islands of Tokyo?'

I confessed my ignorance and he told me that the eighteen islands consisted of land reclaimed from swamp and constituted a vast area used solely for the purpose of prostitution.

That night I accompanied the Professor and one of his students to explore the eighteen islands; we wandered from one street to another, all floodlit with brilliant neon lights, and containing brothels varying according to the price paid for the services of the prostitute.

The lowest priced were housed in small buildings with a lighted shop front window on the ground floor. In front of this posed three or four very attractive young girls in kimonos. The more expensive trade was done in large houses, European in architecture, approached by a short drive; at the entrance to the drive posed a beautiful Japanese girl elegantly dressed in European style. This method of display provided the customer with an opportunity of inspecting a sample of the wares which are for sale inside the establishment. I was told that some dress shops in Tokyo provided the clothes free as this was deemed a fruitful means of advertising in houses patronized only by wealthy clients whose wives might find solace in a new frock or coat.

Having inspected a sample of each we returned to the more modest streets, and the Professor sent the student to interview the 'Madame' of one house, with a request that some social workers would like to have a chat with the girls. 'Madame' made no objection, Provided that she was paid at the usual rates for the girls' time. The Professor therefore paid 1,000 yen, equivalent to £3, the three of us entered the house, climbed a short flight of stairs, and were ushered into a little room furnished in the characteristic Japanese style with cushions on the floor and a small table. 'Madame' bowed and smiled; waved us to the cushions and then brought in tea which she dispensed with the poise of the vicar's wife presiding at a vicarage tea-party. Then the door slid back and there entered three girls, all about twenty years old. They wore kimonos, they bowed and then sat on their heels and 'Madame' indicating that we could ask them any questions we wished, then withdrew. Prompted by my companion each girl told us her story; one had been in the cotton mill, but she found it more congenial to be in the brothel where she earned £5 to £6 a week provided she served about three men a night. Another girl, a former geisha, had lived with a married man who had spent all her savings and then deserted her; the other had been a ballet dancer and was the mother of an illegitimate child.

Two of them said that they sent money home regularly. I asked whether 'Madame' and her husband were kind to them and they replied that they were well looked after provided they did their work properly. They had no complaints except that one said that she found the life boring. As we left I gently held a girl's arm; she looked at me with a completely blank expression and, if she saw any compassion in my face, she did not respond. I reluctantly came to the conclusion that in all probability these girls thought that we were wealthy eccentrics who were prepared to throw our money away for the sake of a little chat, and the Japanese professor agreed.

Neither of us observed anything which might indicate that these girls were conscious of the fact that they were doing something which was morally wrong or that they were being exploited. The economics of the business of prostitution is all cut and dried. The owner of the brothel supplies a girl with her board and lodging and takes 60 per cent of her earnings; while the Government's revenue department ensures that the brothel owner makes a handsome contribution to the treasury.

I had not read the Professor's book but I was inclined to think after this experience that the attractions of prostitution in Japan did not differ fundamentally from those of other countries; the difference lay in the facilities offered in Japan, for these placed few obstacles in the way of a girl who was prepared to earn her living in a brothel. The Japanese show a crude realism in accepting prostitution as a fact, and a strict commercial sense by denying the right of a landlord to enjoy to the full the profits accruing from the trade. Apparently the Government are not squeamish about being the direct beneficiaries of this unsavoury business.

No doubt other countries find it difficult to understand the British attitude to prostitution. The business was driven underground by the 1959 Street Offences Act. The disappearance of the prostitutes from the street has apparently satisfied the moralists, who fail to concern themselves with the manner in which the same prostitutes continue to conduct their business. Although it is illegal to conduct a brothel in Britain yet the various means of living on a woman's immoral earnings, although an infringement of the law, have increased since the Act was passed.

From Japan we retraced our steps to Hong Kong, and there after a rest, with Amah now a little more approachable, we were off to Bangkok and Singapore.

Sir John Nicholls, the governor, invited Aneurin Bevan and me to stay at the massive Government House in Singapore. Conducted by some officials and old European residents I did the sights in Singapore. 'Sights' was certainly the word for some of the conditions I found in Sago Lane and Southbridge Street where the rapacity of the landlords surely cannot be exceeded anywhere in the world. Some dilapidated buildings resembled human warrens; literally every corner was let to some unfortunate human being, even the long entrance passage providing accommodation for about twenty of the near destitute. On visiting one of these houses I noticed in the passage filthy pieces of cloth hanging from a shelf about 2 ft 6 in. from the ground. I lifted one of these to reveal an old woman squatting on her heels. As I lifted the flap which separated her from the ceaseless traffic in the passage she crawled out like some frightened animal. I was told that she would probably pay about 2s. 6d. a week for this accommodation in a building which housed about two hundred human beings. If she became fatally ill, she would then be taken to the death house; a small shabby building where an open coffin in which lay a corpse awaiting burial stood just inside the entrance. Incense was being burnt and at least it did provide an antidote to the stench which met me when I climbed a rickety staircase to the first floor.

In beds ranged round the bare room lay women of various ages in the final stages of some fatal disease. A relation squatted on the floor acting as nurse and occasionally other relations or friends would arrive to say farewell. It is not always easy for a doctor to predict when death will finally supervene and I do not know how long some of these unfortunate women, fully conscious, would have to endure such appalling physical and mental suffering.

Rangoon was our next destination, and we spent a few days in Burma which enabled us to meet members of the Government, and learn more about their social and political problems. At the risk of being charged by the Burmese with adopting a frivolous approach to their country, I have to confess that it was the clothes of the women which made the most striking impression on me.

The Burmese woman is the most elegant in the world. The housewife from a modest home in her longi, an ankle-length skirt of attractive material swathed tightly round her body, a simple blouse, and her hair dressed in a black gleaming chignon surpasses in appearance any wealthy woman I have seen in London, Paris, or New York.

The picture of one of these attractive Burmese women, who throng the streets – for I am speaking of the ordinary woman, not an exceptional national beauty – carrying, not balancing, because it is done with consummate ease, a parasol across her chignon is fascinating.

The Prime Minister, always an early riser, asked us to call at eight thirty in the morning. I had been shown all the buildings and institutions of which undoubtedly he was very proud. When he asked me what I thought of his capital, I had to admit that the women struck me as being more attractive than any others I had encountered. I thought he looked a little disappointed for women in the East, even in Burma where every attempt was being made to catch up with more progressive countries, did not amount to much.

However, perhaps I misinterpreted his expression, because on the morning of our departure the Prime Minister sent me a farewell gift; a length of green hand-woven silk, already cut for a longi and a silver-handled parasol, with a note saying: 'I appreciated what you said about our ladies.'

While I am not greatly influenced by the fashion trends, even I could not defy custom and enter the Palace of Westminster in that beautiful longi, although I would have dearly loved to have done so. I occasionally take it out of a drawer where I keep it carefully wrapped and consider whether I shall use it for some other purpose; then I feel that it would be an unfriendly gesture to the Burmese women to convert their lovely national dress into some trivial passing Western fashion, and so I put it carefully away again.

But when I sit in my sunny garden I sometimes put up my Burmese parasol and dream of a country where the elegance and grace of the women is unsurpassed in the whole world.

We touched down at Calcutta, where Aneurin had an altercation with the medical officer who demanded certain particulars in writing concerning our route. As I had visited a leper colony in Rangoon this did not surprise me. Aneurin regarded this as an unwarranted interference with the liberty of the subject and refused, for some time, to comply with the regulations. I was well aware that, if the request had been made earlier in the day, when we were less tired, the unfortunate medical officer might have been treated with more civility.

We looked forward to a rest in Beirut the capital of the Lebanon, that lovely little country with its terraces and hills thick with olive trees and vines; a country where it is possible to bathe in the Mediterranean and ski in the mountains on the same day.

After our long hot journey I longed for a dip in the sea and no sooner had I expressed the wish than the arrangements had been made by our Arab hosts. As I idly floated I was called and beckoned from the shore. Reluctantly I returned to find myself the centre of a group of young men engaged in a heated discussion on the Arab–Israeli question. Exhausted from my long journey, my bathing-suit clinging to me and my hair becoming loose from under a silk handkerchief nevertheless to these hot-headed youngsters I personified all the forces responsible for the heartbreak of the Palestinian refugees; as such I was to account for my country on that beach there and then. I made the shortest speech of my political life and returned to the warm kind embrace of the Mediterranean.

Later that night the traditional hospitality of the Arab world swept us up to a party in the hills outside Beirut, where congenial companionship accompanied by music and song, calling for no interpreter, made a fitting end to a visit which had taken us half-way round the world.

17

Recollections of Aneurin Bevan

Aneurin Bevan, one of the members of that delegation to the Far East, was undoubtedly one of the most colourful parliamentarians of the twentieth century. If one is to compare like with like, comparisons are difficult to make, for no politician on the Liberal and Conservative benches was launched on a political career with so few educational and social advantages. To me, married to a Welshman, Aneurin Bevan's activities never failed to provide food for thought. We clashed frequently on the National Executive Committee, but he could never rouse any deep antagonism in me; his outbursts always revealed the undisciplined child of promise of a large family struggling to survive in a community stricken with unemployment and its attendant evils. Eloquent with more than the usual Welsh interest in words he had acquired an extensive vocabulary; and he employed this to his own and his listeners' delight with a dexterity which had its origin in a speech defect which he was determined to conquer. Winston Churchill similarly had a defect as a child which he, with an equal tenacity of purpose, but with, I suspect, expert guidance, was resolved to overcome. No doubt history, guided by the written word, will regard Churchill as the greater orator; his written speeches were carefully prepared papers, well rehearsed, and delivered with calculated deliberation. Yet Winston Churchill could not compare with Aneurin Bevan as an extempore speaker. The detailed written speeches which Aneurin delivered were those prepared for him by the department when he was a Minister. While he might equip himself with notes for a speech they rarely seemed to bear the mark of careful preparation. The fact was that he was too lazy to do his homework properly. He liked to talk and to hear himself talking. Sometimes he talked sense; and at other times he would use his vocabulary and his flair for fabricating an attractive phrase to defend some proposition which had been presented to him only shortly before by a complete stranger.

When he was Minister of Health in 1945, I would often chat with him about some aspect of the Health Service and although our talk might have been of a tentative character, I would listen to him a little later hold forth to an audience with complete confidence and with a wealth of language which astonished me. He liked reading books dealing with broad principles and extracting information from all and sundry; so much of his restlessness in the thirties stemmed from his incapacity to get down to the hard, slogging work necessary to acquire a detailed knowledge of a subject.

He occasionally visited us in the thirties, following a phone call to ensure our being at home, and revealed a delightful, simple, uninhibited person as he romped with the children and teased Nana. One Saturday afternoon he arrived and pressed by the children to stay, and provided with clothes by my husband, did not leave until the following Tuesday. It was during this week-end that we all set off for a bathing-pool, Jeffrey driving with Michael next to him and Aneurin between Shirley and me on the back seat. It was a very hot day and I was wearing a thin, sleeveless frock. Suddenly I felt a sting and yelled 'I've been stung'. In a second Aneurin turned, seized my arm, sucked it and spat out of the window. Of course from a therapeutic point of view this was unnecessary, but Aneurin, without a moment's hesitation did what he felt was the right thing, however unpleasant the process.

In the thirties, the Brasserie of the Café Royal served as a meeting-place for politicians, artists and all kinds of people not too well endowed with this world's goods; they had much to say and could say it well. We would sit on the red plush seats, and a sandwich and a lager costing a comparatively small sum would be regarded by the waiter as a purchase sufficient to cover our occupancy of a table until closing-time.

A small orchestra of women would delight us with well-known melodies, and the leader, a thin, fair, dreamy-eyed woman with her violin tucked firmly under her chin would stroll among us; on recognizing the regulars, she would play some tune which we might have asked for on a previous occasion. This setting suited Aneurin for we were prepared to listen, encourage and laugh uproariously at the unending recitals of his experiences or opinions on every subject under the sun.

On one occasion he spent an afternoon at home with us discussing psychology with my husband; it was apparent that Aneurin had read many authorities on the subject for he displayed a knowledge of Freud and Jung which took us by surprise. That night we met some friends at the Café Royal, and politics were hardly mentioned. Psychology was Aneurin's subject, and so brilliantly and wittily did he display his knowledge that the head waiter who always liked to linger by our group, seemed chained to the spot.

The war years changed Aneurin. He grew a little bitter for he believed he should have been given a post in the Coalition Government. He often spoke to empty benches; a passionate torrent of words critical of the administration would pour out, which sometimes only invited ridicule and occasionally a violent denunciation from a Government spokesman. The 1945 Government and his appointment as Minister of Health completely restored his confidence and he slowly gained an ascendency over the house which, despite his long membership, he had never hitherto acquired.

The years were passing and this brilliant, unstable personality knew that there was only a limited time for him to secure the leadership which he so ardently desired. His eloquence made him the leader of a dissident group; but too often his magnetic personality was used by others, whose calculations and designs could only be promoted by a colourful speaker whose powerful oratory, spiced with witty allusion and metaphor, reassured the waverer, and was greeted by thunderous applause from the chronically disaffected.

In the fifties the amusing, kindly, perennially boyish Aneurin of the early thirties had become a moody, introspective politician, aware that men with lesser gifts as parliamentarians, but with a greater stability, had overtaken him in the race. As I sat beside him on the planes and stayed with him in various places on our journey to China and back I failed to recognize in the morose individual whose unpredictable moods puzzled his friends and rejoiced his enemies, the gay laughing Aneurin of the thirties, who romped with Michael and Shirley and whose kind heart prompted him to give me instant first-aid.

18

Some Thoughts on the National Health Service

Two subjects on which I have campaigned with enthusiasm are clean food and the pressures of the pharmaceutical industry. The powerful vested interests of the food industry delayed the introduction of a 'Clean Food Bill' for many years. Finally, in July 1954 an emasculated measure received a second reading but only seven of the original sixty-seven proposals remained untouched and some of the clean handling suggestions were relegated to a 'pious hope'. I expressed the view that, 'It was scarcely possible to believe that in the mid-twentieth century the proposal that persons handling food should not spit, smoke, or use snuff, was not made enforceable.' Apparently you may not spit or smoke in a bus, but to do both while preparing food for the public is not deemed to be an offence. Even Dr Hill, later Lord Hill, the Parliamentary Secretary, made no lavish claims for the measure. He said, 'Don't let us pretend that this Bill does more than provide the fabric for the solution to part of the problem.'

Tinned foods, prepared foods, and concentrated preparations in various forms have undoubtedly relieved the overworked housewife; yet the ingenuity of the chemists has swamped the market with foods adulterated with colouring matter or preservatives; and with inadequately tested drugs which are a menace to the health of the public. Those able to observe the effects of some of the new drugs on patients deplored the failure to exercise greater supervision over the pharmaceutical industry; yet it was not until the 'thalidomide' scandal about 1960 that the whole world was alerted to the dangers inseparable from the fierce competition of the mushrooming drug houses. Women suffering from sickness attendant upon early pregnancy had been prescribed thalidomide which affected the unborn child by arresting the development of the limbs of the foetus, consequently at birth it was found to be suffering from shocking deformities. Thalidomide had been widely distributed in Germany where a large number of deformed babies were born, and while Britain had a considerable number of these unfortunate infants, the United States was spared this tragedy. This was due to the attitude of a woman, Dr Kelsey, attached to the Food and Drug Administration who refused, despite persistent criticism from the pharmaceutical industry, to allow the drug to be distributed, on the grounds that it had been inadequately tested.

One reason for the criticism which has been levelled at the National Health Service by some doctors can be traced to the exploitation of the Service by certain elements in the pharmaceutical industry. 'Free Medicine' has encouraged the manufacture of an ever-increasing number of products, some of them similar in composition but bearing different proprietary names. While in my childhood one trusted representative of a drug firm would call occasionally on my father, today medical practitioners are continually pestered by the glib representatives of the industry and each post contains some advertisement often accompanied by samples of a new drug. There are now more than a hundred and fifty drug firms battening on the National Health Service, all indulging in extravagant advertising for which the state eventually has to pay. The contraceptive 'pill' provided fresh opportunities to the drug houses to compete in a field which offered opportunities for colossal profits. Their customers were to be found among the millions of healthy women in every country in the world anxious to prevent a further pregnancy.

Professor Sir Charles Dodds, the eminent endocrinologist and the President of the Royal College of Physicians, uttered the warning that the human body is a biological clock and if the clock goes well do not try to interfere with it. The *Lancet* said, 'The use of oral contraceptives cannot be contemplated without considerable trepidation; twenty years may go by before we can be sure about the safety of the present oral contraceptive.' Despite the warning, the 'Pill' was widely distributed and even in countries where supervision by qualified doctors was out of the question the 'Pill' is canvassed as being the safe and harmless answer to birth control. Although reports of deaths due to thromboembolic episodes in women taking oral contraceptives gave rise to concern, the pharmaceutical industry was permitted to continue the marketing of oral contraceptives on the grounds that it had not been positively established that the number of deaths was not higher than the number which would occur normally in women of similar ages. Although this exact information was not available and the collection and the assessment of more cases would inevitably take a considerable time, nevertheless the pleas which I made in debates in the House of Lords and which Shirley made in the Commons to withdraw the oral contraceptive from the market pending a decision that it is not injurious to a woman's health fell on deaf ears.

The unremitting commercial pressure of the drug houses encourages a doctor to prescribe costly proprietary preparations in place of the cheaper, but equally effective compounds given in the National Formulary; this comprises a list of drugs distributed by the Ministry of Health to help and inform the medical practitioner. Certain elements of the pharmaceutical industry have used the National Health Service as a milch-cow, consequently in 1965 the cost of drugs to the service is £100 million.

I have raised the matter first in the House of Commons and later in the House of Lords in debates on the National Health Service so often, that a peer who has interests in the pharmaceutical industry refers to my intervention as my 'ritual dance'. The harassed doctor pressed by a patient to prescribe a particular tablet or pill which he asserts another doctor has prescribed for a friend, may comply reluctantly although there is no medical evidence that the patient's condition calls for any drug whatsoever. The practitioner is paid on a capitation basis and if a patient is dissatisfied with the treatment he receives, he can transfer himself and his family to another doctor who may be more disposed to respond to his incessant demands. Younger doctors recognize that a doctor's skill should never be judged by his capacity to attract patients to his list, and that a system which can threaten a doctor's freedom of action is not conducive to the highest professional standards. Good medical practice must be synonymous with the right to be absolutely honest with a patient. A totally different economic barrier has arisen now between the patient and the doctor which often precludes the doctor from giving the patient a frank assessment of his condition.

In the thirties a group of doctors calling themselves the Socialist Medical Association, affiliated to the Labour Party, met regularly at 13 Devonshire Street, the home of Mr Somerville Hastings, an Ear, Nose, and Throat surgeon attached to the Middlesex Hospital. Among them were Dr Charles Brook, a general practitioner, the indefatigable secretary, Dr David Stark Murray, a Pathologist, my husband and myself. Our object was to prepare a blue-print for a National Health Service which could be implemented by the next Labour Government. Exhausted after a hard day's work we would meet about 9 p.m. at Number 13 where it seemed to me that the coffee brewed by Mrs Hastings was the most delicious I had ever tasted.

While the organization of the medical and hospital services undoubtedly offered the most interesting topic for discussion, in retrospect it seems to me that we failed to concern ourselves sufficiently with the more materialistic aspects of the project. We were guided of course by the 1911 National Insurance Act, which assumes that most people on a doctor's list were healthy, and remuneration on a capitation basis was therefore equitable. However, with the introduction of fresh methods of diagnosis and new drugs, together with the emphasis on preventive medicine, the pressure on a general practitioner increased considerably, with the result that there has been a growing revolt against what the older doctors believe is a measure of exploitation.

The Medical Officer of Health has always held a high place in the esteem of the community because it is acknowledged that his concern for the public welfare is entirely disinterested. Never has it been suggested that the salary basis on which he is paid will detract from the value of his services. The medical practitioner should also be freed from all pressures even indirectly related to the profit motive; thus remuneration based on a salary could ensure that the patient would receive the most beneficial advice and treatment.

During the last twenty-five years the use of chemotherapy and antibiotics has changed treatment in a spectacular way, which to some extent has reduced the heavy burden of responsibility carried by the doctor, but at the same time it has severed that close personal tie which existed between the physician and his patient when the prognosis of an illness could not be predicted. Furthermore, the rapid growth of the social services has enabled the doctor to delegate some of the most time-consuming work; this, together with the growing recognition that our ageing population needs the services of social workers who can supplement the doctor's knowledge of the problems of the family, promises to alter general practice radically. The contemporary approach to disease has served to emphasize the importance of the team in our medical services with the result that slowly but surely the single-handed practitioner responsible for the patients welfare from the cradle to the grave is being replaced by the group. The Health Centre which is favoured today and with which younger practitioners in urban areas are prepared to experiment is designed for as many as ten doctors to practise in the same building together with the local authority nurses, midwives, and health visitors. The centre also contains a small laboratory and there is provision for radiography, dental services, speech therapy, and child guidance; and consultative sessions are held by specialists from the local hospitals. This is very similar to the 'policlinics' I have visited in Communist countries in the Soviet Union, China, Rumania, Czechoslovakia, and Yugoslavia. The advantages to the patient with a specific disease are obvious, and although he may have to travel twice as far this is offset by an appointment system for consultations. However, the mobile aged in need of comforting reassurance concerning some painful or disturbing symptom associated with advancing years will find the journey to the Health Centre arduous and perhaps the atmosphere too intimidating. Undoubtedly, the Health Centre will dis-concert the 'chronic' who enjoys a visit to the doctor and a gossip in the waiting-room, and who can dismiss the therapeutic importance of this social contact to the lonely and insecure? In terms of service it rather resembles the introduction of the efficient supermarket at the expense of the little corner shop, and both of course have their place in our modern society.

As statistics reveal that one-third of the patients treated complain of some degree of nervous stress, much of which can be alleviated by an understanding and sympathetic doctor not pressed for time, it is essential that adequate attention is given to the aberrations of the human mind about which, despite spectacular advances in the field of therapy, we still know so little.

19

Life Peeress: Some House of Lords Debates: Abortion Law

In January 1961 I was made a Life Peeress and I took my seat in the Lords, the only other woman on the opposition side of the House was the Life Peeress, Barbara Wootton, the Economist and Sociologist. She and Stephen Taylor, a Life Peer and a doctor of medicine, who had served in the Commons with me for some years, acted as my sponsors. I could not have wished for more appropriate sponsors for they represented fields of work which had stimulated and inspired me throughout my career.

It is customary to arrange a small luncheon party on the day of one's introduction and this included besides my two sponsors my husband, Michael and Shirley, Clem Attlee and Sir George Bellew.

I did not suffer from any feelings of strangeness, or indeed shyness, when I went to the Lords. The Palace of Westminister is one structural unit, and for twenty-three years I had strolled through the corridors and rooms and was familiar with the many officers who had served there as long as I had. Furthermore, when the Commons was bombed in 1944, the Lords offered us accommodation which we gratefully accepted; consequently when I became a Minister in 1945 I not only made speeches from the dispatch-box in the Lords but was subjected to repeated attacks by the opposition there. And nothing can obliterate those memories.

My maiden speech in the Lords did not therefore hold the terrors for me which I had experienced when I made my first speech in the Commons in 1938.

Moreover, many of the faces on the other side belonged to former members of the Commons, whom I had heard on many occasions and therefore I had a pretty thorough knowledge of their attributes and attitudes. Although some of them had adopted different names on assuming a title this presented little difficulty; since the passage of the Life Peerages Act in 1958 new peers are more ready to cling to their old names, which facilitates identification. Custom dies hard, however, and life peers are asked to adopt a place name also. This seems to me to be completely out of touch with contemporary thought on the subject; if we are to democratize the Lords then what is the object of asking a peer to adopt a place name irrespective of whether he wishes to do so or not. The origin of the custom dated from the time when land was allotted according to the service which had been rendered by the recipient. This feudal tribute bears no relationship to the institution of Life Peerages.

Having lived in Highgate on the edge of Hampstead Heath for many years it seemed to me that a part of London which adjoins my home and for which I felt a sentimental attachment and which consequently seemed appropriate for the purpose was Kenwood. It is uninhabited and as far as I know it possesses only one house, Kenwood House, an Iveagh bequest, which was administered by the London County Council and now by the Greater London Council. Garter assured me that this choice was in order and I became without more ado, Baroness Summerskill of Kenwood.

I suggested to many people including the B.B.C that I might retain the 'Dr Edith' by which I was well known but I failed to find any co-operation. Why women Life Members of the Lords should, in the middle of the twentieth century be addressed by the title 'Baroness' has been difficult to discover. Behind the scenes, some decisions are made without sufficient consideration; the same individual responsible for suggesting 'Baroness' might well have been he who coined the ugly 'Dame', the female equivalent of a knighthood for women receiving the honour in their own right. I cannot help associating in my

H

mind, and I do not think I am alone in this, the word 'Dame'
with the Christmas pantomime, and Baroness with the old
French aristocracy, the most Conservative of societies. I
anticipate that the hereditary element in the Lords and the
Lords spiritual will disappear in due course; then perhaps we
may hope that the Members of the House will retain their own
names followed by M.P.L. to indicate the House to which we
belong.

There are some who assert that by making life peerages we
are simply shoring up an anachronism. If there is no necessity
for a second Chamber then clearly the whole *raison d'être* of the
House of Lords has disappeared and the sooner it is abolished
the better. If, however, there are sound reasons for retaining
a revising chamber, and most politicians favour this, then we
may well take the first steps to convert the present institution
into a debating forum which matches the needs of the day.

Nobody can afford to be dogmatic about the constitution of
the House of Lords; it came into being in the most haphazard
manner and for many centuries there was no predestined right
for the members of any stratum of society to regard themselves
as the law makers. According to Pike in the *Constitutional History
of the House of Lords*, the origin of the two titles of Lord and Earl
is lost in the obscurities of an unlettered age and the two words
have become the plaything of rival philologists.

It may well be that the Peerage Act of 1963 will lead to the
abolition of the right of hereditary peers to sit in the House of
Lords, now that a hereditary title is no longer an obligatory
inheritance. As more members of the Lords are those who get
there on merit there may be a growing reluctance on the part
of the new hereditary peers to take their seats.

There are some Members who have accepted a Life Peerage
who find the work of the House uncongenial. This applies to
elderly Members who took their seats late in life and who had
not served in the Commons, for Parliament is an acquired taste
and new habits are not easily established late in life.

The British are masters of improvization. Whereas other
countries abolish existing institutions and start from scratch,
we prefer to adapt to the new circumstances those services and
buildings which have already proved adequate. The debating

chamber of the Lords has excellent acoustic properties, and provides those creature comforts which are not unwelcome in a place where members have to sit for increasingly long hours; and the Member who has already served in the Commons has available for his use all the Commons rooms with the exception of course, of the debating chamber. The Library service is improving rapidly while the clerks at the table are untiring in their efforts to help members who seek their advice.

The Prime Minister on the advice of the leaders of the Parties nominates Life Peers. Undoubtedly the time will come when the hereditary element has been abolished, for members to be nominated or elected by a body which is more representative of public opinion.

It would seem that Life Peers are chosen by reason of some special knowledge which they possess, while the Prime Minister also bears in mind services which they have rendered to the country. It is agreed that since the advent of Life Members the standard of debate has improved, and this may be attributed either to the special knowledge of the new member or to previous experience obtained in the House of Commons.

Commenting on the House of Lords in the mid-twentieth century, Mr Henry Burrows, who served the Lords as Clerk of the House, a knowledgeable and very popular man who gave me invaluable help, wrote in the *Listener* in 1964:

'Three contributions to the reform of the House of Lords have been brought in by Conservative Governments during the last thirteen years. The Life Peerages Act, 1958, provided for the creation of life peerages for men and women, so that the hereditary element in the House of Lords should not contingently be increased whenever a new peerage was created. Forty-five years later than the Commons, their Lordships realized the need for a woman in the House; their sense and sensibility have made a big contribution.'

This is the opinion of an observer at very close quarters; it could be said that habit alone would have made him less favourably disposed to such a revolutionary change and therefore his opinion carries greater weight than that of a new-comer. He says that the House of Lords is less logical than it was and

that it could be made to work better than it does, the problem
of course being how to deal with the hereditary peers; but he
uses this term to denote only the person who succeeds to a
peerage. He does not include the first holder of a hereditary
peerage nor a peer advanced in the peerage for 'the first peer
of a creation should be a person of some distinction, whereas
a successor might be a nonentity or worse.'

What might be regarded as a handicap, namely the provisions
of the 1911 Parliament Act, which deprived the Lords of powers
relating to Finance, has in fact provided more time for debates
on topics of general interest. On the motion of a Member a
debate can be conducted on matters of social and political
significance, some of which are regarded by some members as
unsuitable for public debate in the Commons. I have in mind
the Wolfenden recommendation that homosexual consenting
adults living together should not be subject to legal action, and
also a debate on abortion. No one in the House of Lords need
ever look over his or her shoulder to see how a constituency is
reacting to a speech and no one feels compelled to make a speech
for the local paper in order that his constituents may learn that
he is in his place. The Lords does in fact provide a forum of
debate where social and political philosophies can be thrashed
out without fear or favour by Labour, Conservative and Liberal
representatives.

It is true that debates are conducted in a calmer atmosphere,
but that does not indicate that their Lordships are not without
fire in their aristocratic bellies for Hansard reveals clashes
which are notable for the control which a member exercises in
the use of language. Heat is generated but there are no sudden
verbal explosions, mainly synthetic, which are characteristic of
certain members of the House of Commons, who having made a
particularly noisy and offensive interruption, leave the Chamber
well satisfied with their contribution to Hansard for the day.

About two weeks after I took my seat the Labour peers
moved a vote of censure against the Government on the National
Health Service increases and this enabled me on 13 February
1961 to make a maiden speech on a subject which was very
much my own. It is a little difficult to be non-controversial on
this subject, for a maiden speech is traditionally so; however

by House of Commons standards I felt that I was being sweetly reasonable. I was therefore surprised to find the *Manchester Guardian* report that 'though Lord Taylor tried later to explain that by Summerskill standards Lady Summerskill's had indeed been a non-controversial speech, no Tory peer – to judge from their fierce unsmiling faces – believed him. And when Lord Taylor went on to promise that the Baroness's contribution was "but a small foretaste of things to come" the frost in the House was chilling.'

Whether this was an accurate analysis of the emotional condition of their Lordships is questionable. Patrick O'Donovan put it rather differently in an *Observer* summing-up of the House of Lords in 1964: 'Edith Summerskill, for example, has become a spectacular success in the Lords and the House has not crushed her ebullience or creative impertinence.' I can only say that in the next few years, I made various attempts not unsuccessfully to pilot Private Member Bills and I always found an audience prepared to listen to a sound argument.

As I have said the value of the House of Lords as a debating chamber in which controversial questions can be raised without fear or favour was exemplified in the debates following the introduction of a Bill by Lord Arran to legalise the homosexual practices between consenting adults in private.

The House of Commons has never welcomed the ventilation of social problems which might offend the susceptibilities of the constituents of its members. It avoided any discussion on birth control long after the Lords in 1926 recommended that advice on contraception should be available for married women at the Maternity and Child Welfare Clinics.

'The Sexual Offences Bill' which received its Second Reading in May 1965 embodied a proposal to implement the recommendation of the Wolfenden Committee that, 'Homosexual behaviour between consenting adults in private should no longer be a criminal offence'. The House was full and there was a long list of speakers, for the object was to remove the sanction from something which has been a criminal offence for many centuries. In support of the Bill many speakers drew attention to the fact that the homosexual was a victim of blackmailers. It seemed to me that unless homosexuality becomes accepted as near normal then the risk of blackmail will still exist despite the provisions of the Bill. We were told by a former Home Secretary that according to a report on ninety-six cases of men who were in prison for homosexual offences, a report which covered psychiatric examination, only fifteen out of the ninety-six were genuine inverts. The remaining eighty-one carried out their homosexual practices for other reasons such as a desire for a new sensation and for money.

Viscount Montgomery of Alamein strongly condemned the Bill, which he asserted would undermine the moral fibre of the youth of the nation. He was passionate in his appeal to the House to 'knock this Bill for six right out of the House'. He said, 'What is the greatest single factor making for success in battle and for efficient and well-trained Armed Forces in peace? It is morale. And what is the foundation of morale? It is discipline. If these unnatural practices are made legal, a blow is struck at the discipline of British Armed Forces at a time when we need the very highest standard of morale and discipline throughout the world. If the men know that their officers perhaps are indulging in these practices, it is legal, nothing can be done.' On the other hand the Lord Bishop of Chichester on behalf of the Church gave the Bill whole-hearted support with the proviso that certain other of the Wolfenden recommendations should be included. He said that the moral fibre of the nation may be just as much undermined by heterosexual misconduct as by homosexual misconduct. At this point several peers shouted 'Nonsense'. He went on, 'The present attitude obstructs the very purpose which the law should make possible – namely, the pastoral care and treatment of the offender and the rescue of many would-be offenders struggling, it may be, against a weakness which they have been born with, whose own resistance to the danger at present cannot receive the reinforcement and the counsel which they so desperately need.'

On the Committee Stage, in reply to Viscount Dilhorne, a former Lord Chancellor, who strongly condemned the measure, the Archbishop of Canterbury said, 'Let me say not for the first time that I regard homosexual behaviour as abominable, utterly abominable. I am a supporter of the Bill in the belief that the Bill will help and not hinder the forces making for morality in this respect. . . . The noble and learned Viscount challenged me about the moral relationship between homosexual behaviour and fornication. I think it is extraordinarily hard for any of us to assess the relative sensuality of sins. When we start doing that we get into questions to which the Almighty Himself knows the answer and we do not. I would say that, comparing the two, homosexual behaviour has an unnaturalness about it which makes it vile. On the other hand we are encouraged to measure the vileness of sins by the question of motives and personal circumstances. I think that there can be behaviour of a fornicating kind as abominable as homosexual behaviour and as damaging to the community.'

The Second Reading of the Bill was passed by a large majority, but it was necessary for all the stages to be completed and to be passed by the House of Commons in the same session before it could reach the Statute Book. This is a lengthy process which was not completed before the House adjourned for the summer recess. The Bill was re-introduced in the Lords in the autumn of 1965, but the General Election intervened in March 1966 and the Bill was dropped.

Mr Humphrey Berkeley, the Conservative M.P. for Lancaster, had indicated his intention of piloting a similar Bill through the Commons, but he lost his seat at the General Election and with it his chance of piloting any Bill, at least temporarily. After the election he was asked whether he thought that his support for a Bill of this nature contributed to his defeat. He could not agree with the suggestion.

Also in the autumn of 1965 the House of Lords debated another of those controversial matters which can be discussed there without being deterred by the loud protestations of constituents. Doctors, lawyers, and the victims themselves, are well aware that the Abortion Law does not conform to the needs of our society, yet conscientious and religious scruples, stronger in some regions than others, have always prevented governments from introducing a Bill to reform the law.

In 1965 a National Opinion Poll showed that 72 per cent of the people were in favour of some reform and women's organizations passed strongly worded resolutions focusing attention on the outmoded provisions of the law.

In a recent Government report it was stated that out of 1,000 investigated cases of death at childbirth, no fewer than 345 women were already mothers of six or more children, and in the Registrar General's Report for 1958 it was stated that pregnancy, childbirth and abortion are an increasing cause of death among married women.

In June 1965 Mrs Renée Short the Labour Member of Parliament for Wolverhampton North East introduced a Bill to reform the Abortion Law. She obtained unopposed the assent of the House to its introduction. She said that the Bill would put into statutory form what was now established case law on abortion and would provide that a registered medical practitioner might lawfully terminate a pregnancy at the request of a patient or her guardian when it was necessary for preserving the health or life of the woman, when there was serious risk of a defective child being born, or when the pregnancy resulted from a sexual offence.

The law up to 1803 permitted the medical termination of pregnancy. The law enacted in 1861 made it a felony unlawfully to administer drugs and to use instruments to procure an abortion. For a long time the termination of pregnancy for the purpose of saving the life of the mother had been regarded as the exception to this rule by the courts. In 1939 the case law was extended by the Bourne judgement to include the mother's health as well as her life.

However, many cases had occurred which demonstrated the confusion which existed. While some lawyers might feel that the present case law based on Rex *v.* Bourne was quite clear, there was no doubt that the medical profession required the clarification which a Bill of this kind would bring and that the majority would support it. Mrs Short quoted figures which demonstrated a shift in favour of abortion in both medical and public opinion. The House too, she believed, must give considerable weight to this shift. Unfortunately there was not sufficient time before the end of the session for this Bill to secure a Second Reading.

On 30 November, Lord Silkin moved the Second Reading of the Abortion Bill designed to amend the law to enable a doctor to terminate pregnancy where there is a grave risk of the mother's death, or of serious injury to her physical or mental health; where there is a grave risk of the child being born grossly deformed or mentally or physically abnormal; where the social conditions of the mother make her unsuitable to assume the legal and moral responsibility for a child or another child as the case may be; and where the pregnancy has occurred following unlawful intercourse under the Sexual Offences Act 1956. These offences include rape, sexual intercourse with a child under 13, sexual intercourse with a child over 13 (where the conditions and the penalty are rather different); sexual intercourse with a woman who is insane or mentally defective and sexual intercourse as the result of administering drugs to a woman so as to make her unconscious.

As a mother speaking in this debate my approach was more subjective and forthright than the male speakers. The practice of abortion is as old as pregnancy itself, yet the question still arouses tremendous passion which cannot be countered by rational argument. Consequently, since 1803, when the procuring of an abortion became a statutory crime, society, buttressed by convention, prejudice and theological doctrine, has been obdurate and merciless towards the pregnant woman who seeks relief by abortion.

I was well aware that the opposition to the Bill would be on religious grounds, therefore I felt constrained to ask what right celibate men had to decide the fate of women by pronouncing on abortion law reform. This was a matter in which the voice of British women should be the deciding factor, and not 'the moralizing of men who, in the name of Jesus Christ forget the example He gave and condemn the unfortunate women'.

I showed how historically the opposition to abortion and birth control, like the laws of Moses, which were concerned with elementary hygiene and the safe preparation of food, stemmed from the urgency of the need to decrease the mortality and morbidity rates and to increase the population. In order to ensure the obedience of primitive people these instructions had to be invested in some divine decree. Today, literate people of the space age, in well-populated countries are not prepared to accept taboos without question; and in the matter of abortion the human rights of the mother with her family must take

I

precedence over the survival of a few weeks' old foetus without sense or sensibility.

'I find it difficult to understand,' and I addressed this particularly to the Earl of Iddesleigh, who had strongly opposed the Bill and who had spoken of a woman being tempted 'to kill' the foetus, 'how the Commandment "Thou shalt not kill" is observed by deliberately sanctioning the death of a mother who would otherwise have survived if her pregnancy had been terminated. To my mind, in these circumstances a mother has been killed with the utmost premeditation.'

The debate was not related solely to the principle of abortion, because that had been acknowledged in 1936 following the Rex *v.* Bourne case, which was concerned with the induced abortion of a young girl following rape. In the Alec Bourne test case the surgeon involved, who had defied the law and risked his professional reputation in consequence, was acquitted and the principle established.

The question before the House was whether the practice should be extended to the other categories of women mentioned in the Bill. The provision designed to relieve women where there is a grave risk of the child being born grossly deformed or mentally or physically abnormal would meet the need of women like those who had taken thalidomide during their pregnancy with all its tragic results. To permit science on the one hand to concoct drugs which produced gross deformities in the foetus, while at the same time withholding the skilled hand of the surgeon to relieve the unfortunate mother seemed not only paradoxical and a perversion of science but totally lacking in humanity.

'A girl who has been raped cannot be expected to feel anything but loathing for the man who has assaulted her; her human rights had been violated and when pregnancy results it violates her maternal functions. Can it be argued that it is socially desirable and reconcilable with human rights that she should be compelled to bear and rear a child criminally begotten?' I asked.

I cannot believe that it is desirable to bring into the world a fatherless child who knows he has been hated since his birth. As the law punishes rape as a serious crime should we not help to our uttermost the one who has suffered from the crime? The Government has already established the principle that the State should recompense the victim who has suffered some injury at the hand of the criminal. While it is impossible to recompense a girl for the violation she has suffered, at least she should have the resulting pregnancy terminated.

I was not happy about the clause in which provision was made for a woman to have an abortion if the 'social conditions' were deemed unsuitable. 'Social conditions' could be interpreted to cover such a wide range of circumstances that it would come to be regarded as an alternative to birth control. In 1920, abortion clinics, where a woman could have her pregnancy terminated on demand, were established in the Soviet Union. When I first visited that country in 1932 I asked to see one of the clinics in operation. In a large room six operating tables were being used simultaneously and every few minutes a fresh batch of women was wheeled in. I was reminded very disagreeably of an assembly line in action.

On my last visit I was relieved to find that the Soviet Union in 1936 had rescinded the liberty of abortion on demand, owing to the high morbidity rate among women who had availed themselves repeatedly of this service. In describing these conditions to the House I said, 'I have not to tell this House that I am a champion of my sex, but in seeking to help women we must not establish a service which used indiscriminately, might react to their disadvantage. Safeguards are very important; otherwise the floodgates will be opened.'

I wound up by reminding the House that, 'one function of the law is to uphold the rights of the individual. Roman law gave the husband the power to authorize the abortion of his wife, and a right to damages against a third party who procured her abortion without his consent. That law was designed to safeguard the man's absolute interest in his wife and children as persons subject entirely to his power and control. I am asking that the human rights of a mother must be upheld, and that the law should safeguard her interests above the claims of all others.'

On a division the Bill received the support of the House; sixty-seven voting Content and eight voting Not Content; and the promoter gave an undertaking that it would be amended in Committee to meet some of the objections raised on the Second Reading.

While this was a triumph for humanity and common sense, it also represented the free vote of those unshackled by constituency considerations. The real trial of strength will come when it is taken to the House of Commons where expediency dictates the action of some Members and unremitting pressure from religious groups will be applied to reject the Bill.

Having listened to the Bishop of Chichester and the Archbishop of Canterbury on the Sexual Offences Bill plead on behalf of the Church for the opportunity to exercise pastoral care and to help male offenders in desperate need, I was astonished to find on the 'Abortion Bill' that most of the representatives of the Church in the House of Lords including the Archbishop of Canterbury did not reveal the same humanity and Christian compassion for the completely innocent mother in desperate need.

The controversy arose over whether it should be lawful for a doctor to terminate a pregnancy for a woman who is, or will be, physically and mentally inadequate to be the mother of a child or another child as the case may be. The Archbishop of Canterbury supported the deletion of this part of the Bill. I said, 'I feel, having listened to the most Reverend Primate, and before him, on the Committee stage, to the Right Reverend Prelate the Bishop of Exeter, that the question before us to-day, so far as the Church is concerned, is whether precedence should be given to the wishes of this mother, with her fully developed personality, and with the responsibilities of her children, her husband and her home, or to the survival of a few weeks' old foetus. I have not been favoured with divine guidance. I can speak in this debate only as a mother, and as one with forty years' experience of medical practice during which time I have met very many of these women; I cannot enter into the arena of theological disputation. But I think it should be drawn to the notice of those who might be influenced at this stage by the fact that the name of the Most Reverend Primate appears on this Amendment that I do not think he has received a mandate to speak for the whole Church, or for the mothers of the country.'

I charged the Archbishop of Canterbury with speaking without a mandate because, in *The Times* of 17 February under the heading 'Church Assembly Confusion over Abortion Report' the Church correspondent wrote,

'Attempts by the Church Assembly yesterday to clarify the attitude of the Church of England towards abortion, and at the same time provide a lead to the legislature now considering amendments in the law, did little towards this end. The debate became so confused that the Archbishop of Canterbury, Dr Ramsey, rescued it from – as he said – running into chaos, by rescinding what had been decided and starting again . . . . Confusion arose when five amendments and an amendment to one of them were introduced. The report itself . . . argues that abortion should be allowed if the health or well-being of the mother is endangered. The Rev. D. Stevens, Lichfield, wanted the Assembly to add the words: "Reaffirms that the vital principle involved is the sanctity of human life", and the Bishop of Leicester, Dr Williams, chairman of the board, wanted "Christian compassion" as well as the sanctity of human life.

'Dr Williams said . . . "The Church has erred in the past and can still err." He went on: "We erred over the burning of heretics, and the burning of witches. No doubt many of the arguments heard in this debate were heard then. We had to eat our words, and I think that Rome is showing signs that it may have to eat its words over contraception. Even the Pope has made one exception to the question of abortion, and I think that doctors who have spoken have made it plain that they make exceptions."

'Finally, the Assembly decided that they welcomed the report because it stresses the principle of the sanctity of life for mother and foetus and urges the Church to preserve and demonstrate a balance between compassion for the mother and proper responsibility for the life of the unborn child.'

This debate prompted the *Evening Standard* to devote its leader column on 2 December to the changes apparent in the face of the Lords. It wrote under the title 'Noble Lords':

'No longer speeches which send all but the speaker to sleep. No longer merely a chamber in which obscure backwoodsmen pontificate on trivialities. No longer is the droning debating dialogue in the House of Lords a debate which really doesn't affect the nation at all.

'Gradually the upper chamber is becoming one in which not only the votes, but the debates, count again. In the past year the issue of homosexual law reform was thoroughly thrashed out by the Lords. They made a valuable contribution to the abolition of hanging. And now the illogicalities of the law on abortion are exposed for all to see with the strong discussion of Lord Silkin's Bill.

'Of course, the Lords are in a valuable position as a legislative checkpoint. Their sound consideration of certain bills such as the War Damage Bill and the latest Rent Act have induced the Commons – pressurized into getting laws through on time – to think again. Now with longer discussion of contentious issues, the Lords can, perhaps, induce the Commons not to dismiss them lightly – and think again.

'The House has always been rich in the range of opinion among its hereditary members. They include such controversial figures as Lord Gifford who in his maiden speech attacked the hereditary principle itself, Lord Salisbury, and others.

'More important, however, has been the new blood the House has drawn from experts in a wide range of subjects. Elder statesmen such as Lord Attlee and Lord Butler. Economic experts such as Lord Plowden, doctors such as Lady Summerskill, sociologists such as Lady Wootton, and many more. The upper chamber, in turn, provides them with a valuable platform for a more detailed examination of issues than in the Commons. For long the Lords has been a target for political reformers. But where reforming zeal is concerned – at least on social issues – the Lords may yet prove themselves the peers of political theorists.'

20

Single Women and Married Women

This is a woman's book and I will end it by describing two more women's questions on which I have campaigned and on which much still needs to be done. The first was one which I noticed when still a child and it came to a head while I was still in the House of Commons.

Any organization, provided it is sponsored by a Member of Parliament, is permitted to hold a meeting, to which members of the public may be invited, in one of the committee rooms in the House. The competing claims on a Member's time generally mean that a visiting speaker experiences a sense of shock and profound disappointment – which he effectively conceals – on finding only a handful of Members present to listen to his discourse.

Having in my twenty-seven years at Westminister attended many of these gatherings I strolled along the Committee Room corridor one day in November 1965 to a meeting convened by the Rev. Mary Webster, a Congregational Minister, to launch an organization called the 'National Council for the Single Woman and her dependants'. It was a miserable day and a thin wet fog spread over the Thames almost obliterating the old buildings of St Thomas's Hospital opposite. With the bad weather outside the House and the male preponderance inside, I reflected that Miss Webster would be lucky if twenty turned up to the meeting. I felt very sorry for this was the inauguration of the organization. I knew that for three years she had been working hard to persuade the Charity Commissioners to approve the

Council; and to organize the single women, who were responsible for the care of elderly parents, to make some protest at the failure of the community to recognize the great contribution which their selfless devotion made to the needs of the elderly and infirm.

I was astounded to learn from one of the officials that a room on the Committee Room floor had been reserved for an overflow meeting and that the main gathering was being held in the Grand Committee Room off Westminster Hall, a room big enough to hold eight hundred people if filled to capacity. I lost no time, and on arrival found the Grand Committee Room full, with women standing three deep at the back. Miss Webster, a short, rosy-cheeked, middle-aged woman with twinkling eyes and the unmistakable energy of the good organizer, flanked by a few Members of Parliament among whom I was pleased to see Shirley, gave a brisk, witty, informative address. She said that the problem concerns the last unmarried daughter living at home, caring for elderly and handicapped relatives. Often she has to give up job, friends and pension to stay at home. After years of strain when she is no longer well enough or even qualified to take another job, her dependant dies and she is alone. As I listened my mind went back over the years to a sweet Miss Collins whose life had been devoted to unremitting service to others.

In the 1966 Census a question is included for the first time to find out the number of single women with dependants. The Council will campaign for more equitable tax regulations, for while widows and widowers may claim for a housekeeper, single women may not. It will try to make it easier for single women to get mortgages; it plans to run an advisory service and compile a register of people who could respond to calls in a crisis.

As I looked at this packed gathering of middle aged single women I was struck by the general shabbiness undoubtedly stemming from a life of self-denial; at the sad, unsmiling faces, for a life dedicated to the care of the elderly leaves little room for cheerful social contacts with younger people. When question time came, except for one or two inquiries, the audience remained silent; not because their minds were not crowded with questions which they had asked themselves constantly over the lonely years, but because the silence imposed by habit cannot be easily broken. Aged parents often fail to recognize that a devoted daughter is a grown woman and continue to treat her as a child; their querulous demands on her time and energy must inevitably undermine her will to resist, with the result that she finds in withdrawal her only defence against ceaseless claims on her generosity.

These selfless women are often the butt of cruel music hall jokes; they are called 'old maids' because while women out-number men, marriage cannot be the lot of everybody; the presumption is that sexual attraction is the most important criterion by which the human personality should be judged. Many a devoted single daughter is denied a social life which might have enabled her to meet men and subsequently marry and have children of her own. And who could doubt that with her patience and unselfishness she would have made a wonderful mother.

When I came to move the vote of thanks to Mary Webster, I sought to encourage their campaign with a zest and fervour which reminded me of my early campaigning days.

I had long campaigned against the inequality of the position of wife and husband in marriage and I had an opportunity to continue this when Mr Leo Abse's 'Matrimonial Causes and Reconciliation Bill' came to the Lords in 1963.

Women in two world wars have successfully combined the work of a housewife with work outside the home to which they were totally unaccustomed. After the Second World War they showed a marked reluctance to return to their homes, for while in 1931 only one woman in ten held a job outside the home, by 1951 one woman in every four had taken employment, and by 1961 one in every three married women was at work outside her home.

The most marked increase was among middle-aged house-wives where children had grown up and they refused any longer to be tied to the chores. Now 40 per cent of all wives between forty and fifty-four years of age have jobs outside their home. Perhaps it is the taste of economic independence together with the desire for companionship which has been responsible for a change in the attitude of women towards the institution of marriage. It may account also for the tendency to marry younger; the commonest age for marriage is now twenty-two for men, and twenty-one for women, while the number of teenage marriages continues to increase. Young men and women have been accustomed since childhood to two incomes coming into the home, father's and mother's, and they are prepared to follow the same pattern, consequently early marriage becomes a sound economic proposition.

Those women who have successfully earned their own living experience satisfaction in the sense of independence; and they are not prepared to acknowledge that a marriage has a satisfactory basis in which a man undertakes to endow a woman with all his worldly goods, but in fact never reveals the amount of his income.

Sir Jocelyn Simon, the President of the Probate, Divorce and Admiralty Division of the High Court, in an admirable address to the Holdsworth Club in 1964, put the case well:

'I invite you to accompany me to a village church where a wedding is in progress. The mellifluous cadences of the vicar's voice fall hypnotically on the ear – "honourable estate . . . mutual society, help and comfort . . . comfort her, honour and keep her . . ." Now he has recited the ceremony of the ring. The bridegroom bends a gaze of ineffable tenderness on his bride " . . . with this ring . . . with my body . . . and with all my worldly goods I thee endow". I held my breath, aghast. Will the vicar rend his cassock? Will he sprinkle on his head ashes from the ancient coke stove? Will he hurl the bridegroom from the chancel steps with imprecation and anathema? For the man has committed the most frightful blasphemy. In that holy place, at this most solemn moment actually invoking the names of the Deity, he has made a declaration which is utterly false. He is not endowing the bride, with a penny, a stick, a clod. Nor does he intend ever to do so. And yet the service proceeds as if nothing untoward has happened.'

It is significant that with the slow but undoubted revolt of woman against her dependent role in marriage, the President of the Divorce Court, a former Solicitor-General, with a vast experience of legal work associated with the break-up of marriage, should have denounced in no uncertain terms the age-old wedding ceremony which congregations throughout the land listen to with respectful attention.

This denotes a radical social change; ten years had elapsed since I tried unsuccessfully to pilot the 'Married Women's Disabilities Bill' through the House of Commons with the object of trying to remedy some of the financial disabilities of the wife and mother. If the respect for marriage is undermined by the failure of society to deal equitably with both parties to the contract we should not be surprised to observe certain changes which might stem from this failure.

Can the decline in sexual morality among young people be related in some measure to this? In the 'fifties 30 per cent of all teenage brides were pregnant, as against the Registrar-General's figures for 1939 when some 27 per cent of all brides married before twenty were expectant mothers. Since the mid-fifties one in five marriages of teenage brides has ended in divorce, and each year from 1958 to 1962 there was an increase in the number of divorce petitions filed. It is believed that there are in Britain today some 250,000 women, married, but living apart from their husbands, responsible for the care and up-bringing of some 375,000 dependent children; it is not surprising that marriage and divorce are matters which rouse the keenest controversy.

Divorce is generally available only where a specific matrimonial offence has been committed and to this the only exceptions are the comparatively few cases of incurable insanity and presumption of death. The Morton Royal Commission on Marriage and Divorce in 1956 recommended by an overwhelming majority that divorce should continue to be on the grounds of the commission of a matrimonial offence involving a fundamental breach of the marriage vows. They were against making the criterion for the grant of divorce that the marriage had irretrievably broken down. By a majority they were also against divorce by consent, or by the compulsion of one of the parties after a number of years of separation.

Despite this, a number of people are proposing the extension of divorce facilities. Unsuccessful efforts have been made on previous occasions to extend the grounds for divorce. The unusual claim on this occasion is that by granting divorce without a specific matrimonial offence the family will become a sounder and more stable institution.

At least it is agreed by those who would increase divorce facilities, and by those who oppose this move, that the family is a valuable unit in the community. And who would deny that family life conduces to human happiness? Should divorce be facilitated in such a way that the incentive for mending a marriage is removed, and replaced by a desire to establish a new family? What guarantee is there that the second or third attempt will be more successful than the first?

Every marriage is subject to some stress and strain. Is this a reason why the most solemn obligation should be jettisoned and existing children of the marriage sacrificed to the welfare of the wife and children of a future union? Should the happiness of a husband or wife be bought at the expense of the happiness of their children?

Moreover, should the State, by offering legal aid, subsidize easy divorce? The advocates of easier divorce argue that its denial results in spouses living apart in some illicit union; the provision of easier grounds for divorce would inculcate a greater respect for marriage. Furthermore, that if divorce was granted after five or seven years separation, despite the objection of a substantially blameless spouse, this would enable those who had formed an extra-marital union to marry and thus confirm their faith in the overriding importance of the family as an institution.

It is argued very strongly that increased facilities for divorce and remarriage will result in the children of the extra-marital union being legitimated. However, the figures available do not prove that greater facilities for divorce have meant less illegitimacy.

The man or woman who has left home may have formed some stable union with another person, and these people can agitate through their Member of Parliament for an amendment of the divorce laws to meet their case. But what of the small army of inarticulate powerless children who cannot raise their voices for society to hear their grievances. They are found in the courts, and the doctors' consulting rooms, delinquents, insecure and neurotic.

There are those who believe that a divorce is better than subjecting a child to frequent scenes and quarrels but I am not among them. According to the reports of some Judges sitting in custody, it is at the moment of the break-up of the home that the child shows signs of serious deterioration in bad behaviour and speech defects.

The fact that the divorced wife and children are entitled to a maintenance allowance does not meet the case, for how many men can afford to support two families? It will be the woman who is in possession of the wage earner, who will naturally demand the maximum provision for the second family, at the expense of the needs of the divorced or separated wife and her children.

Apart from the economic argument, is it right, or just, that a woman who has spent her youth and middle age caring for a family should be cast off for a younger woman? This is a frequent pattern in the break-up of marriages.

Some lawyers assert that we have already divorce by consent, because a man and woman often come to some agreement that one shall divorce the other. There are eminent lawyers who say that while this may happen, nevertheless there are powerful sanctions which prevent a deliberate deception of the court. They regard the woman who, it is alleged, sits up all night with a husband in a hotel preparatory to being found by a chamber-maid, so that one can provide the necessary evidence of adultery as a divorce reformer's folk myth.

There are occasions when a wife, desperately anxious to maintain the home, and only too willing to effect a reconciliation is brought under constant pressure to divorce a husband who wishes to remarry; in these cases to provide divorce by consent would weaken considerably the wife's position. How far have we failed to make it clear that marriage should endure; is this one reason why teenagers enter into marriage without careful consideration?

It was in 1963 that Leo Abse, the Labour member for Pontypool, sought to introduce his 'Matrimonial Causes and Reconciliation Bill'. Among other things, it would allow divorce by consent after the couple had been separated for seven years; it would also allow estranged couples to have a three-month trial reconciliation before divorce.

Sir Jocelyn Simon took the unusual step of making a major pronouncement on the law of divorce just when the Bill had completed its committee stage in the House of Commons. He said that 'divorce by the free consent of the parties meant that society was disclaiming concern in the endurance and stability of marriage.

'The truth is that marriage is not purely a private affair of the parties. It is an institution of society, in particular one under which children acquire legal moral and social rights.'

Apart from the moral considerations, the 'Married Women's Association' objected to the Bill on economic grounds. They declared that the second wife would be regarded by the husband as the first call on his income, and consequently the strict observance of a maintenance order would be in jeopardy. And the pension provisions of the Welfare State would be enjoyed by the second wife irrespective of the fact that the first wife might have lived with the deceased man for a far longer period than his new partner.

When the Bill reached the Lords there were powerful forces arrayed against it, consequently the most controversial clause relating to divorce by consent was withdrawn before the second reading. Anticipating that the clause would be reintroduced on the Committee stage I felt it necessary to say: 'I regard the original Bill with the compulsion clause as a husband's Bill, drafted by a man who doubtless meant well, but who failed to recognize that marriage has different values for a man and a woman.

'I am not concerned with the theological approach or the doctrinal pronouncements of the Church, I am concerned with protecting the little earthly paradise, the home – the source of most women's greatest happiness – which they create for their children.

'This I believe could be more easily destroyed if this Bill with the compulsion clause, became an Act of Parliament. Furthermore, with this clause, marriage will be for seven years and not for life; it will encourage young people to treat marriage even more lightly and any beatnik, who marries at nineteen, will know that he can be out of it by the age of twenty-six.'

I also opposed, but unsuccessfully, the three-months' reconciliation clause, called by the popular newspapers the 'Kiss and Make Up Bill', on the grounds that if a man resumed cohabitation for three months there was a likelihood that the wife might become pregnant, and yet, as this was only a trial period, he was under no compulsion to resume permanent cohabitation.

The Lord Chancellor, Lord Dilhorne, supporting me asked, 'Was it really right that in these circumstances the husband could say "I am going to divorce you because of your matrimonial offence committed before this attempt at reconciliation?"'

Lord Hodson, a Lord of Appeal in Ordinary, and the senior man holding judicial office in the country, made his maiden speech on this occasion. He had served as a judge in the Divorce Division from 1937 to 1951 where he said, 'he had the opportunity of listening to people of both sexes, people in great trouble who bore their troubles bravely and with patience and showed that they had done so over many years'.

He told the House that he heartily supported what I had said. Moreover, he said: 'The provision in the Bill which is supposed to provide for a man making provision for his wife's maintenance before he gets this compulsory divorce after seven years was in his submission a quite illusory safeguard. The man will not be able to do it. The woman with whom he is allowed to contract matrimony will get the money and in some cases will get all the money on Friday night, and the deserted wife will get nothing. . . .' 'This seven-year business is going to help only the rich; the poor will not be able to make use of it at all. The odd feature of our law is that well-to-do people can have half a dozen wives all living at the same time and deduct all allowances for surtax purposes.'

The promoter of the Bill, decided not to attempt to introduce the 'Compulsion Clause' on the Committee stage.

On 1 May 1965 Sir Jocelyn Simon discussing divorce law reform at the West Midlands Regional Conference of the Law Society at Leamington made the suggestion that an amendment to the divorce law might forbid divorce between couples with young children but allow it by consent in other cases. He said 'that he drew attention to the proposal partly because it was a compromise and had not had the attention some cruder proposals had received. 'No divorce should be available at all where there were infant children say up to sixteen or seventeen years of age.'

He said that in most cases the break-up of marriage was preceded by some months of ill-feeling and quarrelling between the parents. But unless they are more than ordinarily careless of the effect on their children this period does not seem to do nearly so much damage as the break-up of the family.

We are spending annually through legal aid £4 million on promoting the break-up of marriages. This is about a hundred times more than the sums which, through marriage guidance and education, we are spending to promote the endurance of marriage.

Occasionally a women's magazine asserts that the role of women is changing to the extent that many wives are no longer content with the companionship of one man; and that promiscuity in marriage is necessary for a balanced approach to the various pressures which are inevitable in married life. This represents a perverted form of feminism.

The married woman only wants a second man in her life if the first has failed her in some way. The man who never matures is the chief offender, the husband who seems incapable of emerging from the adolescent state; he is prepared passively to accept his wife as an earner, cook, nurse, laundry maid, odd job man, gardener and the disciplinarian of the children. If she blew up occasionally he might be galvanized into action; but paradoxically, as the burden increases and she recognizes the immaturity of her husband, she becomes less communicative in her attempt to maintain the harmony of the home.

The modern man too often accepts the earning capacity of a wife without being aware that the greater the burden which she carries, the more dependent she becomes on his understanding and help. If he fails as a helpmate, then she is vulnerable to the tender approaches of some more discerning male. On the other hand, the mother of small children who knows that a break-up in the marriage can lead to the loss of her home is too often prepared to suffer in silence a bad tempered and selfish husband.

The Law Commission set up by the 1964 Labour Government is concerned with examining obsolete laws, and Lord Gardiner, a most enlightened Lord Chancellor, is sympathetically disposed to an amendment of the law which deprives an innocent wife of her home on separation or divorce.

Following the General Election of 1966, I had the satisfaction of piloting the Matrimonial Homes Bill, which was designed to remove this injustice, through the Lords. While the Lord Chancellor and Lord Denning, Master of the Rolls, gave me powerful support, the contributions of some of the Law Lords, notably Lords Hodson and Wilberforce, who combined unsuccessfully with Lord Dilhorne, a former Lord Chancellor, to move what was virtually a wrecking amendment, reminded me of the attitude of those opposed to the Married Women's Property Act of 1882.

On the Committee stage of the Bill on 28 June 1966, I said 'Are women asking too much in seeking that it should be inherent in marriage that a wife has some rights in the matrimonial home?' Lord Hodson, a senior Law Lord, warned the House not to get their feet off the ground.

As this book goes to the printers, Mr Robert Edwards, the Member of Parliament for Bilston, an indefatigable champion of women's causes, has enthusiastically undertaken the next legislative stage of the Matrimonial Homes Bill, namely to pilot the Bill through the Commons.

21

The 1966 General Election: Conclusion

I approach every election asking myself the same questions, 'What are the fundamental issues?', 'What glaring injustices should we strive to remedy?'. Undoubtedly in the twenties and thirties I could not fail to recognize them. Hunger, unemployment, sickness waited impatiently on our doorstep demanding attention. Having, since those days, travelled widely and seen misery and suffering far transcending anything we experience in Western countries one frequently ponders on the administration of a country where the low expectation of life denies the majority of the population fulfilment. I am not the first to discover that, while a country cannot provide an adequate diet or a clean water supply for the people, it is compelled to spend vast sums on armaments which may be obsolete in a few years.

Nevertheless, I am still mystified by the inability of mankind, in the light of our brilliant achievements in the field of science, not to have learned through experience the ultimate futility of trying to settle disputes by killing each other.

War, despite the cruelty and waste involved, exercises a fascination for many otherwise intelligent people and consequently the manufacture of armaments offers dazzling rewards to those engaged in the process. While the 1966 election was proceeding in this country a war was being waged in Vietnam in which the modern might of the USA was deployed against the poverty-stricken Vietnamese. The invention of television has enabled us to see what is happening at the ends of the earth and publicity, the enemy of injustice, has rallied to the side of the Vietnamese. While the horrific pictures of a primitive countryside heavily bombed by modern machines outraged those with some semblence of a social conscience every politician knows that memory fades quickly and apathy takes over. The 'I'm all right, Jack' philosophy is hard to counteract. The national problem calling for a solution is how to acquire and retain a world vision. With the world divided into the well-fed and the hungry, it is not surprising that the underfed and illiterate are less concerned with a political ideology than with solving their immediate problems.

It is well to remember that we did not acquire full political democracy in this country until 1928 and we have still failed to achieve economic democracy. There is an unfortunate tendency to dub those who support some movement of an international character as fellow-travellers.

The nuclear disarmers may include Communists, fellow-travellers and individuals motivated solely by idealism or the Christian faith. Whatever their intellectual or political philosophy, their efforts to direct the attention of the country to the inhumanity and colossal waste involved in producing weapons calculated to destroy human life on an unparalleled scale is morally right, and they are to be congratulated on their courage and tenacity of purpose.

Election speeches may start on a high moral note appealing for consideration to be extended in the first place to the underfed millions of a different race and colour whose need is greater than our own, but the response is often lukewarm. The candidate, by the end of the election is compelled to deal with those more mundane matters which are much nearer home and which affect directly the lives of those in the audience.

Mr Edward Heath, the Leader of the Conservative Party, reiterated the need for the Common Market. More experienced politicians of all parties knew that a greatly expanded market for Britain's industrial goods would be given priority in the programme of the next Parliament but that the technicalities of the operation could not be grasped by an election audience. While the Prices and Incomes Policy, designed to steady the economy, was in principle the answer to the intractable problem of rising prices and incomes accompanied by low production, the lowest-paid workers and the women, denied the rate for the job, were not enamoured of a policy which failed to give priority to their legitimate grievances.

The medical profession were inclined to sit on the side lines during the election. Their terms of service were under consideration following very strong protests by the General Practitioners on the conditions of work imposed by out-dated agreements. Their case was a sound one and the rate of emigration of General Practitioners had reached such serious proportions that only the influx of doctors from Commonwealth countries ensured a comprehensive service. Question-time during the election meetings is often the most lively part of the proceedings and protests on the inadequacy of retirement pensions are not unexpected. Although the last Labour Government had given priority to an increase in pension I was surprised that no question was raised on the subject at any meeting at which I spoke. Rather surprisingly a meeting of retirement pensioners concentrated on the increasing crime rate and the consequent threat to the safety of old people living alone. They shared a lively interest in the Act to abolish Capital Punishment piloted through the House by that magnificent, indefatigable reformer, Sydney Silverman, and I was asked to explain why Shirley and I supported such a measure.

In the early 1930's General Management Committees of all parties were extremely reluctant to select women as candidates at Parliamentary elections. They consisted, as now, almost entirely of males, and they genuinely believed that a woman candidate was an electoral liability. Events have convinced them that they were wrong and in 1966 I found that such bias against women hardly existed. Electors are now confronted with the fact that women, when given the opportunity, have succeeded in the professions, in business and in politics. I am afraid, however, that it will be a long time before women are given the safe seats, because these will continue to be cornered by men in whose hands for the most part the power of selection lies.

During my earliest General Elections, my supporters were dismayed because we suffered so much from the shortage of motor-cars at our disposal, while our richer opponents paraded more than they could use. My recent experiences suggest that the Labour Party can now match its opponents in this respect. The flood of cars on the road presents a problem today, but it was pleasant to reflect during March 1966 that the evil was not entirely unmitigated.

On this occasion as in 1964 I was campaigning for Shirley and I made Halifax my base where she was defending a majority of 1,058. I sensed a change in the attitude of the electorate. There was a warmer response from the hitherto uncommitted voter and a quick smiling assurance from our loyal, rugged, Yorkshire supporters that nothing could change their minds. Indeed it was not uncommon for one of these to ask, 'Why are you wasting your time on me?' There was a marked swing to Labour all over the country and Shirley increased her lead to 5,700, a clear majority over her Conservative and Liberal opponents.

The advent of Harold Wilson, with a Grammar school background and an outstanding intelligence and shrewdness which the television cameras brought right into the living-rooms, was partly responsible for this swing, for it effected a remarkable change in the attitude of the business and professional classes. Here was a man with whom they could identify themselves and whose grasp of affairs and political acumen was clearly superior to his Conservative rivals.

Wilson's image reflected that of the scientist, teacher, engineer and technocrat, which now pervaded the Labour Party both inside and outside the House of Commons. His professionalism and self-assuredness in the field of politics dazzled friend and foe alike. Once when asked about the prospects of leading and shouldering the problems of the fifty million people in the United Kingdom of Great Britain and Northern Ireland, Wilson replied, 'If you have the ability and power it doesn't keep you awake.' Mary Wilson, his wife, who probably knows him better than anyone else was asked by a reporter if her husband ever worried and answered, 'Yes, not often. Maybe twice a year. Say twice.' However this question was put to her before Harold Wilson was returned with a ninety-seven majority, and when he could justifiably point to the legacy of debt and muddle bequeathed to him by thirteen years of Tory misrule, and the derisory majority of three with which he was expected to withstand the onslaughts of the Opposition. The question was asked before the cracks of a disintegrating Commonwealth began to appear in Africa, before he and his carefully selected team were exposed to the full rigours of economic competition in a world where rapid industrialization was a mark of progress. Harold Wilson has never sought to disguise his middle of the road philosophy which is as he says, 'essentially a pragmatic conception related to the needs of the age and the world we live in'. This is in line with his decision to quietly drop the Marxist economic outlook and the leftish slogans that have hitherto identified the party.

No Prime Minister at the dispatch-box before his advent has displayed the adroitness and the capacity for a quick retort stemming from a biting and sarcastic tongue supported by a first-class intellect and prodigious memory. His confidence and mastery of the House dispels for ever the myth sedulously fostered by the Tories that only an old school tie confers on a man that self-confidence indispensable to the exercise of power. Winston Churchill once said that Labour was unfitted to run a fried-fish shop. He was saved the discomfort of watching from the Opposition benches a parliamentary performance from a Prime Minister whose Noncomformist background and schooling had nothing in common with the privileged and wealthy upbringing of his Tory predecessors and yet which outclassed them in every way. Labour's decisive victory in 1966 did not appear to trouble the city unduly, although it was whispered in some places that the Prime Minister would be under irresistible pressure from the Left now that his alchemy had transmuted a majority of three into one of ninety-seven and consequently the risk of the Government's sudden collapse had been removed.

Thirty years ago with high unemployment accompanied by demoralizing poverty the Labour Party had argued that a considerable degree of nationalization offered the only cure for the economic ills of the country. The worst social evils have now been overcome in a mixed economy, and unemployment and poverty are now regarded as visitations which can be anticipated and appropriate action taken to prevent the widespread misery associated with the social evils of the past. Even the extreme Left are aware that universal State ownership does not provide a highly efficient economy in every field and they have only to look beyond the Iron Curtain for confirmation. Both efficiency and freedom are safeguarded in an economy which possesses a vigorous private sector.

In the 1966 election steel was the only industry which Labour undertook to nationalize but, on the other hand, no commitment was given that in the event of an industry failing to function efficiently nationalization would be ruled out. Successful exporters have been told repeatedly that the Government attaches great importance to their services and the publicity which their activities have attracted makes it clear that the Government regards them as valuable instruments of a public policy. Not only have export incentives and investment allowances been granted but the Queen has been invited to confer honours on those who serve the country by increasing our export markets. The country was alerted to this new approach to industrial efficiency and the importance attached to the winning of foreign currency by the conferring of the M.B.E. on the Beatles, a group of long-haired young men whose prowess in the field of modern entertainment had resulted in an access of dollars to Britain. The necessity to close the trade gap is so pressing that the industrialistwho increases his exports is recognized as applying himself to a task which is socially desirable, and consequently he is fully deserving of a reasonable profit. Labour's attitude towards the business community in this respect has been responsible for establishing a new understanding based on mutual confidence. The business man recognizes that the Prime Minister has a Nonconformist background from which stems his love of plain living, hard work and shrewd thinking. His attitude has not altered because his majority has increased; it is fundamentally the same as it was in 1964 and indeed all the Government's major policies had been planned long before 1964 when Labour expected to be returned with a good working majority. Harold Wilson is interpreting his Socialist principles in a modern practical manner; he watches the conduct of those other governments which possess mixed economies and like them he aims at creating a society in which the interest of the community prevails over that of any section.

It is sometimes forgotten by the very young in politics that the Labour Parliament of 1945 created a 'Welfare State' and resolved many of the problems stemming from the extreme wealth and poverty of pre-war days, and that before the war unemployment had averaged more than two million, whereas under the Labour Government for the first time in history in peace-time there had been practically full employment even in the pre-war distressed areas from whence came the hunger marches of the thirties.

Between 1945 and 1950 we beat all past records of legislative achievement and fulfilled every promise we made to the electors. We changed the social and economic life of Britain in such a dramatic fashion that the abysmal poverty and accompanying nutritional diseases, which left an unmistakable mark on little children which they carried all their lives, virtually disappeared. It was the signs and symptoms of this widespread misery revealed in the doctor's consulting-room which brought me and my husband into the Labour party. Young, non-medical politicians look a little mystified when I tell them that it is the straight legs of our young people which testify to the success of the 1945 Labour Government.

This was our answer to Winston Churchill who had told Roosevelt during the war that Britain would be bankrupt at the end of it and that the British soldier would have nothing to come home to.

The 1966 General Election changed the Party representation in the House of Commons, but the sex differential had shown little alteration. At the opening of the new Parliament Shirley was chosen to Second the Addresss on the Queen's Speech. Jeffrey and I listened to her with undisguised pride and satisfaction. Having secured a seat herself, with a greatly increased majority she did not fail to recognize that for that very reason she must raise her voice on behalf of her sex. After referring to her other medical colleagues in the House, she said:

'At this point I wish to pay tribute to another small group in this Parliament – the women Members. The psephologists, all of whom seem to be male, have decreed that the swing to female candidates at the Election was greater than that to male candidates. Whatever the reasons for this may be, no Hon. Member would deny that in the Government women are playing a successful part. We have come a long way from the time when militant suffragettes accosted Ministers in Downing Street and demanded the vote.

'But this is not the end of the journey. While the passage in the Gracious Speech concerning the Government's productivity, prices, and incomes policy is a most welcome one, the exclusion of any mention of equal pay for women will not pass unnoticed. I would respectfully remind Right Hon. Gentlemen in the Government that the railings around the Palace of Westminster can be used again.'

At the beginning of the century during the struggle for political enfranchisement there had been many knowledgeable men who had forecast even greater difficulties in removing the economic inequalities from which women suffered. Women had been more sanguine; they firmly believed that the vote was the key to full and immediate emancipation.

As Shirley was speaking I looked up at the spaces at the back of the public gallery from which the iron bars, to which the militant suffragettes had chained themselves, had been removed. These bars had effectively segregated the women enabling them only to glimpse the proceedings on the floor of the House.

We were now finding it more difficult to dislodge the prejudices which were firmly embedded in a self-interest stemming from financial considerations and the conventional powerful masculine desire to assert superiority even at the expense of denying the rate for the job. But we have come quite a long way.

The New Year Honours List published on 1 January 1966 recorded that I had been appointed a Member of the Order of the Companions of Honour, 'in recognition of my political and public services'. My satisfaction on receiving this honour was greatly enhanced by the congratulatory letters I received from my colleagues in the political and medical worlds; but particularly by the messages sent to me by women's organizations whose causes I had helped to promote.

In this recital of some of the events in 'A Woman's World' I have described what has happened to one particular woman. My special hope is that girls who read it may be encouraged to make the best use of those aptitudes which they possess to explore a world which has not always been accessible to women.

Index